RAGGED MOUNTAIN PRESS

Pocket Guide to
WILDERNESS MEDICINE & FIRST-AID

PAUL G. GILL, JR., M.D.

ILLUSTRATIONS BY WILLIAM HAMILTON

RAGGED MOUNTAIN PRESS

CAMDEN, MAINE

International Marine/
Ragged Mountain Press

A Division of The McGraw-Hill Companies

2 4 6 8 10 9 7 5 3 1
Copyright © 1997 Ragged Mountain Press, a division of The McGraw-Hill Companies.

Portions of this book were previously published in *Simon & Schuster's Pocket Guide to Wilderness Medicine* by Paul G. Gill, Jr., M.D.

Library of Congress Cataloging-in-Publication Data
Gill, Paul G., 1948-
    The Ragged Mountain Press pocket guide to wilderness medicine and first-aid. / Paul G. Gill, Jr.
    p.   c.m.
    Completely updated. Originally published under the title: Simon & Schuster's pocket guide to wilderness medicine.
Includes index.
ISBN 0-07-024552-5 (alk. paper)
    1. Mountaineering injuries—Handbooks, manuals, etc. 2. First aid in illness and injury—Handbooks, manuals, etc.   I. Title.
RC1220.M6G547   1997   96-49971
616.02'52—dc21   CIP

Questions regarding the content of this book should be addressed to:
International Marine, P.O. Box 220, Camden, ME 04843, 207-236-4837

Questions regarding the ordering of this book should be addressed to:
The McGraw-Hill Companies, Customer Service Department, P.O. Box 547, Blacklick, OH 43004, Retail customers: 1-800-262-4729, Bookstores: 1-800-722-4726

This book is printed on 55-pound Sebago, an acid-free paper.

A portion of the profits from the sale of each Ragged Mountain Press book is donated to an environmental cause.

This book was typeset in Adobe Minion, BakerSignet, and Zapf.
Printed by R. R. Donnelley, Crawfordsville, IN; Design by Ann Aspell;
Page layout by Deborah Krampf; Edited by Jonathan Eaton, Pamela Benner, Kate Mallien.
Illustrations by William Hamilton.

CONTENTS

PREFACE

The *Ragged Mountain Press Pocket Guide to Wilderness Medicine & First Aid* was written for all who venture into the wilderness, seeking to regain, however briefly, the sense of independence and equanimity that modern life tends to leach from us all. Kayakers, anglers, campers, backcountry trekkers, cross-country skiers, hunters, and modern-day Henry David Thoreaus on a Rocky Mountain Walden Pond will find this book a useful companion when things go wrong. It is the successor to my earlier book on wilderness medicine, *Simon & Schuster's Pocket Guide to Wilderness Medicine*, which was born of the sports medicine column I wrote for *Outdoor Life* magazine from 1988 to 1995. I know how quickly disaster can strike in a remote setting, and how lonely and frightened a person can feel when he suddenly finds himself disabled, in pain, and running out of daylight, warmth, and sustenance. And I know that most individuals who seek out the wilderness are self-reliant, resourceful types who would rather get themselves out of a scrape than accept help from others. And so my articles, and the book, were designed to offer sound, practical medical advice that could be used by men or women on the trail to save life or limb, using the materials they carried with them or could collect from their surroundings.

The responses of readers and book reviewers encourage me to believe that the book succeeds in its objective. Perhaps most gratifying are the many letters I have received from people all over the world, asking for additional copies of the book and telling me how it helped them deal with various wilderness medical emergencies.

I am convinced that a medical book doesn't have to be boring to be useful, and so I have liberally sprinkled the text with anecdotes and literary quotations to make the technical material a little more "digestible." To make the book more comprehensive and to serve a wider audience, the *Ragged Mountain Press Pocket Guide to Wilderness Medicine and First Aid* contains new chapters on abdominal pain and other gastrointestinal problems, pediatric care, and wilderness evacuation techniques, a glossary, and an appendix containing easy-to-access Emergency Treatment Procedures. All the material that appeared in *Simon & Schuster's Pocket Guide to Wilderness Medicine* has been reviewed and updated, and the book is graced by fifty-two pen-and-ink drawings by respected medical illustrator William Hamilton.

I've packed this book with just about all the useful wilderness medical advice that can be squeezed between two covers. There's just one more bit of advice I'd like to convey to the reader: *Primum non nocere.* "First, do no harm."

CHAPTER I

THE BASICS
Shock, CPR, and the ABCs

"Great emergencies and crises show us how much greater our vital resources are than we had supposed."

—William James, *The Letters of William James*

T ravis MacKenzie was picking his way down the back side of Mount Mansfield in the Green Mountains of northern Vermont when he slipped on some loose shale and became airborne. He bounced and rolled several hundred feet down the mountain before his descent was abruptly arrested by a large and unyielding fir tree. Travis slammed into the tree, fracturing several ribs and rupturing his spleen. He lay on the ground, stunned, for several minutes before picking himself up and hobbling back onto the trail. He made it to a cabin halfway down the mountain, where he collapsed.

When hikers found him a couple of hours later, he was barely conscious. He lay shivering on a bunk, a low moan drifting from his bloodless lips with each fitful breath. His face was ashen and dappled with silvery beads of sweat, and his lusterless eyes were sunk into their sockets like pebbles dropped in the snow. A cold sweat glazed his skin, his fingers and nails were blue, and his pulse was a feeble thread. Travis MacKenzie was in shock.

Shock is war. Biologic blitzkrieg. When trauma or severe illness threatens the flow of oxygen- and nutrient-bearing blood to the body's tissues, the body responds with an all-out, banzai counterattack, formally known as *shock*.

As in all wars, the assault may take different forms: bleeding from open wounds, ruptured organs, or fractured bones *(hemorrhagic shock);* fluid loss from crush injuries, burns, heat exhaustion, severe diarrhea, snakebite, or uncontrolled diabetes; "pump failure" from massive heart attack; and vascular collapse secondary to insect sting, overwhelming infection, or spinal cord injury. Virtually any serious injury or illness can lead to shock.

Whatever the nature of the insult, the final result is the same: interruption of the flow of blood to the cells. Each cell in the body houses a miniature power plant where complex chemical reactions generate the energy that keeps our brain cells communicating with one another, the muscle fibers in our hearts contracting, and the rods and cones in our retinas reacting to light impulses. These reactions are fueled by a steady flow of oxygen and nutrients in the blood. When the flow of blood is cut off, the metabolic machinery grinds to a stop, just as an internal combustion engine sputters when it runs out of fuel.

When you think of shock, you think of gory wounds and blood. But internal bleeding can lead to shock, too. You can easily lose a couple of pints of blood from a fractured long bone, and you can bleed to death from a crushed pelvis or ruptured spleen or liver without ever seeing a drop of blood. Crush injuries are doubly dangerous because plasma, the noncellular component of blood, continues to leak from damaged blood vessels long after bleeding is controlled.

THE BODY FIGHTS BACK

The body doesn't take blood loss lying down. The human machine is the end product of millions of years of evolution on a planet where dodging falling rocks and fighting saber-toothed tigers were all in a day's work. The response to blood loss starts when pressure sensors in the aorta and the carotid arteries in the neck detect a drop in blood pressure and alert the vasomotor area of the brain, the shock "command post." The vasomotor area acts quickly to stabilize the circulation by stimulating the *sympathetic nervous system (SNS)*, a special network of nerves sending impulses to the heart and blood vessels. The SNS's response is three-pronged:

1. It stimulates the heart to beat harder and faster so that it delivers more oxygen and nutrients to tissues girding for combat.
2. It constricts the large veins throughout the body that serve as a reservoir for up to 50 percent of the blood in the circulatory tree. This is equivalent to an instant 5-pint blood transfusion.
3. It clamps down on the small arteries in the muscles, intestines, skin, and kidneys, raising the blood pressure and diverting blood to the more vital brain and heart.

Meanwhile, the kidneys do their part by conserving salt and water, and the circulation receives a big boost in volume when fluid in the tissues *(extra-cellular fluid)* passes into the blood vessels.

The body's compensatory mechanisms are very efficient. So efficient, in fact, that a young, otherwise healthy person can lose 25 to 30 percent of her blood volume (1,000 to 1,800 milliliters [34 to 61 ounces] of blood, depending on her size) and show no signs of shock other than a rapid pulse and cool, moist skin. But if she loses even a few more milliliters of blood, she'll be on a slippery slope. Shock will become progressive and irreversible.

DIAGNOSIS

Trauma specialists talk about the "golden hour" in treating shock victims. If shock is not reversed within one hour, the patient will die, no matter what action is taken.

But shock has to be recognized before it can be treated. If your skiing partner takes a bad fall out on the slopes, how will you know if he is in shock? Ruptured spleens don't come with tags and, unless you have X-ray glasses, you can't see a fractured pelvis. But you don't need an M.D. after your name to recognize the classic signs of shock:

Mild Shock

The victim has lost up to a liter of blood, but her body is compensating well and her blood pressure remains normal. (*Beware:* estimating blood loss, especially your own, is like describing "the one that got away"—most people exaggerate.) She is alert, may complain of being cold and thirsty, and may feel weak and light-headed when she sits up. Her skin is pale, cool, and damp, and her pulse is rapid, usually about 110 to 120 beats a minute.

Moderate Shock

Blood loss is substantial, 20 to 40 percent (1 to 2.5 liters/1.1 to 2.6 quarts) of the total blood volume, and the victim is prostrated. She is too weak to move under her own power, her speech is slurred, and she complains of thirst and shortness of breath. Her skin is cold and clammy, her pulse is very rapid and weak, and her urine output scant (less than 30 milliliters/1 ounce per hour).

Severe Shock

The victim has lost 40 percent (2.5 liters/2.6 quarts) or more of her blood, and blood flow to the heart and brain is severely compromised. Her breathing becomes shallow and rapid, her eyes become dull, her pupils dilate, and she becomes restless and agitated, and then lethargic and comatose. Death is in the wings.

✛ Treatment

When shock is your foe, the battle has to be joined early. Once shock has progressed to the "severe" stage, the struggle is lost.

Treatment of the trauma victim starts with the ABCs: airway, breathing, and circulation.

A. *Airway:* If he is unconscious, keep his airway open using the "jaw-thrust" technique: put a hand on each side of his face and lift the jaw up and forward *without tilting the head back,* unless you are sure that he does not have a neck injury (see Figure 1-1).

B. *Breathing:* Check for breathing by listening to his mouth and chest, and observing his chest and abdomen. If you see chest and abdominal movement but don't hear breath sounds, check the airway again. If you still don't hear breath sounds, pinch his nostrils, take a deep breath, seal your lips around his mouth, and give him 2 full mouth-to-mouth breaths; then go on to C.

C. *Circulation:* Put your index and middle fingers over the windpipe, and slide them down alongside the neck muscle; feel between the windpipe and the neck muscle for a pulse. If there isn't one, start CPR (see page 8).

Then do a quick head-to-toe survey for wounds and fractures, and splint any obvious fractures (see Chapter 4). Control bleeding by applying direct pressure to the wounds with any bulky, clean material—use your shirt if nothing else is handy. Bright red blood spurting from a wound is arterial; oozing, dark blood is probably from a vein. Arterial bleeding, especially from the scalp, neck, groin, or shoulder, can be

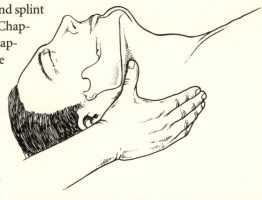

Figure 1-1. Opening the airway using the "jaw-thrust" technique.

difficult to control and can lead to the rapid, complete loss of all the body's blood volume *(exsanguination)*. If firm pressure doesn't stop the bleeding after a few minutes, pack the wound with sterile gauze and cover it with a bulky, firmly applied bandage (compression dressing). To control severe bleeding from a leg wound, push your fist into the abdomen at the level of the navel and press firmly. This compresses the aorta against the spinal column and will control the flow of blood into the legs while you apply a bulky bandage. (This is the only "pressure point" you need to know about.) Tourniquets are dangerous. Don't use one unless you are willing to write off the limb to save the victim.

After you have controlled the bleeding, put the victim in the "shock position" with his legs flexed at the hips, knees straight, feet elevated 12 inches, and his head down. This promotes the return of venous blood to the heart and enhances the flow of arterial blood to the brain. (*Warning:* if the victim has chest injuries, this position may make it hard for him to breathe. In that case, keep him in a semisupine position, lying down with his back at a 45-degree angle to the ground.)

Conserve body heat by bundling him in blankets or an open sleeping bag, and offer him warm fluids by mouth if he is able to swallow.

Move him out of danger if you have to, but avoid rough handling. Check his vital signs every few minutes, including pulse and breathing rate and pattern. Remember, restlessness and agitation may be signs of worsening shock.

Make arrangements for rapid medical evacuation (see Chapter 25). Time is of the essence!

Dealing with shock calls for courage, resourcefulness, and perseverance. General George Patton, "Old Blood and Guts," said it best: "A pint of sweat will save a gallon of blood."

CHOKING

When a diner chokes on a mouthful of filet mignon in a restaurant, it's called a "café coronary." When a backpacker in a remote setting in Montana (or anywhere else) chokes on a mouthful of food, it's called "sudden death"—unless his buddy knows the Heimlich maneuver and acts quickly.

Thousands of Americans choke to death on foreign bodies each year. The "foreign body" is usually a large, poorly chewed piece of meat. Many choking victims had been drinking alcohol or wearing dentures. Both interfere with the normal swallowing reflex.

Airway obstruction is the most acute of all medical emergencies. The metabolic machinery of brain cells is driven by oxygen. If the supply of oxygen is cut off for even a few seconds, it's "lights out." After 3 to 5 minutes without oxygen, the brain cells start to die, resulting in severe and irreversible brain damage.

Tragedy can be averted if you know what to do in an airway emergency and act quickly and deliberately. Your response to a choking emergency has to be reflexive and automatic, the way an experienced grouse hunter reacts to the sound of a bird taking wing. You have to know *beforehand* what you will do in every situation, and then do it without hesitation.

Remember the golden rule of medicine: "First do no harm." If the victim appears to be choking on a piece of food, coughing and spluttering, *leave him alone!* His airway is only *partially* obstructed. Encourage him to cough hard, but resist the temptation to slap him on the back or perform the Heimlich maneuver. If he starts to make a high-pitched noise when he inhales, turns blue, and his coughs deteriorate into feeble grunts, the obstruction is nearly complete. If he can't talk and is clutching his throat with his hands (the "universal distress signal"), the obstruction *is* complete. In either case, it's time for the Heimlich maneuver.

The *Heimlich maneuver* consists of a series of abdominal thrusts that elevate the *diaphragm,* the breathing muscle that separates the chest and abdominal cavities. Elevating the diaphragm causes a sudden rise in the pressure inside the chest cavity and an artificial cough that expels the foreign object. Here are the American Heart Association's recommendations on what to do when someone is choking:

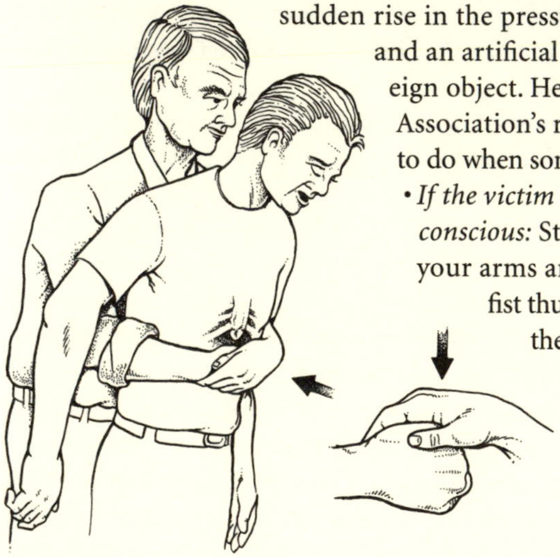

Figure 1-2. The Heimlich maneuver.

• *If the victim is standing or sitting and is conscious:* Stand behind him and wrap your arms around his waist. Place one fist thumb-side in on the center of the victim's stomach, between the rib cage and the navel. Grab your fist with your other hand, and pull up and in sharply, using 5 quick thrusts (see Figure 1-2). Repeat the series of 5 quick thrusts until the airway is cleared or he loses consciousness. If he does lose consciousness, perform a "finger sweep": Open his mouth by grasping the tongue and lower jaw and lifting up (this pulls the tongue out of the back of the throat). Then insert the index finger of your other hand alongside the cheek to the base of the tongue. Hook the finger behind the object and remove it from the mouth. (Be careful not to push the object deeper into the throat!) Then, pinch his nostrils, take a deep breath, seal your lips around his mouth, and give him 2 full mouth-to-mouth breaths. If you can't ventilate the lungs, perform 6 to 10 abdominal thrusts and then repeat the finger sweep and the mouth-to-mouth ventilations. Repeat the sequence of Heimlich maneuver, finger sweep, and mouth-to-mouth breathing until the airway is cleared.

- *If the victim is lying on the ground unconscious:* Place him in a supine position and kneel astride his thighs. Place the heel of one hand against his abdomen just above the navel, and put the other hand over the first. Press into the abdomen with a quick upward thrust. Repeat this supine Heimlich maneuver, the aforementioned finger sweep, and ventilation sequence as necessary. (You can use this technique in the conscious choking victim if your arms are too short to reach around his waist.)
- *If the victim is very obese or pregnant and is conscious:* Stand behind her and wrap your arms around her chest. Place the thumb side of your fist on the middle of the breastbone, grab your fist with the other hand, and perform a series of backward thrusts until the airway is cleared or she loses consciousness.
- *If the victim is very obese or pregnant and is unconscious:* Place the victim on her back, kneel alongside her, and place the heel of your hand on the lower half of the breastbone. Place the other hand over the first, and perform a series of thrusts. As above, repeat Heimlich maneuver, finger sweeps, and ventilations until the airway is cleared.
- *If the choking victim is an infant:* This is the only situation in which back slaps are recommended. If you are sure that the child is choking on an object, and not suffering from a severe upper respiratory infection, position the child's head down so that he is straddling your forearm and deliver 4 brisk blows between the shoulder blades with the heel of your hand. Then turn the infant face up, position him on your thigh with his head down, and perform 4 chest thrusts, as described above for very obese or pregnant victims.
- *If you are alone and choking:* Perform the Heimlich maneuver on yourself.

Make a fist with one hand and place the thumb side on your abdomen just above the navel. Grab the fist with your other hand and press inward and upward in a quick, sharp, thrusting motion. If this doesn't work, press your abdomen across any firm surface, such as a tree stump or rock.

A few caveats: When doing abdominal or chest thrusts, be careful not to place the fist too near the *xiphoid process* (a small piece of cartilage that projects down toward the abdomen from the breastbone) or on the lower margins of the rib cage. Fractures of the xiphoid or ribs can result in lacerations of the liver, spleen, or lungs. Also, abdominal thrusts can result in regurgitation of stomach contents, so try to position the victim so that his head is lower than the rest of the body. That way the stomach contents will drain out of the mouth and not obstruct the airway further.

CARDIOPULMONARY RESUSCITATION (CPR)

If your buddy keels over in cardiac arrest out in the woods, he's going to The Happy Hunting Ground unless you can resuscitate him. The only way to become truly proficient at cardiopulmonary resuscitation (CPR) is by taking a course at your local hospital. When you've taken the course and become certified in CPR by the American Heart Association or American Red Cross, you'll be able to perform the ABCs. Here is a brief review of the techniques:

1. *Airway:* Establish that the victim is unresponsive; place him on his back on a firm, flat surface; and open his airway using the "head-tilt"

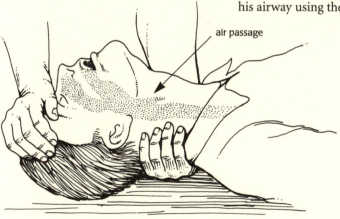

air passage

Figure 1-3. Opening the airway using the "head-tilt" technique.

technique (see Figure 1-3). Place one hand under the victim's neck and the other on his forehead. Then, flex the neck and extend the head.

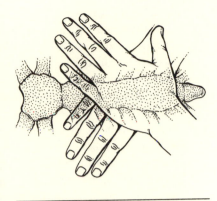

2. *Breathing:* Kneel alongside the victim and check to see if he is breathing by watching for movement of his chest and abdomen and listening for breath sounds with your ear against his chest. If he is not breathing, perform mouth-to-mouth breathing by pinching his nostrils,

Figure 1-4. Proper hand position for chest compression.

taking a deep breath, sealing your lips around his mouth, and giving 2 full breaths.

3. *Circulation:* Feel between the windpipe and the neck muscle for a pulse and, if absent, do chest compressions as follows:

- Place the heel of one hand on the lower half of the breastbone and place your other hand over the first (see Figure 1-4).
- Keeping your shoulders over his chest and your elbows locked, compress the chest at a rate of 60 compressions per minute, stopping every 15 compressions to open the airway and give 2 breaths. The breastbone should be depressed 1.5 to 2 inches with each compression (see Figure 1-5).

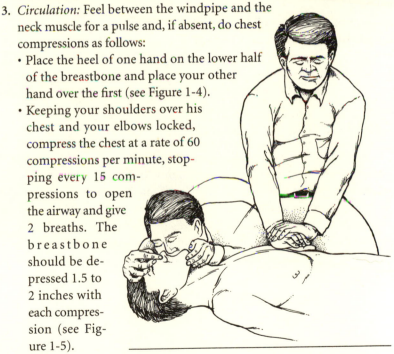

Figure 1-5. CPR.

- *Caution!* Excessively forceful or misplaced compressions can cause fractures and injuries to internal organs. Don't let the heel of your hand slide down over the tip of the breastbone, and keep your fingers away from the chest.

If you *see* the victim collapse, quickly check for a pulse. If there is none, you may be able to restore the heartbeat with a sharp "thump" on the breastbone with your fist.

Continue CPR until

- Breathing and pulse return.
- The rescuers are exhausted.
- The rescuers are in danger.
- The victim fails to respond to prolonged resuscitation (how you define "prolonged" depends on the circumstances; prolonged CPR is more likely to be successful in hypothermia victims).
- The rescuers are relieved by medical professionals.

CPR is not magic. There are situations in which it shouldn't be attempted, including

- A lethal injury (death is obvious).
- A dangerous setting in which rescuers' lives are in danger.
- Chest compressions are impossible; e.g., the chest is frozen or crushed.
- When there is any sign of life (breathing, heartbeat, pulse, movement).
- The victim has stated, in writing, that he doesn't want to be resuscitated.

TRAVIS MACKENZIE, SURVIVOR

Travis was lucky. The hikers who found him recognized the seriousness of his condition and used a cell phone to call for help. While waiting for the helicopter rescue team to arrive, they put Travis into the shock position, covered him with blankets, and built a fire to warm the cabin. When Travis arrived at the hospital, he was given blood transfusions and rushed into surgery. The doctors were able to repair his spleen, and a week later Travis walked out of the hospital, still smarting from his broken ribs, but happy to be alive.

CHAPTER 2

SOFT TISSUE INJURIES
Sprains, Strains, Cuts, and Contusions

"This was the most unkindest cut of all."

—William Shakespeare, *Julius Caesar*

It was opening day of the spring turkey season, and Brian had been walking the ridges of New York's southern Adirondacks since daybreak. He stopped for a moment to rest and wipe the sweat from his brow. He shielded his eyes with his hands and looked up at the sun. The fiery ball was approaching its zenith. Another hour and he'd have to knock off for the day. He picked up his shotgun and headed down the steep, rock-strewn hillside, half-running in his haste to cover as much ground as possible before noon. Suddenly, his right foot went out from under him as he slipped on a rock. He felt an explosion of pain in his right ankle and went down in a heap, landing heavily on his right hip.

Brian saw stars for a few moments. His ankle felt as though it were the top of a ketchup bottle that Hulk Hogan was trying to unscrew. And his hip didn't feel so great either. He pulled up his pant leg, unlaced his boot, and looked at his ankle. There was already a goose-egg–size swelling on the outside of it, but it didn't look broken. He ran his fingers over the bones. He couldn't feel any obvious fractures. If he could just make it back to camp, he'd soak it in some warm water with Epsom salts and he'd be as good as new in the morning. There was no way he was not going hunting tomorrow, especially after being shut out today.

Brian limped back to camp, soaked his ankle in hot water, and slaked his thirst with a couple of cold beers. He would have been better off if he'd soaked his ankle in the cold beer and drunk the water—Epsom salts and all. The beer took the edge off the pain; enough so that he spent most of the afternoon on his feet, hobbling around the camp making repairs. The next morning, his foot and ankle were so swollen they could have belonged to Big Foot. Brian couldn't get his boot on, and his hip was so sore he couldn't raise his leg.

Through his ignorance of the basics of sprain care, Brian converted a minor sprained ankle and contused hip into major, incapacitating injuries that ruined his spring turkey hunting. Treating these injuries is simple if you keep a couple of elastic (Ace) bandages, a roll of tape, and instant ice packs in your pack. But first you have to understand the difference between a sprain and a strain.

SPRAINS

A *sprain* is an injury to the ligaments around a joint. (Knees, ankles, feet, toes, shoulders, elbows, wrists, hands, and fingers can all be sprained. They cannot be strained.) *Ligaments* are bands of tough, thick fibrous tissue that hold joints together. When sufficient stress is placed on a joint, the ligaments will first stretch and then tear as the stress is increased. In a mild to moderate sprain, the ligament is stretched and up to 75 percent of its fibers are torn. In a severe sprain, all or nearly all of the fibers are torn.

Is It Broken?

Whenever you injure any joint, the most important question is: "Is it broken?" If you are 100 miles from the nearest hospital, you'll have to make an educated guess. Here are some tip-offs to fractures:

- Gently press on the bones around the injured joint. If there is a fracture, you may feel and hear the bone fragments rubbing together. This is called *crepitus.*
- A fractured wrist or finger will look deformed, unless the fracture is hairline. If your wrist and hand look like an upside-down fork, the wrist is broken.
- If the joint is dislocated, it will usually be even more deformed.

Swelling alone is not a reliable guide to the severity of an injury. Mild sprains may look much worse than many fractures. You can usually walk, although with pain, on a sprained ankle or foot. If the thin bone on the outside of the ankle (the fibula) is broken, you may still be able to walk on that leg because the fibula is not a weight-bearing bone. The majority of ankle and foot fractures, though, are too painful to walk on. If your wrist is broken, your grip will be weak. You won't be able to hold a cup of coffee in that hand.

✤ Treatment

RICE (not the kind they throw at weddings) is the key to treating sprains. RICE is the acronym for *r*est, *i*ce, *c*ompression, and *e*levation. The objectives in the initial treatment of sprains are (1) to limit swelling and bleeding and (2) to relieve pain. Swelling increases pain and prolongs healing. You've got to move fast to prevent it. A sprained ankle will balloon right in front of your eyes. Reducing swelling after it has already happened is like trying to put toothpaste back into the tube. And the more you move the injured joint, the more it's going to bleed. So rest it.

Ice does two things: It slows bleeding from torn vessels, limiting swelling, and it deadens the sensory nerves in the injured area. There's no better pain killer for a sprain than a bag of ice (a cold mountain stream will do in a pinch). But watch for frostbite: Don't apply the ice directly to the skin. Wrap an elastic bandage around the injured joint or cover it with a towel; then rest the bag on the bandage or towel.

An elastic bandage or towel wrapped around a sprained ankle or wrist provides compression that also prevents bleeding and swelling. Apply the ice over the bandage for 30 minutes; then, remove the ice and bandage for 30 mintues. Repeat as necessary over the next 48 hours. (If you're on the trail and are keeping the ankle or wrist in a cold stream, follow a 30-minutes-in, 30-minutes-out cycle.) Be sure that the bandage isn't wrapped too tightly. If your toes or fingers start to hurt, tingle, or turn white or blue, remove the bandage immediately.

Keep the injured extremity elevated above heart level. (For example, if you sprain your ankle, put a pillow or rolled-up jacket under it while you're lying down.) This reduces swelling by promoting drainage of blood and fluids from the injury.

If there are still pain and swelling after 48 hours of RICE, substitute warm soaks or compresses for ice. Continue to elevate the part as much as possible, and keep it wrapped in a pressure dressing or splint when it's not soaking.

When the pain subsides, start to use the extremity. But be careful! Take those first steps as though you were walking on eggshells. If you overdo it, you will turn your healing sprain into a fresh sprain, and it may never heal properly. You'll end up with permanently stretched, loose ligaments and an unstable joint (*chronic sprain*). When you can walk without pain, or use the wrist, hand or shoulder comfortably, put away the elastic bandage and head back into the field. But be aware that it takes up to six months for torn ligaments to regain maximum strength.

Wrist injuries should be splinted as follows: Put a rolled-up pair of socks in the palm of the hand and rest the wrist and hand (palm-side down) on a 10-inch-long piece of cardboard or wooden slat. Then wrap an elastic bandage around the hand from the knuckles to about 6 inches above the wrist. This is a *"cock-up" splint.* It keeps the wrist bent back in a natural, comfortable position and will prevent the hand from getting stiff. This is also the best way to immobilize a sprained or badly bruised hand. (A word of caution about "sprained" wrists: There is no way that anyone, even a doctor, can tell without X-rays if a wrist is fractured. As soon as you get home, have your doctor look at it. An untreated wrist fracture can result in permanent loss of function of the hand and chronic pain and disability.)

Use the buddy system for sprained fingers and toes. Tape the injured digit to its partner. Then ice and elevate it.

STRAINS

Strains are muscle injuries. Muscles can be "pulled," meaning that the muscle contracts so forcefully during a sudden movement that it either rips the tendon out of the bone or the muscle rips away from the tendon. Or the muscle itself can tear. Strains are every bit as painful as sprains and take about as long to heal. Not surprisingly, the treatment is almost the same: RICE for 24 to 72 hours, followed by range-of-motion exercises in warm water (hydrotherapy) three times a day. The warm water relaxes the muscle and promotes circulation of nutrient-carrying blood to the healing tissues. Continue hydrotherapy until you have regained full, pain-free use of the muscle.

CONTUSIONS

Brian developed a big, tender black-and-blue discoloration on his hip. A deep bruise such as this is called a *contusion.* The force of Brian's weight landing on his hip resulted in a crush injury to the skin and underlying muscle. Blood vessels in the skin and muscle ruptured, causing black-and-blue marks *(ecchymoses)* on the skin and a pool of blood in the muscle, called a *hematoma.* Contusions and hematomas are treated in the same way as strains and take about four to five days to heal. Large contusions can be quite painful and may mask serious underlying injury. A hard blow to the back can cause a contused kidney, usually manifested as blood in the urine. A severe blow to the chest can cause a contused lung, which will cause shortness of breath and coughing up blood.

SUBUNGUAL (FINGER- AND TOENAIL) HEMATOMAS

When you drop a rock on the end of your finger, the nail bed (the tissue under the nail) bleeds into the confined space under the nail. As the pressure builds up under the nail, the nail turns blue and the pain becomes exquisite. The simplest remedy is to clean the nail with an antiseptic solution or soap and water and then drain the hematoma with a hot paper clip. Or you can drill a hole in the nail with a knife or needle point. (First make certain that the end of the finger isn't fractured: push down against the tip—if it is not particularly tender, it probably is not fractured.)

OPEN WOUNDS

"Although Vorg had been knocked loose from his stance, he had fallen only a few feet before the belay piton braked, then held his rope. . . . It was now discovered that Vorg was hurt. When Heckmair's body, sliding feet first, had slammed into him, one of the spikes of Heckmair's crampons had gone through Vorg's mitten and through the ball of his thumb, blood pouring from both entrance and exit holes."

—Arthur Roth, *Eiger: Wall of Death*

Open wounds can be produced by sharp, blunt, cutting, or crushing objects and are characterized by a break in the body's first line of defense against infection, the skin. Regardless of an open wound's size, shape, or location, the objectives in treating them in the wilderness are the same:

- Prevent shock by controlling bleeding.
- Prevent infection by thoroughly cleaning the wound.
- Promote healing by applying sterile dressings and then splinting.

Control Bleeding

Most bleeding can be controlled with firm pressure over the wound or direct pressure with your fingertips over the bleeding vessels (see Chapter 1, page 4).

Cleaning the Wound

After you've stopped the bleeding, the next step is to examine the wound. First wash your hands; then check to see how deep the wound is, and whether there is any damage to deep structures such as bones, nerves, tendons, and blood vessels. Remove pebbles, vegetable matter, and other foreign objects by hand, and then cleanse the wound with the cleanest water available, which in most cases will be your drinking water. Stream water is fine once it has been disinfected (see Chapter 16). Add a little 7.5 percent povidone-iodine solution (Betadine) to make a 1 percent solution, and irrigate the wound liberally, taking pains to wash out grit, soil, and vegetable matter. Use a sterile gauze pad to gently wipe dirt out of the wound. (Scrubbing further traumatizes the tissues, increasing bleeding and the risk of infection.)

The best way to dislodge small dirt particles from the wound is by injecting the solution under pressure with a syringe. Direct the stream into the depths of the wound, under skin flaps, and at any particles that seem to be adherent to the wound. When you're done irrigating the wound, make a final inspection and remove any debris that may be left in the wound.

Closing the Wound

Dirty wounds, and those that are several hours old, are best left "open" in a wilderness setting. No matter how meticulous you are in cleansing the wound, it is virtually impossible to remove all contaminants from a wound when your operating theater is a clearing in the forest and the operating table is a bed of pine needles. Bacteria thrive on the blood and necrotic debris that accumulate in the depths of a contaminated wound. Closing such a wound is a recipe for wound infection. If you leave the wound open, pus can drain freely and won't pool to form an abscess. But each wound has to be treated on its specific characteristics, including location, depth, contamination, and injury to deep structures.

It is generally safe to close facial and scalp lacerations. They rarely become infected, thanks to the rich blood supply to the head. Large scalp wounds usually have to be closed to control bleeding. The simplest way to do this is to tie clumps of hair across the wound until the bleeding stops (hair doesn't hold a knot well, so use double square knots). Most facial lacerations can be closed nicely with skin-closure tapes (e.g., Steri-Strips or Coverstrips) (see Appendix 1). Apply a little tincture of benzoin to the skin on either side of the wound to make the tape stick better (be careful not to get any in the wound itself—it stings!). Then dab a little antibiotic ointment on the wound. When the benzoin has dried, apply several tapes across the wound. The best technique is to first anchor one end of the tape to a wound edge and then pull that edge up snug to the opposite edge, making sure that the wound edges are even. If kept dry, these tapes will stay in place until the wound has healed, usually 5 to 7 days.

Larger lacerations can be closed very nicely with staples. 3M Corporation makes a disposable five-staple device called the Precise Five-Shot. It comes with a device for removing the staples (after 5 days for facial lacerations, 7 days for scalp lacerations, 10 days for upper extremity lacerations, and 14 days for lower extremity lacerations).

Lacerations on the trunk and extremities should be cleaned as well as possible, skin edges stapled together if wound is large and appears completely clean, coated with antibiotic ointment, and covered with a sterile dressing in layers. The first layer should be a sterile, nonabsorbent dressing, such as petroleum jelly. (I recommend Adaptic, from Johnson & Johnson. This is an open mesh fabric impregnated with a petroleum emulsion that allows blood and other fluids to seep through the mesh. It doesn't stick to the wound, so dressing changes aren't painful.) The next layer should be absorbent sterile pads (e.g., Nu Gauze, from Johnson & Johnson), followed by a large surgical dressing (e.g., Surgipad, Johnson & Johnson) if the laceration is large and compression is needed to control bleeding. The dressings can then be taped in place or wrapped with roller gauze or an Ace bandage to apply compression. If you don't have staples on hand, use skin-closure tapes (e.g., Steri-Strips), or simply bandage the wound after dressing it.

If the wound is particularly dirty, wet-to-dry dressings may be the best approach. Apply wet sterile gauze pads directly to the wound and change them twice a day. When the dressing is dry, remove it along with crust and debris. This is an effective way to control infection in any wound. (An antibiotic effective against staph bacteria, such as cefadroxil [Duricef], 500 milligrams [mg] every 12 hours, should be started if the wound turns red and tender, drains pus, or if the victim develops a fever.)

Skin Avulsions and Flaps

When a knife or other sharp object strikes the skin at a shallow angle, it often tears off a hunk of skin. This is called an *avulsion*. Avulsions come in two forms: *partial-thickness*, in which just the top layers of the skin are lost, and *full-thickness*, in which all of the skin and possibly some of the underlying tissue is lost. Fingertips are frequently avulsed when the victim is slicing a loaf of bread or a slab of meat. A glancing blow from an ax may avulse a piece of skin from the leg.

Avulsions are treated in virtually the same way as lacerations, except no attempt should be made to close an avulsion. Since skin is missing, the wound has to heal from the bottom out. All fingertip avulsions heal, providing bone isn't exposed. Exposed bone needs to be covered with a skin graft. And any avulsion larger than a half-dollar will generally require skin grafting.

A *flap* is an avulsion in which the skin and underlying fatty tissue are intact on one side. A flap will often survive if its blood supply is good. A pale flap has no blood supply and can be expected to gradually turn black and fall off. But it can still serve as a "biologic dressing" while the wound heals from beneath. Flaps should be gently cleaned with antiseptic solution and then bandaged. If the wound turns red and starts to drain pus, infection has set in. The flap can be lifted off to promote drainage, and wet-to-dry dressings applied.

PUNCTURE WOUNDS

Puncture wounds can be treacherous. The wound may not look like much, but that rusty nail, thorn, or wood splinter may have driven bacteria and dirt deep into the tissues. It also may have punctured a blood vessel, nerve, tendon, or joint lining. These are tetanus-prone wounds and must be thoroughly irrigated with antiseptic solution, preferably with a high-pressure syringe. Then you can apply antibiotic ointment and a light dressing. (Make sure that your tetanus immunization is up to date before you leave home.)

How to Remove a Fishhook

Here are two good methods:

The String Technique

1. Loop a 12-inch length of string around the curve of the hook, and wrap the ends around your index finger (see Figure 2-1).
2. Push down on the eye and shank of the hook with your free hand to disengage the barb.
3. Align the string with the shank's long axis. Then gently tug on the free ends of the string until the hook comes out through the entrance wound.

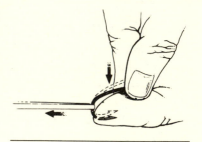

Figure 2-1. Fishhook removal using the "string" technique.

The Push-and-Snip Technique

1. If the barb is protruding through the skin, snip it off and back the hook out (see Figure 2-2).
2. If the barb *isn't* protruding, wash the skin around the wound with antiseptic solution and then numb it with ice. Grasp the shank of the hook with a pair of needle-nose pliers (or hemostat if you've got one) and push the point of the hook through the skin.
3. Snip off or flatten the barb and back the hook out.

push down on shank till barb protrudes

grab shank of hook and push barb through skin

snip barb

back out hook

Figure 2-2. Fishhook removal using the "push-and-snip" technique.

How to Remove Splinters

Splinters are always harder to remove than you think. And your best shot at removing a splinter is your first. The more you poke at it, the more fragmented it becomes, the farther you push it into the wound, and the less cooperative is the victim. So sit him and yourself down, shine some light on the wound, and get out your finest tweezers. Before you start, press on the skin around the entrance wound, and get a feel for the orientation of the splinter under the skin. Put your finger against the point of the splinter that is embedded in the skin and push it toward the entrance wound. Then, get a good hold of the exposed portion of the thorn or splinter with your tweezers and pull in the opposite direction to that in which it entered the skin. After you get the splinter out, wash the wound with antiseptic solution and apply antibiotic ointment and a dressing.

Large impaled objects should be left in place, especially if they are in the eye, neck, chest, or abdomen. In the old westerns, they were always in a big hurry to pull the arrow out of the cavalryman's back. In real life, that's a big no-no. That arrow, stake, or what-have-you may be the only thing preventing catastrophic bleeding from a perforated blood vessel. Instead, stabilize the object by wrapping it in a bulky bandage and evacuate the victim to a hospital (see Chapter 25).

ABRASIONS

An *abrasion* is what you get when you skin your knee or elbow, or scrape the superficial layer of skin over any bony prominence, such as the front of the leg, knuckles, or chin. Dirt may be ground into these wounds, so you need to spend some time washing them, using either a mild soap or an antiseptic solution. Small abrasions can be covered with a transparent dressing, such as Bioclusive (from Johnson & Johnson) or Tegaderm adhesive dressings (made by 3M). These are waterproof dressings that "breathe." They keep water out but allow oxygen to penetrate to the healing tissues, and they can be left on for several days. Larger abrasions should be bandaged the same way as a laceration—with antibiotic ointment, a nonabsorbent dressing, and a few layers of absorbent gauze for compression. The dressing should be changed daily until a firm scab forms (resist the temptation to pick off the scab—it's a natural dressing).

CHAPTER 3

BURNS

"The full shock . . . hit Corti, who was almost pulled from his stance with the
dead weight of the 200-pound Longhi's falling body. Still, Corti managed to
break the fall. Grabbing the rope with both hands, he saw smoke rise from
the gloves he had on. The friction of the rope burned right through the
gloves and into the skin of Corti's palms, burned to such a depth that his
hands would bear the grooved scars for months afterwards. Yet somehow
he slowed the smoking rope, then held his falling partner."

—Arthur Roth, *Eiger: Wall of Death*

There are three things you can always say about burns: they nearly always
are preventable; they nearly always happen at an inconvenient time; and
they usually cause more pain than permanent injury.

Whether the result of fire, chemicals, friction, electricity, or exposure to
hot water or steam, burn injuries are entirely preventable, *especially* in the field.
If your cabin or duck boat catches fire, chances are it's due to some mistake
on your part rather than arson.

GRADING BURNS

Presumably, you put out the fire and removed the smoldering clothing from
the burn victim before you picked up this book. The next step is to remove all
clothing and jewelry from the burned area and evaluate the severity of the
burn. This is determined by the depth, size, and location of the burn and the
age of the victim.

Partial-thickness burns are red and painful and may have large blisters. If
they are red and painful without blisters, they are first-degree burns. Blisters

indicate second-degree burns. With first- and second-degree burns, the hair follicles and nerve endings are undamaged and sensation is preserved. If infection is kept at bay, these burns will heal.

Full-thickness (third-degree) burns have a charred, leathery, or waxy appearance. Ironically, since the skin is destroyed, so are its nerve endings, and full-thickness burns are virtually painless. Full thickness burns larger than a silver dollar usually require skin grafting.

The size of the burn is expressed in terms of the percentage of body surface burned. The easiest way to do this is to use the "rule of nines." The head is considered to be 9 percent, the front and back of the torso each 18 percent, each upper extremity 9 percent, each lower extremity 18 percent, and the genitals 1 percent of the body surface area (see Figure 3-1).

Partial-thickness burns involving less than 10 percent of the body can be considered *minor* and treated with the materials on hand in your medical kit. Apply cool compresses for a few minutes to give immediate relief of pain. Then, gently clean the burn with disinfected water and a mild soap or antiseptic solution, using a cotton ball to remove dirt and debris. An intact blister is sterile and should be left alone. Once it is opened, it is vulnerable to infection. All burns with blisters, open or closed, should be covered with a thin (⅛-inch) layer of antibiotic ointment or silver sulfadiazine (Silvadene) cream and covered with Spenco 2nd Skin (if it is a small burn) or a fine-mesh roll gauze bandage and then bulkier dry (e.g., Kling) gauze bandage. Fingers and toes are bandaged individually. The dressing should be carefully loosened with warm water and removed daily, the burn washed with mild soap

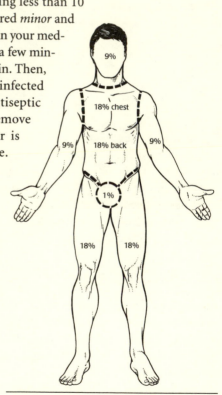

Figure 3-1. The "rule of nines."

(Dial or Ivory), and then re-dressed. By changing the dressings daily, you remove accumulated pus and necrotic debris and keep the wound clean. If you don't have any ointment or dressings, simply allow the burn to scab over. The scab will help to protect it against infection.

A partial-thickness burn will heal if it doesn't become infected, usually within 7 to 10 days. Burns are tetanus-prone wounds, so make sure your tetanus booster is up to date. Ibuprofen, up to 2,400 mg a day, or Darvocet N-100, 1 every 4 to 6 hours, will take the edge off the pain of an extensive burn. (Note: Do not apply Silvadene to the face.)

The following types of burns are considered major burns: second-degree burns covering more than 10 percent, or third-degree burns over more than 5 percent, of the body; most burns involving the face, eyes, ears, hands, feet, and genitals; circumferential burns (burns involving the entire circumference of the limb); burns associated with fractures and other significant trauma; and less severe burns in anyone younger than 5 or older than 60. Victims of major burns should be rapidly stabilized and evacuated to a hospital (see Chapter 25). When the body is denuded of a significant amount of its covering, shock from fluid loss and overwhelming infection is inevitable unless fluid is replaced and the burns covered with sterile dressings. While awaiting medical evacuation, keep the extremities elevated to promote drainage, and encourage the burn victim to take fluids by mouth if she is alert and in no respiratory distress.

CHEMICAL BURNS

There is a long list of caustic chemicals that can cause serious burns, but the outdoors enthusiast in the field is not likely to come into contact with any of these except the sulfuric acid in a car or boat battery—and then only if the battery explodes through the improper use of jumper cables. (Always first connect one end of the red cable to the positive terminal of the good battery, the other end to the positive terminal of the dead battery. Then connect one end of the black cable to the negative terminal of the good battery, and the other end to the engine block of the vehicle with the dead battery.) Skin that has been exposed to the 28 percent solution of sulfuric acid in 12-volt batteries has a red appearance, signifying first-degree burns. When the eyes are exposed to the acid, they become red and teary and the lids swell. Treatment of battery burns consists, first of all, of removing all wet clothing and then thoroughly washing all burned areas with voluminous amounts of water. A thin layer of Silvadene cream is soothing and will help prevent infection. (Note: Do not apply

Silvadene to the face.) If the eyes are burned, they should be washed under running water for at least 15 minutes. Flip up the lids and thoroughly irrigate the recess where the lid meets the eyeball. Then patch the eye and head for the nearest hospital (see Chapter 25 for evacuation procedures). Time is of the essence if permanent scarring of the cornea is to be averted.

Hot gasoline and kerosene can cause painful, scaldlike partial-thickness burns when spilled on exposed skin. Treatment is the same as for sulfuric acid burns.

A pot of boiling water can be knocked off a campfire or portable stove just as easily as off the kitchen stove back home. The result is the same, of course: partial-thickness burns with large blisters, or full-thickness burns. Treat them the same as any other thermal burn.

ELECTRICAL BURNS

Portable gas-powered generators have become popular among those who hunt or fish in remote areas. These units can really turn on the juice (120 volts, the same as house voltage), and must be handled with respect. *Flash burns* are partial-thickness burns that result from exposure to an electrical flash or explosion. They are treated just like any other partial-thickness burn. *Arc burns*, which result when the electrical current directly contacts the skin, are horses of another color. They are far more serious, and result from electric current passing through the body from a point of entry to a point of exit. In the low-voltage arc burns that usually result from these generators, current accumulates at the points of entrance and exit, and these two areas are more badly burned than underlying tissues. If entrance and exit wounds are on either side of the chest or on the hands, the current may have taken a path through the heart, possibly injuring it. And it may have caused serious thermal injury to blood vessels, nerves, bones, and other structures in its path. Since arc burns are almost always full-thickness, they must be treated at the nearest hospital. The best way to avoid electrical burns from these generators is to become thoroughly familiar with their operation before leaving home. Never try to hook them up in the dark.

FRICTION BURNS

Friction, or "rope," burns can range from mild superficial abrasions to deep thermal burns and shredding of the skin of the palms of the hands or other unprotected body parts. They are treated in the same manner as other burns. Always pack a pair of rawhide work gloves.

A WORD ON SPACE HEATERS

Gasoline heaters are intended for use only in well-ventilated areas away from combustibles. Kerosene heaters used to heat cabins or tents are economical and efficient. They are also dangerous. They can start a conflagration if knocked over (although newer models have automatic fuel-shutoff features), and emit dangerous concentrations of toxic gases. They should only be operated in well-ventilated structures, and the fuel supply should be kept outside.

CHAPTER 4

FRACTURES AND DISLOCATIONS

"While accompanying a hunting party on her estate in Scotland, Queen Elizabeth II was hit—by a falling grouse.

Shot by one of the hunters, the two-pound fowl plunged from the sky and struck the Queen's shoulder, cracking her collarbone. Her Royal Highness is expected to make a full recovery."

—*Sports Afield*, February 1996

Rick skied up to the edge of the ice-covered ledge, leaned forward on his ski poles, and took a long look at the narrow, chutelike trail that snaked around the mountain and down into the valley far below. Then he adjusted his goggles, took a deep breath, and pushed off on his poles, launching himself down the mountain. He telemarked through a tough mogul field at the top of the hill, and was descending quickly over a smooth stretch of trail when disaster struck. He caught the inside edge of his right ski on a small bump and went airborne. He somersaulted as he flew through the air, and when he landed thirty yards down the mountain, his left arm was levered violently backwards. He cried out in anguish as his shoulder popped out of joint like a cork out of a bottle.

Mac, Rick's partner, skied down the mountain right behind him and was at his side in seconds. Rick was lying on his back moaning, his left arm sticking out from his side at an odd angle. Mac loosened Rick's jacket and shirt and ran his hand over Rick's shoulder. It was dislocated. His eyes wandered down to Rick's arm and hand. They were cold and blue. He quickly felt the wrist for a pulse. There was none.

Can you imagine lying in the snow on some remote mountainside with a dislocated shoulder? If you were fortunate, you'd have a partner who could pop it back in for you, if he knew how. Otherwise, you'd be in tough shape. Fractures and dislocations are big-time injuries. They should ideally be treated by a physician. But if you're in some wilderness area, you won't want to wait several hours to be helicoptered to a distant hospital before getting your hip put back in socket. And if your dislocated shoulder is pressing on nerves and blood vessels, causing your arm to turn blue, you need help fast.

EVALUATING THE INJURY

The first step in treating a fracture in the wild is to check the circulation, motor function, and sensation *(CMS)* of the limb beyond the injured area. After all, a fracture is nothing more than a soft-tissue injury complicated by a broken bone. How you handle an injured extremity depends primarily on the results of this initial exam. If you find a loss of motor function, sensation, or circulation in the limb, then the bone ends are pressing on the vessels or nerves at the fracture site; gangrene or permanent paralysis could result if you don't remedy the situation. Here's how you do a CMS exam:

1. *Circulation:* Gently remove the boot and sock, or glove or mitten, and feel for pulses. Feel at the wrist on the thumb side, and right behind the inner knob of the ankle, or on the top of the foot between the first and second *metatarsals* (long bones). Then check the warmth and color of the fingers and toes. They should be pink. If they are blue or pale and cold, the circulation is impaired.

2. *Motor Function:* Ask the victim to wiggle his fingers or toes and to flex and extend his wrist or ankle.

3. *Sensation:* Check for perception of light touch, pressure, and pinprick.

The next step is to make an educated guess as to whether you *are* dealing with a fracture or just a bad sprain, meaning that the bones are intact but the ligaments around the joint are torn. (By the way, a "fractured" bone is the same as a "broken" bone.) A sprained ankle can swell to the size of a grapefruit in a matter of minutes. And a badly bruised shoulder or thigh can look for all the world as though it's broken. But you don't need a portable X-ray machine to diagnose a fracture. Press gently on the bone. If it's broken you'll feel a crunchy sensation *(crepitus)* as the bone ends rub together (and you'll elicit some colorful language from the victim). Compare the injured limb to its opposite.

Do they look the same? Can the victim move the limb through a full range of motion? If so, it's probably not fractured.

Next, check the skin over the fracture. If bone is protruding from the skin, you are looking at an *open fracture*. Put the cleanest possible dressing on the wound before you do anything else. Then splint the limb, and give the victim cefadroxil (Duricef), 1 gram immediately and 500 mg every 12 hours. There is a danger of bone infection *(osteomyelitis)* and gangrene in any open fracture, and these people have to be evacuated to a hospital as quickly as possible (see Chapter 25).

If the bones are bent at an odd angle, you need to bring them back into alignment. Here is why it's important to set, or *reduce,* an obvious fracture:
- To relieve the pressure of bone ends pressing on nerves and blood vessels.
- To stop bleeding at the fracture site.
- To prevent a closed fracture from becoming an open fracture.
- To relieve pain.
- So that you can apply a splint to the limb.

After stabilizing the fracture, you'll have to make a decision regarding evacuation. Some fractures can be definitively treated in the field. Others will be angulated and require reduction under anesthesia. Reduction of uncomplicated fractures can be put off for up to 7 days without jeopardizing the final result. But any open fracture or fracture associated with significant blood loss, spinal cord injury, or nerve or circulatory impairment must be evaluated quickly by trained medical personnel.

SPLINTS AND SLINGS

You can't apply a cast, obviously, but you *can* effectively immobilize most fractures with splints made from rope, brush and tree branches, metal pack frames, rifles, shotgun barrels, arrows, pack straps, sleeping pads, newspapers, and maps. On a long trek, you'd be smart to bring along a selection of wire or padded aluminum splints. Splinting the fracture in the functional position will decrease bleeding and damage to soft tissues, prevent stiffness, and make the victim more comfortable. The splint should immobilize the joint above and the joint below the fracture. It should provide some compression, but not so much that it cuts off the circulation. Loosen any compressive bandages or wraps every 2 hours to check CMS, and don't forget the RICE: rest, ice, compression, and elevation (see page 13).

FRACTURES OF THE UPPER EXTREMITY

Collarbone

Fractures of the collarbone are usually obvious. After a fall onto the shoulder, you'll have swelling and crepitus over the middle of the collarbone and pain on upward movement of the arm. Treatment consists simply of wearing a sling for 10 to 14 days, or until the patient feels comfortable without it (see instructions on how to make a sling under "Shoulder").

Shoulder

A hard fall on the side or back of the shoulder can crack the upper arm bone (*humerus*) near the shoulder. There will be marked swelling and inability to use the arm. A fractured shoulder blade is just one of the injuries you can get when a tree jumps out in front of you while you're cross-country skiing. A violent impact against the shoulder blade will crack it like an eggshell. Both of these fractures do well in a sling and swathe. You can make a sling out of a triangular bandage, a shirt, or a large piece of cloth. Rest the injured arm in the sling, keeping the hand free so that you can check the pulse periodically, (see Figure 4-1)and strap it against the chest with an elastic bandage or any material that you can wrap around the arm and chest. This will hold the arm in a comfortable position.

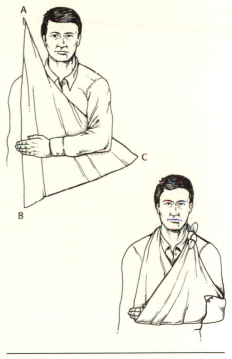

Figure 4-1. Making a sling. A goes behind neck then ties to B; fold C over and pin.

Upper Arm

Fractures of the mid–upper arm are problematic. These are unstable fractures, and muscle forces cause the fracture to bow forward. A common complication of mid-humerus fractures is *wrist drop*, inability to extend the wrist or fingers due to pressure on the nerve that supplies the wrist and finger extensor muscles. Immobilize these fractures by firmly applying wood slats or similar materials to both the inner and outer aspects of the upper arm and securing them with an elastic bandage. Then put the arm in a sling and swathe. If there is wrist drop, splint the wrist in a position of function with a cock-up splint (see under "Wrist").

Elbow

The elbow doesn't have much padding. If you slip on a rock and land on your elbow, it's not the rock that's going to crack. Immobilize fractures of the elbow in a sling with the elbow flexed to a right angle.

Forearm

Fractures of both bones in the forearm are unstable and should be firmly splinted and then put in a sling. If the forearm is badly deformed and CMS is impaired, take hold of the arm by the wrist and apply steady, gentle traction. When the arm looks straight, splint it and put it in a sling. Sure, it'll hurt a little. But reducing the fracture will do wonders for the circulation to the arm and hand, and your buddy will be much more comfortable when the fractured wing is splinted and resting in a sling. Be sure to check the CMS of the fingers at regular intervals after you reduce the fracture. Loosen the splint if the pulse is weak, if there is any loss of motion or sensation in the fingers, or if they turn blue or white.

Wrist

If, after a fall on the outstretched hand, the wrist and fingers look like an upside down fork, the wrist is fractured. But one of the small bones could be fractured and not produce a deformity. If there is any question of a fracture, make a cock-up splint: Put a rolled-up pair of socks in the palm of the hand and rest the wrist and hand, palm-side down, on a 10-inch-long piece of cardboard or wooden slat. Then wrap an elastic bandage around the hand from the knuckles to about 6 inches above the wrist. This will keep the wrist and hand in a natural, comfortable position and prevent them from getting stiff. (This is also a good way to splint a sprained or badly contused hand.) If you can't find a pulse at the wrist, or the fingers are cold and blue, you may be dealing with a fracture-dislocation. Reduce it by grasping the victim's hand in yours, handshake fashion, and pull straight out until the deformity is corrected. Check the circulation and then splint as described above.

Hand

Fractures of the long bones of the hand are usually stable and require nothing more than an elastic bandage or a cock-up splint. Reduce angulated fractures of the fingers by pulling straight out on the injured digit. Splint the finger with an aluminum splint or by taping it to the adjoining finger *(buddy splint)*. Crushed fingertips should be thoroughly cleaned, dressed, and then protected with a short splint applied to the distal third (toward the tip) of the finger.

FRACTURES OF THE SPINE AND LOWER EXTREMITY

Back

Most back injuries are due to twisting, bending, or lifting movements that injure the muscles, ligaments, and discs of the lower *(lumbar)* spine. These generally respond to a day or two of bed rest, along with warm compresses and analgesics (e.g., ibuprofen, acetaminophen).

> *"Then the great tree, burdened with its weight of years and snow, played its last part in the tragedy of life. He heard the warning crash and attempted to spring up but, almost erect, caught the blow squarely on the shoulder. . . . Mason was terribly crushed. The most cursory examination revealed it. His right arm, leg, and back were broken; his limbs were paralyzed from the hips; and the likelihood of internal injuries was large. An occasional moan was his only sign of life."*
>
> —Jack London, "The White Silence"

Falling off a cliff never hurt anyone. It's those hard landings that will get you every time. Rapid deceleration produces tremendous compression forces that can crush the vertebral bodies, usually in the midback area. A severe injury will result in fracture-dislocation of the spine. In a situation like this, you have to assume that the spinal cord is injured until you find evidence to the contrary (see Chapter 5). If the victim has to be moved, logroll her to avoid further injury to the spinal cord. Then do a quick neurologic exam: Check her grasp strength, then ask her to wiggle her toes and bend her knees and hips. Check to see whether she can feel light touch, pressure, and pinprick over the arms, legs, and trunk. If her motor strength and sensation are normal, roll her onto one side and check for fractures by gently thumping over the entire spinal column. If you find a tender area, you can assume that there is a compression fracture at that level. Gently roll her onto her back, check for other injuries, and arrange for medical evacuation (see Chapter 25). If the neurologic exam is normal and you don't find any tender areas in the spine, you can assume that there is no serious spinal injury and tend to her other injuries.

Pelvis, Hip, and Thigh

Fractures of the hip, pelvis, and thigh bone *(femur)* are potential killers. You can easily lose a quart of blood from one of these fractures. Pelvic fractures are frequently multiple and can result in massive blood loss, shock, and tears in the bladder. Such injuries in the wilderness will challenge your resourcefulness and will. Here is how you handle them: if a fractured pelvis or hip is suspected and weight bearing is painful, place the victim on his back. If he complains of pain in the groin, and the injured leg appears shorter than the other and is rotated outward, he probably has a fracture of the hip. Splint the fracture by strapping the legs together. Make a litter or sled, put him on it, and head for home (see Chapter 25). (A roll under the knees will make him a little more comfortable during the trip.) Stop periodically and check for signs of shock: pale, cool, wet skin, rapid, thready pulse, and agitation (see also pages 3–4).

Fractures of the shaft and lower end of the femur are more problematic. Powerful muscles attach to this bone, and spasm of these muscles cause the sharp bone ends to pierce muscle and other soft tissues, causing heavy bleeding. These fractures must be immobilized immediately. If there are extra hands, have one person apply steady traction to the leg by pulling on the foot while another person applies countertraction to the pelvis. Pull until the pain is relieved (this will usually require a force of about 10 percent of the victim's body weight), and maintain traction on the leg while a splint is being applied. One simple technique is to secure the broken leg to the uninjured one. Or you can strap a tree branch, oar, or some other long object

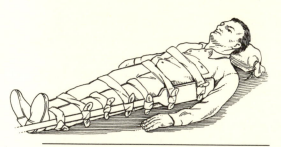

Figure 4-2. Splinting a fractured leg.

to the leg from chest to ankle (see Figure 4-2). But make sure there is padding over all bony prominences, such as the knee and ankle. And put a soft roll under the knee so that it's flexed about 5 or 10 degrees.

If there are 6 or more people in your party, you can consider transporting the victim out overland, although a litter-borne evacuation can be conducted more safely with 12 or more people. If you don't have enough people, send someone for a helicopter rescue crew (see Chapter 25).

Kneecap

This is another one of those unpadded bones. A fractured kneecap can be hard to distinguish from a bad bruise. If there is a lot of swelling over the front of the knee and you feel crepitus when you press down on the kneecap, it's probably broken. The best treatment is a cylindrical splint from groin to ankle. A rolled-up foam sleeping pad will do nicely. Climbing will be almost impossible with this injury, but the victim can walk over gentle terrain with the help of a walking stick.

Lower Leg

A fall from a height may result in a fracture of the upper part of the leg bone (*tibia*). These fractures usually involve the knee joint, and bleeding will cause the knee to swell like a balloon. Fractures of the shaft of the tibia are frequently angulated and open, and the thin bone that runs alongside the tibia (*fibula*) is usually broken also. If the leg is deformed and CMS is impaired, realign the bones by grasping the ankle and applying steady traction along the long axis of the bone until it straightens out. Then splint it. If the bone is protruding, wash the fracture site with antiseptic solution (or soap and water) and apply a sterile dressing or the cleanest cloth bandage available. Then reduce and splint the fracture.

Ankle

Ankle fractures and sprains are often indistinguishable: a swollen, tender ankle could as easily be fractured as sprained. Run your fingers over the bony knob on each side of the ankle, feeling for deformity and crepitus. If you find none, call it a sprain and apply the RICE technique (see page 13). If ice isn't available, cold water or snow will help to reduce swelling and alleviate pain. The victim may be able to walk with some help. If there is no deformity, it may be better to leave the boot on. It will make an excellent splint, and you'll never get it back on once it has been off for a while.

Fractures of the ankle often come as a package deal with dislocations. These are usually obvious, with the foot discolored and bent at a weird angle. This puts the stretch on the blood vessels in the area, and prompt reduction is necessary to save the foot. Grasp the foot with the heel in one hand and the other hand over the top of the foot; then pull steadily toward you. The ankle will slip back into place with a "thud," and a nice pink color will return to the foot as the circulation resumes. A pillow, down parka, or other soft, bulky object wrapped around the ankle and pinned in place makes an excellent splint.

Foot

Jumping from a height and landing on the feet is a recipe for a fractured heel or long bone of the foot *(metatarsal)*. Fractures of the heel are often associated with compression fractures of the spine, so make sure that you examine that area also. Splint suspected fractures of the heel area as you would an ankle fracture (see above). A stiff-soled boot makes a good splint for metatarsal fractures.

Fractured toes heal nicely if you just tape them to their buddies. Put a little cotton between the toes to absorb moisture and prevent skin breakdown *(maceration)*. There is a great deal of pressure on the big toe during the toe-off phase of walking, so fractures of this digit can be disabling. Stiff-soled boots help to take some pressure off the fracture, especially if you tape four or five tongue depressors across the sole at its widest part.

DISLOCATIONS

Reducing a dislocated joint can be like trying to put "Jack" back in the box. It's a tough job, but someone has to do it. And quickly. If you don't pop that shoulder (or elbow, finger, or hip) back in right away, swelling and muscle spasm will make the job next to impossible. And reducing the dislocation provides instant pain relief, takes the pressure off the nerves and blood vessels around the joint, and allows you to splint the injured limb in a comfortable position. A wound over a dislocated joint constitutes an *open dislocation*. Clean the wound thoroughly and apply a sterile bandage before attempting to reduce it. *Always* check CMS before and after reduction.

Here are some of the common dislocations encountered in the wilderness and how to handle them:

Shoulder

Every outdoors enthusiast should be able to recognize and treat a dislocated shoulder. This is a common injury and is relatively easy to reduce. It usually is the result of a backward force on an elevated arm, as illustrated by Rick, the skier discussed at the beginning of this chapter. *Warning:* Before you start yanking on that "dislocated" shoulder, make sure that it really is out of joint. Unless you carry X-ray glasses in your pocket, this can be tricky. But you can be reasonably sure of your diagnosis if

- The shoulder has an unnatural, "squared-off" appearance.
- The arm is held out from the body.
- Using the injured arm, the victim can't reach his hand across to touch the opposite (uninjured) shoulder.

Here is one way to reduce a dislocated shoulder: Have the victim lie prone on a ledge or other flat surface with the dislocated arm hanging over the edge. Use strips of cloth or other material to secure a weight of 10 to 15 pounds to the wrist (see Figure 4-3). Then take a short hike. When you return in 10 minutes, the shoulder will be back in joint.

Here is another technique: Position the victim as above, with the injured arm hanging over an edge. Sit or kneel next to him, wrap your hands around his upper arm, and gently pull down on the upper arm. Gradually increase the downward force on the arm until you feel the shoulder slip back into joint.

You'll know when it's back in when you hear the victim give a huge sigh of relief, and a beatific smile spreads across his face.

Immediately after reducing the shoulder, put the arm in a sling and swathe, keeping the hand and wrist free so that you can check the circulation at regular intervals.

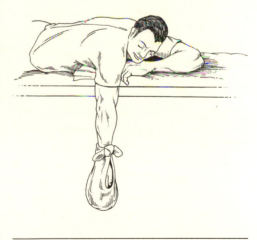

Separated Shoulder

It is common to mistake a "separated" shoulder for a dislocation. A *separation* is generally caused by a fall directly onto the shoulder, causing disruption of

Figure 4-3. Reducing a dislocated shoulder.

the ligaments that connect the collarbone with the shoulder blade *(scapula)*. In a *partial separation,* the ligaments are only partially torn, and you will find swelling and tenderness over the end of the collarbone. In a *complete separation,* the ligaments are totally disrupted, and the end of the collarbone is elevated an inch or more. (You can distinguish between a separation and a fractured collarbone by pressing over the end of the collarbone. If it feels "springy," you are dealing with a separation. If the collarbone is very tender and feels "crunchy," it's fractured.) Separated shoulders should be immobilized in a sling.

Elbow

You will know a dislocated elbow when you see one. A hard fall on the arm drives the forearm bones backward and out of the elbow joint. These dislocations can be tough to reduce, but it's worth a try if you are more than a few hours from help. Pull slowly and steadily on the forearm while an assistant pulls in the opposite direction on the upper arm. You will feel the elbow go back in, and the victim will be able to bend it to 90 degrees. If one or two good efforts fail to reduce the dislocation, put the arm in a sling and hit the trail. Undue force will only result in unnecessary pain and damage the joint and nerves and blood vessels.

Finger

Dislocations of the first joint of the finger are common on wilderness treks, usually the result of the finger being struck and bent back by a thrown object. A dislocated finger is always obvious. Reduce it by pulling straight out on the deformed digit with one hand while pushing the base of the dislocated bone back into joint with the thumb of your other hand. Then splint the finger to its buddy.

Hip

It takes a fall off a cliff or a similar violent injury to dislocate the hip, a very stable ball-and-socket joint. Either the thigh will be sticking out at an odd angle or the leg will be shortened, rotated inward, and crossed over the uninjured leg.

While reducing a dislocated hip in the wild is no mean feat, it should be attempted. The longer the hip is out of socket, the greater the risk of complications, including damage to the sciatic nerve and necrosis of the ball part of the joint. Lay the victim on her back on the ground and slowly bend the knee and hip to 90 degrees so that the knee and foot are pointing up. Have an assistant push down on the hips while you straddle the victim, place her leg between your thighs, and wrap your hands behind her knee. Then pull up hard on her thigh while you gently rotate the leg first one way and then the other. When you feel the hip go in, splint it to the other leg with soft padding between the knees. If you cannot reduce it, splint it in a comfortable position and arrange to evacuate the victim (see Chapter 25).

Kneecap

Scrambling down a rocky mountainside can cause a sudden twisting motion of the knee that can dislocate the kneecap. A direct blow to the inner side of the kneecap will do the trick, too. The kneecap will be displaced laterally, and the knee will be flexed 45 or 60 degrees. These dislocations can usually be reduced by slowly straightening the knee. You may have to gently nudge the kneecap back into place by pressing laterally on it with your hand. When it's reduced, apply a cylindrical splint to keep the knee in a fully straightened position. Walking may be a little painful, but it is safe.

AMPUTATIONS

Amputations are treated the same way as an open fracture. Control bleeding by holding firm pressure over the stump with a bandage or rolled-up clothing. Then irrigate it with disinfected water before applying a sterile dressing secured with an elastic bandage. The amputated part should be cleaned and transported with the victim (see Chapter 25). Cover it with a moistened, sterile bandage, and put it in a plastic bag, filled with ice if possible.

CHAPTER 5

HEAD AND NECK INJURIES

"'Suddenly Bayley's foot slipped under him, and before he could recover himself he had fallen . . . like a flash he shot down the mountain, disappearing in an instant from the horrified gaze of his companion, to be found an hour later, over two thousand feet below, on a narrow ledge seventy feet down in a crevasse. . . .

"'My body just slid over the surface for the first 1,500 feet. Then . . . I shot 500 feet further, was hurled across a crevasse over twenty feet in width, striking the opposite side with a crash that knocked me senseless on a narrow ledge. . . .'"

—From the *Oakland Enquirer*, 1883, as quoted by Evelyn Hyman Chase, in
Mountain Climber

It had been a long hike up the old logging road to the pristine lake high in Idaho's Salmon National Forest. But it had been worth it. Jim and Ron had landed a half dozen goldens in the first hour after sunrise. But now it was time to return to camp on the Lehmi River, 2,000 feet below. They dreaded the long hike: the trail was a tedious series of switchbacks, like a long row of ribbon candy stretching down the mountain. So, they opted for a dangerous but much quicker trail along the boulder-studded back side of the mountain.

Picking his way down the precipitous rock face, Jim slid on the seat of his pants down the side of one large boulder, and sat on a ledge and waited for his partner. He didn't have to wait long. Ron lost his footing and let out a blood-curdling yell as he went tumbling head over heels down the mountainside. He came to a stop 60 bruising yards later at the bottom of a steep defile. Jim leaned over the ledge and peered into the gorge. All he could see was Ron's legs. They weren't moving. Jim's eyes moved farther down the slope where, well below, he could just make out a narrow ribbon of whitewater: the Lehmi River. It was a long way off.

Jim is caught on a rock in a high place. His buddy just took a bad tumble and is either unconscious, paralyzed from a spinal injury, or both. And he may have fractures and internal injuries as well. Jim has to get Ron out of there, but if he tries to move him without immobilizing his neck, he could do irreparable harm to Ron's spinal cord. So what should he do? Would you know what to do? Let's go through the systematic series of steps that you would need to take to get your partner and yourself off that mountain.

BACK TO BASICS

The approach to the badly injured person has got to be streamlined and efficient. Start with the ABCs: *a*irway, *b*reathing, and *c*irculation, as described in Chapter 1 (page 4). Once you have attended to any immediately life-threatening problems, assess his mental status by evaluating the following areas:

1. *Eye opening:* Does he open his eyes spontaneously, or only on command or in response to a painful stimulus?
2. *Verbal response:* Is his speech understandable, and does he make sense? Or is he confused and disoriented, or talking gibberish?
3. *Motor response:* Does he obey simple commands? Does he withdraw from a painful stimulus?

Then check the pupils. They should be symmetrical and react to light by constricting. Confusion, lethargy, garbled speech, and unequal or unreactive pupils are all signs of possible brain injury.

The next step is to resuscitate the trauma victim with the materials at hand. He might need oxygen, intravenous fluids, blood transfusion, antibiotics, and a urinary catheter, but if it's just you and him on a rocky crag, you're not going to be able to do much more than to make him comfortable and perhaps give him a drink of water. (And if he has a serious head injury, fluids by mouth are out because he could breathe them into his lungs.)

CHECK THE SPINE

As you do your head-to-toe exam, check for signs of spinal fractures. Remember: any blow to the head, face, or neck and any fall from a significant height can produce a spinal injury. The golden rule of spinal injuries is: every trauma victim has one until proved otherwise. And if he does have a fracture or fracture-dislocation of the spine, the slightest movement can drive sharp fragments of bone into the spinal cord, resulting in permanent paralysis or death.

Ask the victim if he has pain in his neck or back. Then, without moving him, slip your hand between the ground and his back and run your fingers down his spinal column from the base of the skull to the base of the spine, feeling for tenderness or any abnormal prominence. If there is any sign of a neck injury, immobilize the neck by applying "sandbags" (sacks stuffed with dirt or tightly bundled clothing) around his neck, head, and shoulders. The sandbags can then be anchored in place with rocks, or a strip of adhesive tape can be drawn across his forehead and secured to the bags on either side (see Figure 5-1). If you suspect a back injury, keep the victim on his back.

After immobilizing the spine, look for a *spinal cord injury*. These are the signs:
- Pain in the neck or back radiating down the arms or legs.
- Numbness or tingling in the hands or feet.
- Loss of sensation in the arms or legs.
- Paralysis of the arms or legs.
- A sustained penile erection *(priapism)*.

Note: It's possible, though highly unlikely, that someone could fall a great distance, injuring her spine, and end up on her stomach. In this case, *do not* roll the victim over. Leave her as she is, but try to follow the procedures outlined above.

HEADS UP

With head injuries, what you see is not always what you get. It's hard not to get excited when your buddy hits his head on a rock overhang and lays his scalp open down to the bone. The bleeding can be horrendous, and he may turn pale and feel punk for a while. But that doesn't mean that he has a brain injury. On the other hand, he could have serious bleeding *inside* his skull with nary a mark on his scalp. Of far greater importance than the appearance of the scalp is his mental state. Was he knocked unconscious? Is he awake and alert now? Is he oriented to his surroundings, or does he think he's on the planet Tralfalmador? Determine whether he

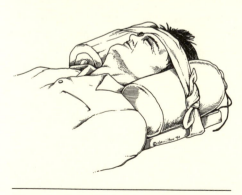

Figure 5-1. Immobilizing the neck.

knows who he is, where he is, and what day/year it is. Then decide whether he has one of the following injuries:

Concussion

You don't have to be a neurosurgeon to treat most brain injuries in the wild. That's because most of these injuries are simple concussions. A *concussion* is a transient disturbance of brain function following a blow to the head. The hallmark of a concussion is a brief loss of consciousness, often followed by a period of mild confusion, memory loss, headache, and perhaps some nausea and vomiting. These symptoms resolve within a few hours or days at the most. The victim will feel better with a day or so of rest, and acetaminophen for the headache.

Intracranial Bleeding

You *do* have to be a neurosurgeon to treat a blood clot on the brain (*subdural* or *epidural hematoma;* see Figure 5-2). Any blow to the head, especially over the relatively thin part of the skull just above the ear, can cause a tear in the vessels in or under the covering of the brain *(dura)*. Because the skull is a rigid compartment, there's no room for expansion. So when a vessel on the surface of the brain bleeds, it forms a clot that increases the pressure within the skull. When the pressure becomes great enough, blood flow to the brain ceases and the brain dies. It's "thanks for the memories," unless something is done to relieve the pressure. That means immediate evacuation to a hospital (see Chapter 25).

A person who develops a blood clot on the brain may be knocked unconscious and never regain consciousness. Or he may regain consciousness for a brief period (the *lucid interval*), only to lapse back into unconsciousness. And occasionally (especially in older people) there is no initial loss

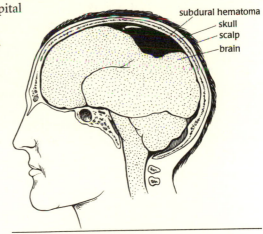

Figure 5-2. Subdural hematoma.

of consciousness, but increasing confusion and lethargy progress to coma some hours or days after the injury.

How do you know when your buddy has a life-threatening clot on the brain? Unless there's a CT scanner there in the woods, you won't know. You're going to have to keep a close eye on him for at least 24 hours, observing for:

- Personality changes.
- Vomiting.
- Increasing headache.
- Unequal pupils. If one pupil becomes widely dilated, he has a very serious problem. The brain is being squeezed out of the skull, and the situation is desperate.

Other things to look for include:

- Dropping pulse rate. As the pressure in the head rises, the blood pressure goes up and the heart rate slows.
- Blood or clear fluid draining from the ears or nose. This may be a sign of a fracture of the base of the skull.
- Obvious fracture or indentation of the skull. Run your fingers through the hair, feeling for fractures, depressed areas, and lacerations.
- Bruises behind the ears and "raccoon eyes" (also signs of a fractured skull).
- Spinal injury. Fifteen percent of victims of severe head injury also have a broken neck. If the victim is unconscious, assume he has a broken neck and immobilize his head.

Scalp wounds can bleed like Old Faithful. The best way to control the bleeding is to sew them up. If you don't have the wherewithal, here's an alternative that doesn't require needle and thread: Clean the wound, irrigating it with the cleanest water available, and pick out dirt particles, sticks, and so on. Then moisten the hair on either side of the laceration and twist small clumps of hair into braids all along the wound edges. Tie these braids across the wound until it's closed up tight. Then apply a turban dressing with a few rolls of gauze or cloth. The wound will have to be explored and closed under sterile conditions later, but this technique will control bleeding in the meantime. (*Warning:* If there is an obvious skull fracture, *don't* irrigate the wound. That would only drive dirt and bacteria into the brain. Just apply a sterile dressing and a bulky bandage. If there is a ski pole, rock, or other foreign object embedded in the skull, *don't touch it!* Doing so could result in catastrophic bleeding into the brain. Apply a bandage to the wound with the object in place.)

EVACUATION

When do you evacuate the head-injury victim? You can best make this judgment by assigning him to one of three risk groups:

1. *Low risk:* The victim has sustained a mild blow to the head but had no loss of consciousness and complains only of a minor headache and dizziness. He may have a small laceration or bruise on the scalp, but his pupils are symmetrical and he has no paralysis, loss of sensation, or other sign of neurologic injury.

2. *Moderate risk:* The victim has had a brief loss of consciousness, vomiting, persistent or worsening headache, and amnesia for the events immediately following the injury.

3. *High risk:* The victim was knocked unconscious and now has a depressed level of consciousness or loss of sensation or strength on one side of the body. Anyone who has fallen more than 15 feet, who has sustained a high-energy blow from a falling rock or other object, or has suffered a skull fracture or penetrating injury to the skull should be considered at high risk, even if there was no loss of consciousness or other sign of brain injury.

Those who fall into the low-risk group can be expected to do well but should be watched carefully for 24 hours. They will need to be evacuated if they develop signs of lethargy, drowsiness, personality change, forceful or persistent vomiting, or abnormal gait or speech. Those in the high-risk category need to be evaluated in a hospital, and must be evacuated as quickly as possible (see below, and Chapter 25). The disposition of those in the moderate-risk group depends on a number of factors, including other injuries and evacuation time. Generally, anyone in this group who also has spinal or other injuries should be evacuated at once.

How about the person with a neck or spinal injury? If he has only minimal pain in the neck or back and there's no sign of paralysis, he can safely walk out under his own power. If he has significant pain but no sign of a spinal cord injury, keep him immobilized and recheck him every 20 minutes. Subtle signs of spinal cord injury may only become apparent after repeated exams. If there are *definite* signs of a spinal cord injury, go for help. Any attempt to move the victim at this point can result in catastrophe.

Evacuating an unconscious person from the mountains or deep woods can be one of the Labors of Hercules, so hit the trail while the victim is still awake and able to cooperate in his evacuation. If he is reasonably alert, he can walk without assistance. But keep a close eye on him, especially when going over rough terrain that may require above-average balance and judgment.

If you have enough strong people in your party, it may be best to evacuate an unconscious person yourselves. But make sure that his neck is rigidly immobilized if there is any possibility of spinal injury. Carry him on his back on a litter with his head slightly elevated to help increase the drainage of venous blood from the brain and to reduce swelling. If he vomits, lower his head and turn him on his side so that he doesn't breathe the vomited material into his lungs. (If his spine is immobilized, logroll him onto his side.) And make sure that you put padding under his shoulders, elbows, buttocks, and heels to prevent pressure sores.

Rescuing a head- or neck-injured victim in the wild may be the toughest challenge you will ever face. It calls for all the stamina, courage, and ingenuity you possess, but your buddy will thank you.

CHAPTER 6

CHEST AND ABDOMINAL INJURIES

"The horse stumbled and Paul hurtled into the air. He came crashing down onto a log, landing on his right shoulder and hitting his head. . . . Dazed, Paul felt waves of nausea sweep over him. Jolts of pain stabbed his body. A cut over his eye was bleeding. Horrified, he saw that the blood pouring out of his mouth was foamy pink, which meant it came from his lungs. *Oh, God,* he thought as he fought to stay conscious, *I don't think I am going to make it.*"

—Sara Jameson, "Fight for Life in the Bitterroot Mountains," *Reader's Digest*, May 1996

Paul was is in trouble, and he knew it. Any serious chest or abdominal wound spells trouble in the wilderness. When he landed on that log, Paul fractured his collarbone and most of his ribs, and a rib fragment penetrated the lining of his lung, causing the chest cavity to fill up with blood and air and his lung to collapse. As bad as it was, it could have been worse—blunt chest trauma can also cause flail chest (see "Flail Chest," later in this chapter), rupture of the great vessels in the chest, and any number of other complications, including a lacerated liver or spleen. It's not hard to slip while crossing mountainous or rocky terrain, and it seems as though there is always a tree stump, tent pole, ice ax, or some other pointed object waiting to skewer you in the chest or abdomen as you tumble to the ground.

Many blunt or penetrating chest and abdominal injuries are life-threatening and require immediate evacuation. But some can be treated adequately in the field. Let's talk about how you size up such injuries in the wild and what you can do to treat them or stabilize them while preparing for evacuation.

CHEST INJURIES

The chest is a bellows, which *Webster's* defines as "a machine that by alternate expansion and contraction draws in air through a valve or orifice and expels it through a tube." When the chest muscles and *diaphragm* (the broad, flat muscle that separates the chest and abdominal cavities) contract, the chest expands, creating negative pressure in the chest cavity. Air rushes into the lungs through the mouth and respiratory tree for a few seconds and then is expelled as the chest muscles relax. Chest injuries have to be understood in terms of their effect on the chest bellows. Any injury that violates the integrity of the chest wall or causes an obstruction of the respiratory tree will make breathing difficult or impossible, and then it's "curtains for certain," unless you intervene to set things right in a hurry.

Evaluating Chest Injuries

You're going to have to rely on your senses of sight, touch, and hearing to evaluate a chest injury in the wild. But the signs of serious chest injury are rarely subtle. Physical diagnosis is based on the examiner's ability to inspect, feel, *percuss* (tap; see below), and listen for signs of disease or injury. Here's a crash course in the examination of the chest:

Inspect. As with any trauma victim, first check to make sure that she has an adequate airway and that she is breathing (see ABCs, page 4). Count the number of breaths per minute and note the breathing pattern. The normal breathing rate at rest is 12 to 20 breaths a minute. Very slow, fast, or irregular breathing denotes trouble. How is her color? If she's blue, she's not breathing effectively. Look at the neck. Are the veins distended? That may be a sign of a tension pneumothorax (see "Tension Pneumothorax" later in this chapter). Is the windpipe *(trachea)* in the center of the neck or pushed over to one side (another sign of tension pneumothorax)? Expose the chest and look for abrasions, lacerations, puncture wounds, or asymmetrical movement.

Feel. Gently run your hands over the chest, from the collarbones down to the abdomen, and from the breastbone to the backbone. Take note of any tender areas, signifying broken or contused ribs or breastbone. If there is a crunchy feeling (crepitus) over the bone, it's probably fractured. A bubbly feeling under the skin *(subcutaneous crepitus)* is a sure sign of a collapsed lung. What you're feeling is air that has leaked out of the lung and passed into the tissues under the skin. You might feel crepitus anywhere from the neck to the groin.

Percuss. Place the long finger of one hand at various points on the chest wall and tap the end of that finger with the long finger of your other hand. You should hear a slightly hollow sound from the collarbones to about the sixth ribs in the front, and from the shoulder blades to about the tenth ribs in the back. Don't worry about the exact pitch of the sound you hear as you percuss. The important thing to look for is marked differences from one side to the other. A *very* hollow percussion note indicates collapse of the lung, while a very dull sound indicates a chest cavity filled with blood *(hemothorax)*.

Listen. Put your ear to first one side of the chest, and then the other, and have the victim take several deep breaths. You should hear the sound of air moving into and out of each lung. A loud, harsh sound on one or both sides indicates obstruction of the upper airway. A wheezing or rattling sound suggests blood or fluid in the bronchial tubes or air sacs. The absence of sound on one side means that air is not moving into that lung, either because of a collapsed lung or a chest cavity filled with blood.

Blunt Chest Injuries

Rib Fractures. A fall onto a rock, log, or other hard surface can crack a rib or two. These are painful injuries that hurt more with deep breathing. Run your fingers over the injured area. A tender area with underlying crepitus most likely represents a fractured rib. You can confirm the diagnosis by pressing down on the breastbone with the victim lying on her back. If she complains of pain in a rib, it's fractured.

An uncomplicated rib fracture is a painful but not disabling injury if the pain can be controlled. But be wary of fractures of the first three ribs and the lower ribs on either side. They are often associated with injuries to the great vessels and liver and spleen respectively. And multiple fractured ribs should alert you to the possibility of serious underlying injury to the lung, heart, vessels, or abdominal organs. Victims with these injuries need to be evacuated (see Chapter 25).

Treatment of a simple rib fracture requires nothing more than a bottle of aspirin or some other analgesic. Rib belts and taping the ribs are helpful but should only be used intermittently. They restrict movement of the rib cage, causing underventilation of the lung, which can lead to pneumonia and other complications.

Separated Cartilage. The ribs don't join directly to the breastbone. Instead, they connect to a short segment of cartilage that then joins the breastbone. A hard blow to the front of the chest can cause a disruption of this rib-cartilage junction, or *separated cartilage.* These are very painful injuries and are hard to distinguish from fractured ribs. Treatment is the same as for a rib fracture.

Fractured Breastbone. It's not easy to break the breastbone. It requires the kind of high-energy impact you'd get from falling off a cliff or ramming a snowmobile into a tree at high speed. There will be tenderness and crepitus over the breastbone, and the chest may have a caved-in appearance. These are serious injuries and are often associated with contusions of the heart and lacerations of the lung. Attend to the ABCs and arrange for rapid medical evacuation (see Chapter 25). The victim will be able to breathe more easily in an upright position (this is true with any chest injury).

Flail Chest. When three or more consecutive ribs are each fractured in two or more places, there will be an unstable segment of chest wall. This is known as a *flail chest.* You can diagnose this injury by looking for paradoxical movement of the chest wall in the area of the injury: When the rest of the chest is expanding, the negative pressure in the chest cavity will pull in on the "floating" flail segment, and positive pressure will cause it to move outward with expiration. Obviously, this interferes with normal breathing. And the lung tissue under the flail segment is often contused or lacerated. Classically, these injuries are tolerated fairly well for a day or two, and then the victim goes into respiratory failure, often requiring artificial ventilation for a while. Old medical textbooks recommend splinting and bolstering the flail segment with tape, hooks, and sandbags; but these just make things worse. Give the victim analgesics and evacuate him before he deteriorates.

Pneumothorax. When air enters the chest cavity through a hole in the chest wall, or a fractured rib pokes a hole in the lung, pressure rises in the chest cavity until the lung collapses. This is a *pneumothorax.* The victim will be short of breath, breath sounds will be diminished on the affected side, and you'll hear a hollow sound when you percuss over the collapsed lung. These are painful injuries, but the victim may be able to walk out of the woods under her own power. All but small pneumothoraces require insertion of a chest tube to drain air from the chest cavity. You won't be doing this in the wilderness.

Tension Pneumothorax. When air leaks from a punctured lung into the chest cavity but can't escape, that side of the chest will fill up with air. The pressure increases to the point that the heart, great vessels, windpipe, and other midline structures are pushed over to the opposite side of the chest. The great veins in the chest become kinked, and venous blood can't return to the heart. The victim turns blue, the neck veins become engorged, and cardiovascular collapse ensues. This is called a *tension pneumothorax*. Death is imminent if the chest isn't decompressed immediately. (*Warning:* This technique requires a large, sterile needle and proper training.) The needle is inserted into the space between the second and third ribs at any point lateral to the nipple. Guide the needle over the top of the third rib and then perpendicularly down into the chest until you hear a gush of air as the needle enters the chest cavity. The victim's appearance will improve dramatically after this procedure, but she's still not out of the woods. Leave the needle in place and make arrangements for a hasty evacuation to a hospital (see Chapter 25) where a chest tube can be inserted.

Hemothorax. Rib fractures can cause bleeding from the artery that runs along the undersurface of the rib or from a punctured lung. The blood collects in the chest cavity, causing a *hemothorax*. The victim will be hurtin' for certain, and short of breath. If you tap over the affected side, it will sound dull. An isolated hemothorax is not an immediate life-threatening injury. Blood loss into the chest cavity is rarely enough to cause shock, and respiratory distress is usually not severe. There's nothing you can do for the guy with hemothorax except to make him as comfortable as possible while awaiting evacuation.

Penetrating Chest Wounds

A ski pole through your chest can ruin your skiing season. Reports of skiers impaling themselves on poles during a bad fall are not uncommon. Other outdoors enthusiasts transfix themselves on ice axes, arrows, or tent poles. This is serious business. Even if the offending object misses the heart, lungs, and great vessels (an unlikely proposition), at the very least it's going to poke a hole in the chest wall and create a pneumothorax or *hemopneumothorax* (blood and air in the chest cavity). And if it punctures the chest below the nipple line, there's an excellent chance that it will skewer the liver, spleen, or other abdominal organs.

In the old Indian movies, they'd just yank an arrow out of the guy's chest and he'd be all set to return to the action. That's *not* the thing to do. The impaling object has created a channel through the tissues. But as long as it occupies that channel, bleeding will be controlled by the "tamponading" effect it has on torn blood vessels. Always leave the arrow, pole, or what have you exactly where it is.

One of the most dangerous chest wounds is the *sucking chest wound.* If the hole in the chest wall approaches the diameter of the windpipe, it becomes impossible for the bellows mechanism to create negative pressure in the chest cavity, and the lungs won't expand. Instead, air is sucked through the hole in the chest into the chest cavity. It's like trying to run a vacuum cleaner when there's a large hole in the canister (see Figure 6-1).

You have to act fast when confronted with a sucking chest wound. Cover it with the cleanest bandage available—a shirt, towel, or even your hand if necessary. After the victim is stabilized you can take the time to apply a sterile, petrolatum gauze dressing (Adaptic, for example) right over the wound, and cover it with a sterile 4 × 4 gauze pad. Tape the pad on 3 sides, so that air can escape but not enter through the wound. (If you seal it up tight, you'll create a tension pneumothorax [see page 49]—a dangerous situation.) As with any chest wound, these people have to be medically evacuated ASAP (see Chapter 25).

ABDOMINAL INJURIES

Blunt Abdominal Injuries

Blunt abdominal injuries are rarely as dramatic or immediately life-threatening as chest injuries. But they can be just as deadly. It's rare for a chest injury to lead to hemorrhagic shock. But you can easily lose a couple of quarts of blood from a ruptured spleen or liver. As blood collects in the rigid chest cavity, the pressure within the cavity increases until the bleeding vessels are "tamponaded." But as blood collects in the abdominal cavity, the abdominal wall stretches, and impressive amounts of blood can be lost before pressure rises within the cavity. By then, it may be too late to do anything about it if you're in the wilderness.

The tricky thing about blunt abdominal injuries is that they are rarely obvious. These injuries are hard enough to diagnose in a hospital setting with high-tech diagnostic equipment, let alone in the deep woods when all you have to work with is your brain, your eyes, and your hands. The key is to know when to look for these injuries and then to examine the victim carefully at repeat intervals. Obviously, if your buddy slips and falls belly-down on a tree stump, you're going to think about blunt abdominal trauma. But you should also think about blunt abdominal trauma if he cracks his breastbone or a few lower ribs. Pain in the abdomen referred to the left shoulder should alert you to a ruptured spleen.

First, look for signs of shock: thready pulse; blue fingertips; cold, clammy skin; agitation; and rapid breathing. Then, if you have no reason to suspect a spinal injury, gently roll

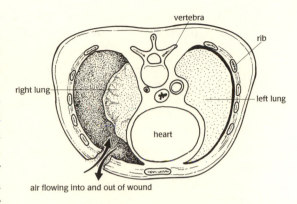

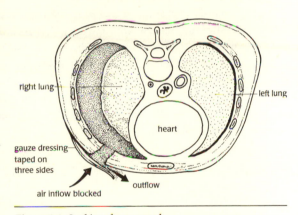

Figure 6-1. Sucking chest wound.

him onto his back and expose his abdomen. Note any bruises or discoloration and check for rib fractures. Is his belly soft, or are his muscles rigid? Gently press under the rib cage on the right (liver) and left (spleen), the pit of the stomach, and both lower quadrants. A bruised abdominal wall may cause localized tenderness, but if you find persistent rigidity and tenderness, along with signs of early shock, you've got to assume that he has a blunt injury. Treat him as you would any shock victim (see pages 4–5) and prepare to evacuate him. (A swollen, tight abdominal wall is a very late sign of abdominal bleeding and will be accompanied by signs of late shock.)

A blow to the flank or the back can injure the kidneys. The hallmark of a contused or ruptured kidney is blood in the urine *(hematuria)*. If the kidney is just contused, the hematuria will stop within a few hours. If the kidney is lacerated or ruptured, it may continue to bleed, causing persistent hematuria and, eventually, signs of shock. Treat the shock and prepare to evacuate the victim.

Penetrating Abdominal Injuries

You don't have to be a surgeon to diagnose a penetrating abdominal injury. There are usually plenty of clues. These are the important things to keep in mind:

- Any wound from the nipple line to the groin can involve the abdominal contents.
- Gunshot exit wounds are larger than entrance wounds. Look for exit wounds by examining the back, chest, and legs.
- A shotgun blast at close range can create a big defect in the abdominal wall, causing bowel to protrude through the wound. *Don't replace it!* Stool will soil the abdominal cavity, causing peritonitis. Just cover eviscerated bowel with moist dressings.
- These injuries need prompt surgical exploration and repair. Apply sterile dressings to all wounds and evacuate the victim as quickly as possible (see Chapter 25).

PAUL DAFFER, TRUE GRIT PERSONIFIED

After being thrown from his horse and making a grueling three-day hike through the Selway-Bitterroot Wilderness, Paul stumbled out of the woods and drove himself to a ranch house. He was taken by ambulance to a hospital fifty miles away, and then flown to a trauma center in Boise, Idaho, where he was treated for multiple rib fractures, a hemopneumothorax, and a fractured clavicle.

CHAPTER 7

EYE, EAR, NOSE, AND THROAT PROBLEMS

"A small hurt in the eye is a great one."
 —English proverb

THE EYES HAVE IT: EYE INJURIES IN THE WILD

Poets call the eye the "window to the soul." True enough. But the eye is much more than that. It's also a sophisticated camera, with a dust cover (eyelids), a lens system, a variable aperture system (pupil and iris), and "film" (retina). We're not talking Instamatic here. The human eye is "high tech," with features you won't find in those fancy Japanese cameras—such as automatic focus, depth perception, an automatic light meter, and voluntary and involuntary fixation systems and "pursuit movement" that allows us to (1) look for a red-crested warbler in a barberry thicket, (2) keep an eye on it while it decides whether to sit tight or fly away, and (3) lock onto the bird when it takes to the air.

You've got to take care of optical equipment like that when you're running around out in the woods. And there's a lot more to it than dodging swinging branches. Your eyes are vulnerable to a wide range of injuries in the outdoors, everything from frozen corneas to solar retinitis. Let's take a look at a few of these ocular hazards.

Corneal Foreign Bodies and Abrasions

These are the most common eye injuries in the wild. The *cornea* is the clear membrane that overlies the *iris*, the colored part of the eye. The nerve endings are packed in there like fly fishermen on a prime trout stream on opening day, making it the most sensitive structure in the human body. When the wind blows a grain of sand in your eye, that grain can feel like a boulder. It will make your eye water and the lid snap shut like the jaws of a bear trap. Most often, tears will wash out sand and other foreign bodies. That's the good news. The bad news is that they are sometimes caught under the upper lid and are dragged back and forth across the cornea a few times before they are washed away, leaving you with a painful corneal abrasion. The important thing to know about a corneal abrasion is that it feels *exactly* like a corneal foreign body.

Here is what you do if sand, grit, or embers blow into your eye: Have your partner take a good look at the eye. She should first check the shape and symmetry of the pupils and do a rough vision check (she should ask you to count fingers or read newsprint). Then she should search carefully for foreign bodies, checking the cornea, under both lids, and in the corners. (Use a cotton swab or a match stem to invert the upper lid, a favorite hiding place for grit.) If she sees something, she should try to flush it out with a gentle stream of clean water. If that doesn't do it, she should pull the upper lid down over the lashes of the lower lid. Or she can use a cotton swab or the corner of a piece of cloth to lift a piece of sand off the cornea (see Figure 7-1).

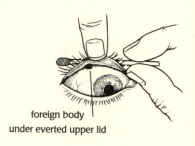

foreign body
under everted upper lid

cornea

sclera covered

If the pain persists, you probably have a corneal abrasion. Cover the eye with a tight eye patch for 12 to 24 hours and avoid bright light. If the eye is still painful after being patched for 24 hours, there may be a small particle embedded in the cornea. It will have to be removed by a physician as soon as possible.

Blunt Injuries to the Eye

The eye is set back in a protective bony casement, but swinging branches, flying rocks, and fists all can inflict devastating damage. Lacerations, puncture wounds, and contusions are usually obvious. *Hyphema* is bleeding in the front chamber of

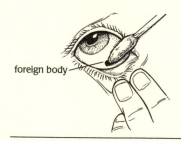

foreign body

Figure 7-1. Removing a foreign body from the eye.

the eye, just behind the cornea. It can lead to glaucoma and bloodstaining of the cornea. Fluid in the back chamber of the eye seeping through a tear in the *retina* (the light-sensitive membrane lining the inner eyeball) causes the thin retina to peel off the back of the eye like loose wallpaper. This is known as a *detached retina*. A *dislocated lens* is usually pushed backward, but you may see it in the front chamber of the eye.

These are all severe, vision-threatening injuries. There is not much you can do about them except to gently wash dirt and debris away from the eye with disinfected warm water, cover *both* eyes with opaque eye shields (to minimize eye movement), and evacuate the victim to the nearest medical facility (see Chapter 25). Never attempt to remove a foreign body that is embedded inside the eyeball. If a fishhook, thorn, or some other large object is embedded in the eye, do *not* attempt to remove it. Prevent further damage by taping a Styrofoam or paper cup over the eye and then evacuate to the nearest hospital.

Snow Blindness

Snow blindness is sunburn of the corneas. You're more likely to get it at high altitudes, where ultraviolet radiation (UVR) is more intense (UVR intensity increases 4 percent for each 300-meter [984-foot] increase in altitude) and where snow and ice reflect up to 85 percent of incident UVR into your eyes. UVR in the range of 280 to 320 nanometers (known as ultraviolet B, or UVB) is absorbed by the thin layer of cells on the surface of the cornea. These cells swell and rupture, and the cornea becomes hazy. You won't realize what's going on for 6 to 12 hours. Then your eyes will begin to water and redden, your lids will swell, and you'll feel as though you have hot cinders in your eyes. UVR in the range of 320 to 400 nanometers (ultraviolet A, or UVA) is transmitted to the lens, where it can cause cataracts over a period of time.

Snow blindness is temporary, and the corneas heal spontaneously in about 24 hours. But there are some things you can do to relieve the pain. First, remove contact lenses. Then, apply cold compresses to the eyes and take an analgesic tablet (e.g., acetaminophen, ibuprofen). Avoid the problem altogether by wearing sunglasses (more on eyewear later). If you forget your sunglasses, you can fashion a crude pair by cutting narrow slits in cardboard or some other material and strapping it to your head with string or elastic.

Frozen Cornea

This is a windchill injury. You can get it by trying to force your eyes open while walking into a stiff breeze on a very cold day or while riding a snowmobile.

The symptoms are similar to those of a corneal injury or snow blindness: blurred vision; red, watery eyes; lid spasm; and sensitivity to light. There is no pain, however, until the corneas start to rewarm. Treatment consists of rapid rewarming with warm (104°F/40°C) compresses.

Solar Retinitis

Solar retinitis is what you get when you stare at the sun, especially during a solar eclipse. The lens of the eye acts as a magnifying glass, focusing an intense beam of light on the retina. It can actually burn a hole in the retina, causing a permanent blind spot in the center of your visual field.

Contact Lenses

Contact lens wearers know about the contact lens corollary to Murphy's Law: Anything that *can* go wrong with contact lenses *will* go wrong at the worst possible time. Like the lens that pops out when you're trying to land a trophy lake trout, or the lens that becomes "lost" somewhere in your eyeball just as your kayak approaches a rough stretch of whitewater. But you shouldn't have any problems if you remember the basics of contact lens care and handling. Always wash your hands before handling the lenses, store them in the prescribed manner, don't wear them for longer periods than you would at home, and don't put a scratched or damaged lens in your eye.

The first place to look for a "lost" lens is in the eye. It may drift off the cornea and under one of the lids. If you don't see it, it's not in the eye. (Contrary to common belief, contact lenses can't slide into the back of the eyeball and pass into the brain. The *conjunctiva,* the clear membrane that covers the white part of the eye, folds back on itself at the periphery of the eyeball, forming a *cul-de-sac,* or blind pouch, that prevents this from happening.)

The cornea gets oxygen directly from the air, so if you are rock climbing in the high Rockies, or fishing for golden trout in some high lake in the Sierra Nevada where the air is thinner, you may have to cut back on your wearing time.

It is important to remove contact lenses from the eyes of anyone who is unconscious. Remove a soft lens by gently pinching the lens between two fingers and lifting it off. Remove a hard lens by placing a finger on the skin at the outer corner of the eye and pulling outward. The lens will pop out.

Sunglasses

Before you go out and buy those new hiking boots or spinning rod, invest a few bucks in the health of your eyes. Get yourself a good pair of sunglasses to protect yourself from snow blindness, cataracts, wind, dust, and glare. You'll need a pair that blocks 85 to 95 percent of visible light and close to 100 percent of UVR. Glass, polycarbonate, and plastic each have advantages and disadvantages you can discuss with your optician. You can also ask him or her about "gradient" and photochromic lenses. Polarizing lenses reduce the glare from snowfields and lake surfaces. Lens color is a matter of personal preference. The frames should be metal, silicone-graphite, nylon, or Lexan— not plastic. Side shields and nose protectors are recommended for desert travel and alpine trekking.

And don't forget your regular glasses. Plastic lenses absorb 90 percent of UVR, glass lenses about 80 percent. That's good, but you can now buy lenses that block out virtually all UVR. Or you can have your optician treat your current lenses with a UVR filtering dye.

EAR, NOSE, AND THROAT DISORDERS

Swimmer's Ear

This is a bacterial infection of the outer ear canal. It is common during the summer months because heat and constant moisture break down the natural barriers to infection in the inner part of the external ear canal. Swimming, frequent showers, and mechanical trauma all predispose to infection with strep and pseudomonas bacteria. Swimmer's ear can cause a sense of fullness in the ear, diminished hearing, intense earache, and a soupy yellow-white discharge. Pulling on the ear lobe causes intense pain.

Treatment of swimmer's ear starts with careful irrigation of the canal with sterile water and instillation of several drops of vinegar or Burow's solution 4 times a day. Cortisporic otic solution (available by prescription) is even better, if you happen to have a bottle. You can avoid swimmer's ear by keeping the ears dry, not using earplugs or cotton swabs, and by instilling a little vinegar and rubbing alcohol in your ears after each swim or shower.

Dizziness

"Dizziness" means different things to different people. But if you feel as though you have been on a merry-go-round *(vertigo)* every time you lift or turn your head, there is a good chance that you have *labyrinthitis*. This is a short-lived disorder of the organs of balance in the inner ear. It usually lags a head cold by a few days, and may be accompanied by nausea and vomiting. Meclizine, 25 mg 3 or 4 times a day, is the treatment of choice.

Ruptured Eardrum

It's not hard to get poked in the ear with a branch while working your way through dense vegetation. If the branch perforates your eardrum, you will have sudden, intense pain in the ear, vertigo, hearing loss, and bleeding from the ear. The branch may have damaged the small bones *(ossicles)* in the middle ear, so the ear should be examined by a physician as soon as practicable.

If you get cuffed on the ear during a tussle with your buddy and notice bleeding from the ear and a loss of hearing, the eardrum is probably perforated. In these situations, the eardrum usually heals nicely if left alone. Never put *anything* in the ear if a perforated eardrum is suspected.

A blow to the ear can cause a pool of blood *(hematoma)* to collect under the skin of the *auricle* (the large, projecting portion of the external ear). A large hematoma will lead to "cauliflower ears" if it is not drained. Cleanse the skin with antiseptic solution and then insert a sterile needle into the center of the hematoma. Drain as much of the blood as possible. Apply a compression bandage and an icebag to the ear.

Few things are as maddening as the feel and sound of an insect crawling around inside your ear. Resist the temptation to squash the bug with a cotton swab. That just creates a mess and can lead to a ruptured eardrum. Instead, take the kinder, gentler approach: Have a buddy flush the critter out with warm water.

Nosebleed

Most nosebleeds will stop if the patient sits up, leans forward, and squeezes the soft part of her nose for 10 or 15 minutes. If that doesn't work, have her clear her nose. Then use a penlight to try to identify the bleeding site. Usually it will be in *Kiesselbach's area,* an area in the front part of the septum where there is a rich supply of blood vessels (see Figure 7-2). Once you have found the bleeding site, cauterize it with a silver nitrate stick. If the bleeding persists, coat a nasal tampon (I recommend Merocel brand) with antibiotic ointment, insert it into the nose, and drip water on its end until it is fully engorged with water. The tampon will

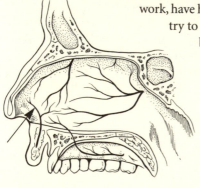

Figure 7-2. Kiesselbach's area.

impede sinus drainage, so administer amoxicillin, 250 mg every 8 hours, to prevent sinus infection. If blood is draining down the back of the throat and you can't find a bleeding site, the victim may have a *posterior nosebleed.* Insert a Merocel nasal tampon as above. If that doesn't control the bleeding, you need to get her to medical help ASAP (see Chapter 25). If the tampon *does* control the bleeding, leave it in place for 3 days and then remove it after first making certain that it is engorged with water.

Food Caught in the Throat

We talked about "café coronaries" in Chapter 1. A piece of meat can go down the right way and *still* give you fits. Large pieces of meat or bread can get hung up in the esophagus and cause terrific spasms. More than one patient has been admitted to the hospital with the diagnosis of heart attack, when all he really had was a hunk of filet mignon stuck in his esophagus.

If you have a piece of meat or some other food stuck in your esophagus, you may choose to ride it out if it's not interfering with your breathing and you're still able to swallow. The food will plop down into the stomach within a few hours. A few sips of water or a cup of gelatin, yogurt, or some other semi-solid food will stimulate the swallowing reflex and help to push the food down into the stomach.

If you are drooling and your chest feels as though you swallowed a keg of nails, you have an obstructed esophagus and need to get to a hospital right away. This is a dangerous situation. An obstructed esophagus may perforate, and you might breathe food and saliva into your lungs. If nothing else, you will become dehydrated from lack of water.

Adolph's meat tenderizer is a traditional remedy for food caught in the esophagus. There's no doubt that it works. The problem is, it can burn a hole in your esophagus. Save it for the roast.

Fish and chicken bones can get hung up in the upper esophagus. They are not big enough to obstruct the airway, but they can make swallowing a real pain. Have your buddy shine a bright light into the back of your throat. He should be able to see the bone overlying one of the tonsils and remove it with a cotton swab.

Here are some tips to keep you from biting off more than you can chew:

- Cut your food into small pieces and chew slowly.
- Don't laugh and talk while you're chewing.
- Ease up on alcohol before and during meals.

CHAPTER 8

HYPOTHERMIA

"A certain fear of death, dull and oppressive, came to him. This fear quickly became poignant as he realized that it was no longer a matter of freezing his fingers and toes, or of losing his hands and feet, but that it was a matter of life and death with the chances against him. This threw him into a panic, and he turned and ran up the creek bed along the old, dim trail. He ran blindly, without intention, in such fear as he had never known in his life. . . . Without doubt, he would lose some fingers and toes and some of his face; but the boys would take care of him, and save the rest of him when he got there. And at the same time there was another thought in his mind that said he would never get to the camp . . . that it was too many miles away, that the freezing had too great a start on him, and that he would soon be stiff and dead."

—Jack London, "To Build a Fire"

A few years ago, during the spring salmon run on Lake George, a man capsized his small aluminum boat while trying to land a large fish. He was in the frigid water for an hour before he was rescued. It appeared that he was going to do alright when he climbed on deck and went below to warm up. He collapsed in the cabin and died of hypothermia.

Cold is a relentless enemy. You don't really defeat it, you survive it. If you're lucky. It cannot be denied, only stalled. If you're exposed to it long enough, it will beat you. Probing with icy fingers, it finds a chink in your armor and exploits the breach in your defenses until it has sucked the warmth out of your marrow, dooming you to the fate of the man in Jack London's classic story.

Whether you are bobbing in the chilly waters of Lake George or stranded in a snowstorm on a Rocky Mountain peak, your body is going to be under siege from the cold. It will mount a feverish struggle to preserve warmth, but once your core temperature drops below 95°F (35°C), you're hypothermic. Then you are on a slippery slope, and it's only a matter of time before your body's caloric reserve is depleted, your internal organs shut down, and your heart stops beating.

MECHANISMS OF HEAT LOSS

Actually, there isn't any such thing as "cold." What we perceive as cold is merely the absence of heat. But it is convenient to think of cold as a kind of magnet that pulls the heat out of your body through the following mechanisms:

- *Conduction:* The direct transfer of heat from the body to a cooler object. Normally not a major mechanism of heat loss, it is *the* major cause of heat loss during cold-water immersion.
- *Convection:* The loss of heat by circulation of the air or liquid in which the body is immersed. Movement of the medium breaks up the thin layer of warm particles on the surface of the body. A fan cools by convection, and windchill plays a big role in cooling on windy days.
- *Radiation:* The loss of heat through emitted energy. It normally accounts for over half of the body's heat loss.
- *Evaporation:* Heat lost when sweat or water on the body's surface is changed into steam. For each gram of water that evaporates from the skin, 580 calories of heat are lost. Perspiration increases evaporative heat loss, as does wet clothing on a windy day.

RISING TO THE CHALLENGE

Humans are warm-blooded animals. We keep our internal temperature right around 98.6°F (37°C). We even have a thermostat, a part of the brain called the *thermoregulatory center.* When "cold" signals arrive from the millions of thermal sensors in the skin and elsewhere in the body, the thermostat, acting through the sympathetic nervous system (see Chapter 1, page 2), does a number of things to increase heat production and decrease heat loss:

1. The muscles start to shiver, increasing heat production five-fold. Vigorous exercise increases heat production by 1,000 percent.
2. Blood vessels in the skin and limbs constrict. This limits radiant heat loss from the body surface, but even more importantly, it preserves the flow

of warm blood to a core of vital organs (brain, heart, lungs, and digestive organs), and shunts blood from the cold shell of skin, muscle, and fat.
3. The heart beats faster and harder.
4. Sweating stops, decreasing evaporative heat loss.
5. The metabolic rate increases up to six-fold, increasing the heat generated by the chemical reactions in each cell.

THAT SLIPPERY SLOPE

The body's furious response to the cold is like turning on your car heater when you're stranded. It's great while it lasts, but sooner or later you're going to run out of gas. When that happens, the situation deteriorates in a hurry. Eventually, the muscles become too tired and too energy-starved to shiver. They become stiff and sluggish when the core temperature drops below 90°F (32.2°C). And the heart and metabolism slow, fluid shifts out of the circulation into the spaces between the cells, fluid is lost through the kidneys, and the blood pressure drops. With further cooling, the brain becomes sluggish, and the heart becomes irritable. Below 80°F (26.7°C), you become stiff and unresponsive and have no detectable pulses. You may mistakenly be declared dead.

PREDISPOSING CAUSES

Here are some of the things that can help to turn you into Frosty the Snowman:
- *Exposure to the elements:* You can become hypothermic in the Yukon Territory just about any day, and you can become hypothermic in Georgia or anywhere else when the conditions are right. That means cool temperatures (not necessarily below freezing), high wind, and low humidity.
- *Cold-water immersion:* Water is a much greater heat conductor than air, and you'll cool at least 100 times faster in water than in air at the same temperature. This effect is compounded by movement and exposure of areas of high heat loss, such as the head, neck and face.
- *Immobility:* A fracture or other disabling injury is a double whammy: not only does it interfere with one of your first lines of defense against hypothermia (increased muscle activity and shivering), it also makes it harder for you to get out of the cold.
- *Drugs and alcohol:* Alcohol and cold are compatible—if you are a lizard. Lizards and other cold-blooded creatures don't have to worry about a thermostat. They just go with the flow. Alcohol screws up the thermo-

stat, inhibits shivering, impairs judgment, and dilates the blood vessels in the skin. Those Saint Bernards they used to send out with the whiskey barrel around their necks always came back alone.

HOW TO RECOGNIZE HYPOTHERMIA

To diagnose hypothermia, you have to think of it. If your partner has been buried under an avalanche, you are going to be thinking about it. If she's been sitting out in the bay in a kayak on a cold, blustery day, you may not. But you should always be thinking "hypothermia" whenever one of the predisposing factors is in play.

The most reliable sign of *mild hypothermia* (core temperature 93.2°F to 96.8°F [34°C to 36°C]) is shivering. But you must be sensitive to some of the more subtle signs, such as thick or slurred speech, confusion, difficulty keeping up with the group, and incoordination. The victim of mild hypothermia may have trouble buttoning a shirt or hammering tent stakes into the ground, and her skin may be cool to the touch.

A person who has been shivering, but has stopped and now is confused and indifferent to her surroundings, has moderate hypothermia. Her core temperature is between 86°F and 93.2°F (30°C to 34°C), and her skin is cold to the touch, and pale or blue. She's forgetful and neglects to cover up from the cold, leaving her jacket unzipped and her mittens and hat off. She may even undress or make other dangerous errors in judgment. She may become apathetic or stuporous, and she is clumsy. If she becomes severely hypothermic (core temperature falls below 86°F/30°C), she will lose all voluntary motion and reflexes, and will not respond to pain. Her blood pressure plummets, her pulse slows, and she is at great risk for ventricular fibrillation (a lethal, chaotic heart rhythm). The lowest core temperature recorded in an accidental hypothermia survivor was 60.8°F (16°C).

✦ Treatment

When a person is drowning, get him out of the water first and then worry about resuscitating him. It's the same story with hypothermia. The first order of business is to get the victim out of the cold and wind, remove any wet clothing, and take measures to limit further heat loss. Cover up his head and neck and make sure he's not in contact with the cold ground.

The next priority is to estimate the severity of his hypothermia. (This is not an academic distinction. If you try rewarming a victim of severe hypothermia in the field, you may kill him.)

If he is suffering from *mild* or *moderate hypothermia,* give him dry clothing and have him crawl inside a sleeping bag, either alone or with someone else. Or, you can throw a blanket around him and let him sit by the fire. Hot toddies are out, but you can give him a cup of hot cocoa or cider and some high-carbohydrate food to stoke his metabolic furnace.

The victim of *severe hypothermia* has to be handled the same way you'd handle an angry porcupine: *very gently.* The heart becomes irritable when it's cold. Physical exertion can cause cold, acidic blood in the cold shell to surge into the heart, causing it to fibrillate. Get him out of the elements, but don't let him get up or move around. Gently place him in a sleeping bag or under a blanket with one or two other people (with his chest in contact with his rescuers' chests) while you arrange for medical evacuation (see Chapter 25).

If evacuation isn't feasible, you will have to rewarm him in the field, using the radiant heat from a fire, chemical "hot packs" if you have them, hot-water bottles, warmed stones, or other warmed objects. Hot baths are not a good idea for a victim of severe hypothermia. They cause the blood vessels in the skin and extremities to dilate and fill with warm blood from the core. The blood volume is already compromised by loss of fluid into the tissues and from the kidneys, so this leads to *rewarming shock.* And when the now-cold blood returns to the heart, it can cause a paradoxical temperature *afterdrop* and fibrillation.

CPR and Hypothermia

The victim of hypothermia may be stiff, unresponsive, and pale, and may have fixed and dilated pupils. But he is not dead until he is warm and dead. Do CPR *unless* he has a lethal injury, his chest is frozen, he is breathing or moving, or doing CPR would put his rescuers in danger (for CPR procedures, see pages 8–10).

You may elect *not* to do CPR if his core temperature is below 82.4°F (28°C) and equal to the ambient temperature, he's been immersed in water for more than 50 minutes, or you are more than four hours from a hospital.

PREVENTING HYPOTHERMIA: DRESS FOR SUCCESS

Your body may be a temple, but it is also a heat-generating machine. If you are physically fit, you will be able to maintain your body heat longer on the trail, and you'll have a better chance of getting to shelter if the weather turns nasty. Get yourself into shape with a good aerobic and muscle conditioning program before you answer the call of the wild in winter.

Drink plenty of fluids when you're out in the cold. Your metabolic furnace cannot run at full capacity if you are dehydrated. And dehydration increases the risk of frostbite.

You should also keep that metabolic furnace stoked with plenty of calories, especially the carbohydrate variety. And make sure you bring some snacks along with you on the trail.

When it comes to hypothermia, clothing choices are critical. Exercise is great, but jumping jacks alone aren't going to do it. Clothing can dramatically decrease conductive and convective heat loss. Air is a great insulator, so the key is to maintain multiple layers of warm air around your body. And the best way to do that is by wearing multiple layers of clothing, which you can shed or add to as weather conditions change. The last thing you want to do is to sweat excessively. That accelerates evaporative heat loss. You can doff hat and gloves when you start to feel warm, and then loosen up your collar or take off your jacket and one or two underlayers as conditions dictate.

The best cold-weather materials are wool (which retains its insulating properties when wet), down, foam, Orlon, Dacron, polyester, Gore-Tex, Thinsulate, taslanized nylon, and polypropylene. Cotton wets easily, and its "wicking" action causes rapid cooling. You'd survive longer stark naked than in wet cotton in the cold.

Your cold-weather wardrobe might look something like this: wool underwear (polypropylene, Capilene, or olefin are good choices if you anticipate working up a sweat); wool pants and shirts; a wool sweater; a jacket or vest filled with down, Quallofil, or some other lofting material and having a two-way zipper; a hooded nylon or Gore-Tex parka or windbreaker; windproof and water-repellent wind pants; two pair of socks (polypropylene liner and wool); a wool stocking cap or balaclava; wool or wool-lined polypropylene mittens with nylon or Gore-Tex shells; and rubber-soled, leather climbing boots or winter mountaineering boots with a felt or foam inner lining and a leather, plastic, or nylon outer shell. Select boots with thick soles and insoles to impede conductive heat loss through the feet, and plenty of toe room. Tight boots cut off the circulation to the toes, and leave no room for a layer of insulating air between sock and uppers.

IMMERSION HYPOTHERMIA

Cold water is a relentless killer. It knifes through your clothing, overwhelms the insulating capacity of your subcutaneous fat, and sucks the warmth out of your very core. And water doesn't have to have ice floes in it to qualify as "cold water." You can become hypothermic in 77°F (25°C) water. Most American coastal waters and lakes are cooler than that *year-round,* even the waters off Honolulu and San Diego.

There is a common misconception that falling into frigid water is tantamount to instant death. Actually, that's rare. When it happens, it's because the *gasp reflex* causes you to inhale air and drown. The fact is, you can survive for several hours in 50°F to 60°F (10°C to 15.6°C) water, depending on your body type and other factors. The body's core temperature remains stable for 15 minutes in cold water—time enough to save yourself, if you know what to do.

Here's what happens when you fall into cold water:

1. The cold water on your skin stimulates the respiratory center in the brain, causing you to gasp and then hyperventilate for a minute or two. All that respiratory stimulation diminishes your breath-holding capacity to 15 to 25 seconds—not good if you're trapped underwater.

2. The blood vessels in your skin and muscles constrict, shutting off blood flow to the periphery and forming that cold "shell" insulating a warm "core." Your skin turns blue, you break out in goosebumps, and your movements become sluggish, making it harder for you to pull yourself out of the water. Fine motor tasks, such as operating a radio and using signaling devices, become impossible.

3. You begin to shiver. Shivering is the body's main defense against hypothermia in air, but in water it's a mixed blessing. It increases metabolic heat production by 500 percent, but it also increases the flow of water between skin and clothing, accelerating convective heat loss (the "flushing effect").

4. As your core temperature drops below 90°F (32.2°C), you stop shivering and you start to get a little wacky. You become confused, your judgment becomes impaired, and you may even hallucinate. Immersion victims have been known to remove their personal flotation devices (PFDs) and clothing, or attempt to swim for shore, even when shore is not in sight.

Because of its greater thermal conductivity and specific heat, you cool 100 times faster in water than in air at the same temperature. The head and extremities cool most rapidly because of their greater surface-to-volume ratio, but heat loss from the trunk is more critical to survival. Heat escapes quickly from the groin and neck, where blood passes through large vessels immediately under the skin's surface.

Not everyone who goes into the drink cools at the same rate. How fast a person cools depends on several factors:

- *Body fat:* This is *the* most important factor. Eskimos know what an excellent insulator blubber is. The fatter you are, the slower you cool in water.
- *Body type:* Big people cool slower than smaller people, and kids cool faster than adults. Women have more fat but usually are smaller, so they cool at the same rate as men.
- *Physical fitness:* A double-edged sword. Cardiovascular fitness may help you to handle the stress of cold-water immersion, but this benefit is outweighed by the fact that fit people have less subcutaneous fat for insulation. So the fat and unfit probably have at least as good a shot at surviving immersion as the triathlete.
- *Water temperature:* The colder the water, the faster you cool.
- *Clothing:* Conventional thermal clothing, designed to take advantage of the insulating effect of pockets of air trapped between skin and garment, is of little value in water. These air pockets are history as soon as you hit the drink. But protective clothing has been developed that minimizes the loss of trapped air.

  "Wet" garments trap air in bubbles in tight-fitting wetsuits or in loose-fitting coveralls or flotation jackets. Insulated coveralls are a good choice for recreational fishermen and kayakers in cooler waters. They have nylon covers, closed-cell foam insulation, foam neoprene hoods, reflective tape, 29 to 38 pounds of buoyancy, and fit like snowmobile suits. They are easy to put on, don't hinder movement, and provide protection from cold air as well as cold water.

  "Dry" garments (survival suits) have watertight wrist, ankle, and neck seals that keep covered areas dry. They provide twice the insulation of insulated coveralls, and their effectiveness isn't diminished in rough seas. (The cooling rate in "wet" garments nearly doubles in rough water due to the "flushing effect.") Although drysuits are cumbersome for recreational anglers, kayakers and canoeists paddling cold waters depend on them.
- *Alcohol:* If you have been drinking alcohol, you are more apt to fall off a dock or out of a boat. In that case, you're more likely to drown than die of hypothermia. And while alcohol doesn't significantly increase your

cooling rate in water, it may impair your judgment and coordination to the point that you can't do the things you need to do to save yourself.

Figure 8-1. The HELP (Heat Escape Lessening Posture) position.

- *Behavior:* Swimming and treading water increase the flow of warm blood from the body's core to the muscles, breaking down the "shell" insulation and increasing the cooling rate 35 to 50 percent. Exercise also accelerates cooling by increasing the flow of cold water under protective clothing. If you are wearing a PFD, you won't have to tread water or swim.

If you go in the drink, stay with the boat, and get out of the water if you can. At least pull yourself as far out of the water as possible. Try to conserve energy and body heat, and exercise as little as possible. Avoid the open body position in the water, cover the sides of the chest and groin, and go into *Heat Escape Lessening Posture (HELP)* position (see Figure 8-1). A group of people should huddle in a tight circle, with children in the center. Remember, 75 percent of heat loss is from the head; cover it and keep it clear of the water.

The best way to rescue a person who has fallen through the ice is to assume the prone position and reach out to her with a stick. Keep your feet anchored on the shore so that you aren't pulled into the water (see Figure 8-2).

When the rescue boat pulls up and plucks you from the lake, you may be out of the water, but you're still not out of the woods. The fisherman who collapsed after being pulled out of Lake George died of vascular collapse. Walking or any other physical exercise, jarring movements, rewarming shock, and core temperature afterdrop can all cause sudden death. That's what happened to the salmon fisherman when he walked across the deck of the rescue boat.

The cold-water immersion victim has to be handled very carefully. *Move him as little as possible.* Keep him horizontal, do CPR if necessary (see

Figure 8-2. Rescuing someone who has fallen through the ice.

pages 8–10), and keep him from getting any colder by *gently* removing wet clothing, drying his skin, and keeping him out of the wind. Then apply warm compresses (soak towels in warm water) to the neck, sides of the chest, and groin. Or take your clothes off and get into a sleeping bag or under some blankets with him. A hot bath or shower, if available, is fine for moderate hypothermia. If he has severe hypothermia, arrange for medical evacuation (see Chapter 25).

CHAPTER 9

FROSTBITE AND OTHER COLD INJURIES

"... Already all sensation had gone out of his feet. To build the fire he had been forced to remove his mittens, and the fingers had quickly gone numb. His pace of four miles an hour had kept his heart pumping blood to the surface of his body and to all the extremities. But the instant he stopped, the action of the pump eased down. The cold of space smote the unprotected tip of the planet, and he, being on that unprotected tip, received the full force of the blow. The blood of his body recoiled before it. The blood was alive, like the dog, and like the dog it wanted to hide away and cover itself up from the fearful cold. So long as he walked four miles an hour, he pumped that blood, willy-nilly, to the surface; but now it ebbed away and sank down into the recesses of his body. The extremities were the first to feel its absence. His wet feet froze the faster, and his exposed fingers numbed the faster, though they had not yet begun to freeze. Nose and cheeks were already freezing, while the skin of all his body chilled as it lost its blood."

—Jack London, "To Build a Fire"

FROSTBITE

During its disastrous invasion of Russia in 1812, Napoleon's Grand Armée was devastated by cold injury. This was due in no small part to the fact that soldiers with frostbite spent their nights thawing their frozen limbs over roaring fires, only to refreeze them the next day.

On the Eastern Front in World War II, the winter of 1941–42 was the coldest in over a century. The Russians, with the help of their two greatest commanders, "General January" and "General February," dashed Hitler's hopes for a quick victory over the Soviet Union by repelling the Nazi invaders on the outskirts of Moscow. German casualties from frostbite numbered 112,627.

A few winters ago, a fisherman froze his feet while ice fishing on a lake in Minnesota. He built a fire and thawed them out, then refroze them while hiking back to his car that evening. He eventually lost eight toes.

Whether you wage your winter campaigns on the Russian steppe or on ice-covered lakes in Alaska or Minnesota, your real enemy is frostbite. This is one foe you don't want to underestimate. It'll sneak up and nibble at your fingers and toes, turning them into so many links of frozen sausage. But you can turn the tables on the cold and nip frostbite in the bud, if you know its modus operandi.

Predisposing Factors

Frostbite is tissue injury or death caused by exposure to subfreezing cold. Predisposing factors include:

- *Ambient temperature:* Frostbite is more likely to occur in temperatures below 20°F (−6.7°C).
- *Windchill:* A cold wind whipping across your face will take the color out of your cheeks in no time, as convection accelerates the cooling process. Tissues don't become cooler than ambient temperature, but they cool faster.
- *High altitude:* Because it's colder up there, mainly. But the thinner air also seems to aggravate cold injury, and the storms are more violent.
- *Alcohol and drugs:* You won't know enough to come in out of the cold, or pull on a hat and mittens, if you're sloshed. You're also more likely to fall and break an arm or leg, increasing your risk of hypothermia and frostbite.
- *Conduction injury:* You remember that old story about not touching cold metal with exposed flesh—how your finger or tongue would freeze to the metal? It's true. Metal and most other materials are much better heat conductors than air. On a cold day, a sled runner or ice ax extracts heat from your hand the way a magnet attracts iron filings. So does water. The freezing point of gasoline and other volatile hydrocarbons is slower than that of water; it's −70°F (−56.7°C). Spill some on your hand on a cold day and it's instant frostbite.
- *Fatigue:* Vince Lombardi said, "Fatigue makes cowards of us all." It also makes us candidates for hypothermia and frostbite by depleting our energy reserves.

- *Underlying illness:* Diabetes and circulatory disorders impair the circulation to the extremities, setting the stage for frostbite.
- *Tobacco:* Nicotine puts a vise-grip on the small arteries in the skin and extremities, opening the door for cold injury.
- *Previous frostbite:* Once you've been initiated into the Frostbite Club, you're a lifetime member, and always vulnerable to repeat cold injury.
- *Deep snow:* Standing or walking in deep, loose snow will cool your piggies real quick. It is much colder deep down in the snow than on the surface.

Mechanism of Injury

Here's what happened to the ice fisherman in Minnesota. After sitting out in the open on a frozen lake for several hours, he became mildly hypothermic. The blood vessels in his skin and extremities clamped down in order to minimize further heat loss. The ice he was standing on drew the warmth out of his feet, and the skin and subcutaneous tissues of his toes froze. Chilled arterioles just beneath the frozen tissues reflexively constricted, the blood in the capillaries became more viscous, and the flow of blood through these capillaries slowed nearly to a halt. The blood became thick and syrupy and clots formed, blocking the capillary bed and depriving the tissues of badly needed oxygen and nutrients. Shunts running from arterioles to venules then diverted blood away from the capillary beds. These shunts opened and closed in cycles, like the valves on a steam pipe, allowing waves of warm blood to surge into the feet from time to time. When the fisherman's core temperature dropped further, these shunts stayed open for good, and the tissues began to freeze.

As the tissues cooled, ice crystals formed in the spaces outside the cells. These crystals then pulled water out of the cells, dehydrating them, disrupting their cell membranes, and throwing a monkey wrench into their metabolic machinery.

The original frostbite injury to the fisherman's toes was severe enough. His tootsies got the knockout punch when they were refrozen on the hike back to his car. I hope he at least caught some fish.

✤ Signs and Symptoms

Because of their distance from the warm core, and because of their large surface-to-volume ratio, which predisposes to more rapid cooling, the feet, hands, ears, and nose are most vulnerable to *frostbite.* There have been reports of frostbite to the penis in joggers, but we can only speculate whether that is attributable to the part's distance from the core or an unusually high surface-to-volume ratio.

The first response to cold is usually a stinging pain, followed by numbness and blanching of the tissue. This is known as frostnip. It looks like a small white patch on the cheeks, nose, or ears. Frostnip is easily treated by immediate rewarming.

Frostnip that is ignored progresses to *superficial frostbite*. This involves frozen skin and subcutaneous tissues. The skin remains bloodless, pale or gray, and cold to the touch. The tissue beneath the surface remains soft and pliable. A day or so after the injury, large blisters pop up like mushrooms. After a few days, the blisters heal, and a hard, dry *eschar* forms. This is a thick, black scar that separates from the underlying tissue in a few weeks and is replaced by new, red skin that eventually takes on a normal appearance.

"There was very little skin to the face. The face, for that matter, sunken and emaciated, bore little likeness to human countenance. Frost after frost had bitten deeply, each depositing its stratum of scab upon the half-healed scar that went before. This dry, hard surface was of a bloody-black color, serrated by grievous cracks wherein the raw flesh peeped forth."
—Jack London, "An Odyssey of the North"

Deep frostbite implies freezing of superficial as well as deep structures, including nerve, muscle, tendon, and even bone. The part is purple or red, cool to the touch, and anesthetic. The limb is as hard as a piece of wood. In contrast to superficial frostbite, in which the injured part is sensitive, warm, and pink after rewarming, the part remains cold and blue after thawing. Small blood blisters may form after one to three weeks, and the part may remain swollen for months after. Eventually it will mummify and fall off.

✤ Treatment

You can treat frostnipped hands anywhere, anytime, by breathing through cupped hands or by putting your hands in your armpits. But there's a time and a place for the treatment of frostbite. The place is *indoors* and the time is when you are sure there is no chance that the thawed part will be refrozen. Avoid the freeze-thaw-refreeze cycle at all costs. It is infinitely better to walk out of the wilderness on frostbitten feet than to thaw them out and risk the chance of their refreezing later. Before you start out for the warming hut, first remove and replace all wet clothing and tight boots. And stay away from campfires and car heaters and mufflers en route.

Start thawing the injured part as soon as you get to a secure shelter. The key to recovery from frostbite is *rapid rewarming*. Fill a large container with water heated to between 104°F to 108°F (40°C to 42°C) and immerse the part in it. Make sure that you remove all jewelry and constrictive clothing and don't allow the part to rest on the bottom or sides of the vessel.

That frozen foot or hand will cool the bath as a block of ice would, so you'll have to add warm water at frequent intervals. Ensure against scalding insensitive tissues by never using water warmer than an uninjured hand can tolerate and by thoroughly stirring the water before reimmersing the limb.

Rewarm until the skin becomes soft and flushed. This should take no more than 30 minutes. And don't forget to warm the whole person! There is no point in rewarming a frozen foot if the circulation to the foot is still shut down due to hypothermia.

After the Ice-out. When you are done rewarming the limb, gently dry it with a clean towel. Place sterile gauze or cotton between the digits to absorb moisture and apply aloe vera or antibiotic ointment to the damaged skin. Then elevate the injured part on a pillow and leave it open to the air.

Bathe the frostbitten part in a warm bath with mild soap twice a day. This cleans the debris from the wounds, reduces the chance of infection, and stimulates the circulation. It's also a good time to do gentle, active range-of-motion exercises to prevent stiffness in the digits. But try to resist that primitive human urge to pop the blisters. They will go away bye and bye on their own.

One or two aspirin or ibuprofen tablets twice a day may improve the microcirculation and enhance healing. A few extra glasses of water or fruit juice each day will aid in rehydrating the frostbite/hypothermia victim and give the circulation a big boost.

✤ Prevention

A few words to the wise:

- Eat mountains of nutritious food in cold weather to keep that metabolic furnace stoked. (You'll get more bang for the buck from fats at low altitude.)
- Don't set out on a long trek too early in the morning or when the weather threatens to turn nasty.
- Tight boots have caused more cases of frostbite than the arctic express. Shun constrictive clothing, plastic boots, and tight crampon straps.
- Dress for success. Keep your head, neck, and face covered. On extremely

cold days, tie a cloth over your face below your eyes and let it hang loosely. It will allow you to breathe and yet keep your face warm. Wear mittens instead of gloves and keep them attached to a string draped around your neck. Keep your socks dry and wrinkle-free. Always bring along extra socks and mittens. You can stick a few feathers or some dry grass or moss inside your shoes for extra insulation.

- Wash your hands, face, and feet sparingly in cold weather. Soap and water remove protective oils; shaving removes the layer of dead cells that protect against the wind and cold. You want skin like a shark's in rough weather.
- Never touch metal with your bare hands in cold weather. Metal parts that must be touched with the bare hands should be wrapped with adhesive tape.
- Keep your fingernails and toenails trimmed.
- Allow several hours to recover from mild hypothermia.
- Treat alcohol and tobacco as though they were bad for you.
- No matter what happens out there, don't panic. Remember, sweat accelerates evaporation and heat loss.

OTHER COLD INJURIES

Trench Foot (Immersion Foot)

Trench foot is so-called because it was a common injury during the trench warfare of World War I. It is caused by *vasoconstriction* (constriction of the blood vessels) secondary to prolonged standing or walking in cold water. After sloshing around in cold puddles for a few hours or days, the feet become cold, pale, waxy, pulseless, and numb. Upon rewarming, blood flow returns with a vengeance, and the foot becomes hot, red, and swollen, not to mention painful. The swelling eventually subsides, but the foot remains weak, sweaty, and sensitive to the cold for years.

Prevention of trench foot is simply a matter of avoiding prolonged walking or standing in marshes, bogs, and streambeds, and avoiding tight boots or shoes.

Treatment consists simply of removing wet boots and socks and rewarming the feet with warm blankets or by resting them in a buddy's armpits. Avoid weight-bearing for a day or so after the feet are rewarmed.

Chilblains (Pernio)

When I think of chilblains, I think of one of those nineteenth-century English novels, like *Great Expectations* or *Wuthering Heights*, in which someone is always running across the moor, exposing her skin to the wet and wind. When the arms, shins, knees, hands, or cheeks are exposed to raw, wet weather (such as prevails in England and northern Europe), the skin becomes red, itchy, warm, tender, and swollen. Chronic exposure to such weather conditions can produce skin that is red, rough, and cool to the touch.

Warm, protective clothing protects the skin from chilblains. A bland moisturizing ointment is as good a treatment as any.

CHAPTER 10

SOLAR INJURIES AND HEAT ILLNESS

"Mad dogs and Englishmen go out in the midday sun."

—Noël Coward, *Mad Dogs and Englishmen*

Chicken Little was right. Sort of. The sky isn't exactly falling, but it has sprung a leak. There's a big hole in the ozone layer over the South Pole, and it's getting threadbare everywhere else. All those chlorofluorocarbons, atmospheric pollutants, and jet aircraft are destroying ozone molecules. The less ozone there is up there in the ozonosphere, the more destructive ultraviolet radiation (UVR) strikes the earth's surface. And that's bad news for mad dogs, Englishmen, and those who love to recreate outdoors.

THE ELECTROMAGNETIC SPECTRUM

The sun's rays contain a broad spectrum of electromagnetic radiation, ranging from cosmic rays to radiowaves (see Table 10-1). Two-thirds of this radiation is absorbed, scattered, or reflected by the atmosphere. Ozone absorbs UVR with wavelengths in the range 220 to 290 nanometers (nm), called *UVC*. But significant amounts of ultraviolet B (*UVB;* 290 to 320 nm wavelength) and ultraviolet A (*UVA;* wavelength 320 to 400 nm) penetrate the atmosphere. UVB causes sunburn, tanning, premature aging, and skin cancer. UVA is responsible for "sun cataracts" and sun allergies.

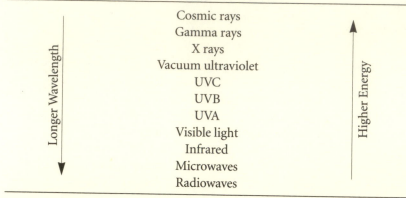

Table 10-1. The Electromagnetic Spectrum

Sunlight is like cholesterol. A little bit is not only good for you, but essential for life. In fact, UVB converts a form of cholesterol into vitamin D in the skin.

HOW MUCH SUN CAN YOU HANDLE?

How much UVR you can take before your skin turns to burned leather depends on a number of factors. The most important of these is your skin type (see Table 10-2). Whether you tan or burn depends on the number of pigment particles *(melanosomes)* in the pigment-producing cells *(melanocytes)* in your epidermis. And that is genetically determined. Melanocytes produce *melanin,* the dark pigment that causes tanning and blocks transmission of UVB into the deeper layers of the skin. Blonds and redheads with blue or green eyes have relatively few melanosomes, burn easily, and almost never tan.

TYPE	BURNING/TANNING CHARACTERISTICS	EXAMPLES
I	always burns, never tans	blonds and redheads, blue eyes
II	usually burns, tans after many hours in the sun	fair skinned, blonds
III	burns and tans moderately	most Caucasians
IV	burns slightly, tans well	Hispanics and Asians
V	almost never burns, tans darkly	Middle Easterners, Indians
VI	burns only with very heavy exposure	Blacks

Table 10-2. Skin types

DETERMINANTS OF UVR INTENSITY

You are stuck with the skin you were born with, but you do have control over some of the other factors that determine your exposure to UVR. It helps to be familiar with the *solar zenith angle*—the angle at which the rays strike the earth's surface. The sharper the angle, the greater distance they have to travel through the atmosphere, and the more UVR is absorbed. The solar zenith angle in turn is a function of the *time of day, time of year,* and *latitude.*

Do you remember how the sheriff (Gary Cooper) couldn't get anyone to come outside and help him fight the bad guys in the movie *High Noon*? Those people weren't afraid of the gunslingers. They just didn't want to get roasted in the noonday sun. The sun is most directly overhead at noon. Sunlight passes through the atmosphere most directly then, so less UVR is absorbed. You can get deep-fried between the hours of 9 A.M. and 3 P.M. That's when 80 percent of the UVB for the day strikes the earth's surface. (UVA intensity, on the other hand, remains almost constant throughout the day.) And sunlight is most intense during the summer months, when the sun traverses a more northerly (or southerly, if you live in the southern hemisphere) route in the sky. Your UVR exposure per unit time is much less on a sunny winter day than on a summer day. If you are smart, you will apportion more of your outdoor activities to the winter months.

The third determinant of the solar zenith angle is *latitude.* The sun's rays strike the earth perpendicularly at the equator and more obliquely with increasing latitude. The solar zenith angle and intensity of solar radiation decrease as you travel farther north or south of the equator.

Altitude has a lot to do with the amount of UVR you are exposed to. The atmosphere is thinner at higher altitudes and there is less water vapor, smoke, and dust to filter UVR. Figure on 4 to 5 percent more UVR for each 1,000 feet of elevation. And glaciers and snowfields reflect 85 percent of the ultraviolet radiation that strikes their surfaces, adding to the already considerable direct light.

Atmospheric conditions effect the intensity of UVR. Smoke absorbs UVR. Dust and water scatter it. On the other hand, UVR penetrates the densest cloud cover, while heat-carrying infrared waves are filtered out. That makes cool, overcast days dangerous. Because it's not warm and "sunny" out, you don't appreciate the intensity of the sun's rays and you fail to cover up. And you can't hide in the shade on such days; the sun's rays are "bent" by the haze and reflected into shady areas.

Wind and sun are a potent combination. Together they cause windburn. Wind dries the skin, removing urocanic acid, a natural skin protector, and irritates sunburned skin.

Even people with skin types III and IV will be sunburned after spending a day out on the water. That's because sunlight bounces off the water's surface and into the face. This is called *reflectivity*. Substances have different reflectivities. Water is 100 percent reflective at noon but only 10 percent reflective in the early morning and evening. (Choppy water is much more reflective than calm water.) Snow is highly reflective (85 percent), while sand has a reflectivity of 20 percent, and grass 2.5 percent. You'll get less UVR in the high desert in the winter than on a snowfield at the same elevation and latitude.

PHOTOSENSITIVITY REACTIONS

UVR can get to you in many different ways. It can combine with certain chemicals, known as *photosensitizers,* to cause an exaggerated response to sunlight. Photosensitivity reactions can take the form of a severe sunburn (*phototoxicity*) or an allergic reaction resulting in an eczemalike rash (*photoallergy*). A burn that continues to worsen over a period of days is probably a phototoxic reaction. They are caused by both UVA and UVB radiation and are quite common. Photoallergic reactions are triggered by UVA radiation and are uncommon.

A partial list of photosensitizers includes food additives (cyclamates and saccharin), shaving creams and aftershave lotions, sulfa antibiotics, certain antihistamines and tranquilizers, oral diabetes medications and diuretics, tetracycline antibiotics, benzocaine (used in most spray anesthetics), barbiturates, biothionol (used in soaps and first aid creams), green soap, some sunscreens, and certain plants.

A twist of lemon can brighten your drink. Skin contact with lemon, lime, parsley, celery, parsnip, fig, carrot, and other plants, followed by a dash of UVR, can light up your skin in a type of photosensitivity reaction called *phytophotodermatitis*. You may get a fierce sunburn or (rarely) an allergic rash resembling poison ivy.

SKIN CANCER

Skin cancer is a recreational hazard for outdoorspeople. "The sun is the cause of at least 90 percent of skin cancers," according to the Skin Cancer Foundation. They predict a worldwide epidemic of skin cancer in the coming years if the current growth rate continues. They also predict that "during the next decade, 5 million men and women in the United States will learn that they have skin cancer . . . 90 percent of those cancers will appear on the face and other exposed parts of the body. Hundreds of thousands will be disfigured through the total or partial loss of noses . . . eyes . . . lips . . . ears . . . 50,000 will die of the disease or its complications."

Basal cell carcinoma, the most common skin cancer, is a painless, smooth, waxy thickening of the skin. It's easy to ignore. It grows very slowly but it will bore straight down through the skin, muscle, fat, and even bone. It can kill you if you let it.

Look at the tops of your hands. Now examine your face in a mirror. Do you see any scaly, rough thickenings—white things that you've picked at that won't go away? These may be *solar keratoses,* the product of chronic exposure to the sun. They won't hurt you, usually. But every once in a while, a solar keratosis turns into a *squamous cell carcinoma*—painless, red nodules with scales. They are highly curable if they are removed before they spread to other parts of the body.

Malignant melanoma, the deadly "black mole," was a rare cancer 50 years ago. It now strikes more than 23,000 Americans each year, and by the year 2,000, 1 out of every 100 Americans can expect to be diagnosed with malignant melanoma at some time in their lives. Skin types I and II are especially vulnerable to melanoma. Early detection is the only hope for a cure.

PREVENTING SOLAR INJURY

The only sure way to avoid sunburn and sun-damaged skin is to join the submarine service. But there are a few things you can do short of that.

- *Limit your exposure.* Time your forays into the outdoors carefully. Stay in the shade during the hours of maximum sun intensity, 9 A.M. to 3 P.M.
- *Wear protective clothing.* Tight-mesh clothing blocks nearly all UVR when dry. Wet or loose mesh clothing transmits a significant amount of UVR. Wear a long-sleeved shirt and long pants and a broad-brimmed hat or a baseball hat with a "Foreign Legion" flap in the back to protect your neck.
- *Use sunscreens and sunblocks.* Sunscreens are creams, gels, oils, or lotions containing chemicals that absorb ultraviolet radiation. They can help to prevent sunburn, photosensitivity reactions, and skin cancer. Since sunburn is caused by UVB, and most photosensitivity reactions are triggered by UVA, you should choose a sunscreen containing either benzophenone or anthranilate, chemicals that absorb both UVA and UVB.

Sunscreens are rated according to their *sun protection factor* (SPF). If you are wearing a sunscreen with an SPF of 5, you could, theoretically, stay out in the sun five times longer before burning than you could if your skin was unprotected. If your skin burns moderately, you should use a sunscreen with an SPF of 6 to 8. If you have fair skin, you should use a sunscreen with an SPF of at least 15. Liberally apply the sunscreen to all exposed skin 30 minutes to 1 hour prior to exposure so that it can penetrate to the deep layers. And reapply it after swimming or sweating, even if you are using a "waterproof" brand. (*Warning:* Reapplying sunscreen doesn't extend the total time that you can safely spend in the sun.)

Many of the chemicals used in sunscreens, including cinnamates, oxybenzone, and para-aminobenzoic acid (PABA), can cause rashes and photosensitivity reactions. If you are sensitive to these chemicals, you can use physical sunblocks. These are opaque creams or pastes that block transmission of all types of solar radiation. Examples of physical sunblocks include talc, zinc oxide, titanium oxide, icthammol, calamine, kaolin, red veterinary petrolatum, and red ferric oxide. Dab a little on areas that are especially likely to burn, such as your nose, ears, cheeks, lips, and neck. If you are caught out in the sun without a sunscreen, try axle grease, charcoal or wood ashes, or a paste of clay. If you are at the seashore, you can make "sunburn powder" of lime. Burn seashells or coral over an open fire and pulverize them into a powder. Then, make a paste by mixing the powder with oil or water, and apply it over all exposed skin. Or, expose coconut meat to the sun to make a coconut oil sunscreen.

✤ Treatment

There's nothing new under the sun in the treatment of sunburn. The pain and redness peak in 24 to 36 hours and resolve in 2 to 3 days. Cool compresses with milk and water or Burow's solution, or just lying in a cool stream, can provide merciful, if temporary, relief from the pain of sunburn. Soothing mentholated lotions and creams help, and aspirin, acetaminophen, or ibuprofen can be counted on to take the edge off the sting.

Anesthetic sprays offer short-term relief at best and usually contain benzocaine, which can cause a rash or act as a photosensitizer.

Tannic acid (tea bags), calamine, aloe, oatmeal, baking soda, cornstarch, and talcum powder have all been touted as sunburn remedies, but there is no evidence that they are efficacious.

If you have skin type I or II, or spend a lot of time outdoors, have your doctor check you for skin cancer at least once a year. He can show you how to check yourself at monthly intervals. Remember, it's your hide!

HEAT ILLNESS

Handling the Heat

The body combats heat stress in two ways. Sweating is the first line of defense. The human body can withstand extreme heat and humidity as long as the sweating mechanism is intact and the salt and water lost in sweat is replenished. Heat is lost as sweat evaporates from the skin's surface. As the body adapts, or acclimatizes, to heat and humidity, it develops the ability to produce sweat with a lower concentration of sodium chloride. And the acclimatized individual can produce a greater quantity of sweat. Acclimatization generally takes 4 to 7 days.

The body's other major defense mechanism against heat stress is the dilatation of blood vessels in the skin. This allows for greater dissipation of heat through convection, radiation, and conduction.

Heat Cramps

Most people who develop heat cramps are in good physical condition. They get into trouble when they engage in vigorous exercise or hard physical work on an unseasonably hot day. Because they are not acclimatized to hot weather, their bodies can't handle the extra heat their muscles generate under such conditions. As a result, they sweat profusely and lose a large amount of salt (sodium chloride) in their sweat. The decreased sodium concentration in the blood causes their muscles to become more contractile, to the point where they go into spasm and cramp up. Unlike heatstroke victims, they sweat normally and their body temperature doesn't rise.

Heat Edema

Hormonal fluctuations and dilation of the blood vessels in the extremities and skin cause an expansion of the blood volume, which leads to edema (swelling) of the hands, feet, ankles, and legs. This is typically seen in unacclimated persons and the elderly. No treatment is needed, as the edema goes away in a few days.

Heat Syncope

In military circles, this is known as "the parade ground faint." The classic case is the recruit who faints after standing at attention for a prolonged period on a hot, humid day. This can happen to a fly fisherman or any unacclimated person under the right environmental conditions. There are several causes:

- Loss of blood volume due to excessive sweating.
- Pooling of blood in the extremities after long periods of standing or sitting.
- Dilation of the blood vessels in the skin and extremities.

The heat syncope victim doesn't really need treatment. He usually comes to after lying on the ground for a few moments. You can avoid heat syncope by avoiding prolonged sitting or standing in hot weather.

Heat Exhaustion

Heat exhaustion (heat prostration, heat collapse) is the most common form of heat illness. Classically, it afflicts unacclimatized people who exercise hard during periods of high temperature and humidity (temperatures over 90°F/32.2°C, relative humidity over 60 percent), sweat profusely, and do not replace their water and electrolytes losses. But it also can strike sedentary individuals who sweat "insensibly" while sitting in the hot sun on a breezy day. Older people on diuretics and the obese are prime candidates for this syndrome.

Heat exhaustion usually develops over a period of days. Headache, confusion, and drowsiness or euphoria are the usual harbingers, followed by a variety of symptoms that may include weakness, dizziness, nausea, vomiting, sweating, muscle cramps, chills, goose bumps, and loss of coordination. The victim may collapse and his skin is cold, clammy, and ashen-gray. His temperature may be normal or up to 104°F (40°C). He'll recover in a few hours if you lie him down in a cool spot and give him cold water to drink.

Heatstroke

Classic Heatstroke. Classic heatstroke is what kills the elderly and the chronically ill during a big-city heat wave. The victim sweats profusely at first, but if her heat-dissipating mechanisms become overwhelmed she may experience headache, confusion, or drowsiness and then start to convulse or lapse into coma. Her body temperature soars, and once it exceeds 106°F (41°C), the blood and internal organs—especially the brain, heart, kidneys, and liver— start to bake.

Exertional Heatstroke. Exertional heatstroke afflicts endurance athletes and others engaged in strenuous physical exercise in hot weather. The victim's pulse will be very rapid and her blood pressure low. Lung congestion, hyperventilation, vomiting, and diarrhea are common symptoms. The brain, which is exquisitely sensitive to heat, becomes swollen and congested when body temperature climbs during extreme conditions of heat and exercise. The victim may become agitated or delirious, lose muscle tone and control, and hallucinate or have a seizure before losing consciousness.

✤ Treatment

Only heroic methods can prevent death. Keeping the ABCs in mind (see page 4), stabilize the victim as well as you can, taking special care to protect her airway if she is unconscious. Then cool her as rapidly as possible. Remove her clothing and place her in an ice-water bath, if possible, or some other cool place, such as a lake or stream. If a bath or body of water isn't available, apply ice packs to her neck, groin, armpits, and chest and cover her with cold wet towels. After her temperature has been lowered to 102°F (38.9°C), place her in a cool, well-ventilated place and massage her skin. This stimulates the flow of cool blood from the skin to the overheated internal organs and the return of warm blood from these organs to the skin, where its heat is dissipated. As soon as she is alert, give her cold fluids by mouth. Then arrange for speedy medical evacuation (see Chapter 25).

✤ Prevention

Here's how to stay cool when the going gets hot:
- Take a few days to become acclimatized to a hot climate before embarking on an arduous hike or climb.
- Stay hydrated. You can easily lose 2 or 3 quarts of sweat an hour while exercising in a hot, humid environment. And you will lose even more after you acclimate. Furthermore, studies have shown that people never voluntarily drink as much water as they lose and usually replace only two-thirds of their net water loss. You cannot rely on thirst as a guide to replacing fluids on a hot day. If you haven't made a conscious effort to drink more water than you wanted, consider yourself dehydrated. To prevent dehydration, drink 8 ounces of water before exercising and 8 to 12 ounces every 20 to 30 minutes during exercise. The sodium, chloride, and potassium lost in sweat are generally adequately replaced with meals or snacks. Gatorade and similar commercial solutions are good rehydrating solutions, but no better than water. Let your urine be your guide to your level of hydration. If you are voiding good amounts of clear urine at regular intervals, you are replacing fluids adequately. If you are producing scant, dark urine, you are dehydrated and need to get with the program.

- Wear absorbent, light-colored, loose-fitting clothing. Light colors absorb less light, and flowing clothing allows maximal evaporative heat loss. Did you ever see a Bedouin wearing tight-fitting, black clothing?
- Take frequent dips in cold-water streams or lakes.
- Accelerate evaporative heat loss after exercising in hot weather by dipping your clothes in water.
- Remain in a cool environment as much as possible, and avoid the midday sun.

CHAPTER II

LIGHTNING INJURIES

"It is the mountaintop that the lightning strikes."
—Horace, *Odes*

W*e had barely turned off the ridge . . . when it was on us in a blinding tormente of snow and hail, snarling wind, and crashing thunder. The charged clouds were blown at great speed against the mountain and . . . discharged their electrical energy. . . . There was a blinding glare and a terrible explosion. I received a stunning blow on the head. . . . For a second or so I was . . . knocked out, and but for the rope . . . I might have fallen and dragged the party to disaster.* —Frank Smythe, "A Bad Day in the Schreckhorn," in *Peaks, Passes and Glaciers,* edited by Walt Unsworth

Does lightning strike twice? You bet. Shenandoah National Park ranger Roy Sullivan was zapped 7 times in 35 years. He survived all 7 strikes, but lightning blew off one toenail, vaporized his eyebrows, ignited his hair (twice), and once blew him out of a moving car. No one knows just why Roy was a human lightning rod, but being an outdoorsman had something to do with it. Most lightning strikes occur in rural areas, and hikers, campers, and other outdoor recreators are on the receiving end of most lightning injuries.

Hurricanes and earthquakes hog the headlines, but year in and year out, lightning accounts for more weather-related deaths than does any other natural disaster. Lightning strikes hundreds of people in the United States each year, killing as many as 300. When you consider that there are 50,000 thunderstorms and 8 million lightning strikes (100 each second) each day around the world, it's a wonder that more of us aren't struck by lightning.

Lightning is an awesome force, capable of generating up to 300,000 amps of current and 2 billion volts of electrical potential. That's enough power to shift a 5-ton boulder or blast a Douglas fir into toothpicks. You can imagine what it can do to a human being.

LIGHTNING MYTHS AND SUPERSTITIONS

- *"The safest place to wait out a lightning storm outdoors is under a tree."* Only if you're in the mood for a little cosmic electroshock therapy. Lightning tends to strike the highest object in an area. If the tree you're standing under is hit by lightning, you're going to get zapped, too.
- *"You'll always be safe from lightning in a car."* Only if it's a hardtop. All-metal cars deflect the charge around the metal skin and down into the ground. Open-frame vehicles and convertibles won't protect you from lightning.
- *"Lightning never strikes on a clear day."* Lightning can strike during a snowstorm, a sandstorm, a volcanic eruption, or seemingly "out of the blue" when a long horizontal flash turns earthward miles from the cloud that spawned it.
- *"Lightning strike is usually fatal."* Wrong. Lightning kills only about 30 percent of its victims, and timely CPR would save most of them.
- *"If you hear thunder, you're safe from a lightning strike."* Well, for a while, anyway, since thunder follows lightning after several seconds. But you won't hear the one that hits you.
- *"It's dangerous to touch a lightning strike victim."* Yes, if the victim is a rattlesnake. Otherwise, there is no problem. The electric current passes through the victim's body in a fraction of a second and is gone.
- *"Lightning injuries are no different from other electrical injuries."* Lightning usually passes outside the body, so injuries are usually less severe than those caused by generated electricity, which traverses the body and damages internal organs.
- *"Lightning victims are in a state of 'suspended animation' and may be revived after prolonged resuscitation."* You're thinking of cold-water immersion. Lightning confers no protective effect on brain metabolism. Breathing and heartbeat have to be restored within minutes to allow any chance for survival in a person who has been "struck dead."

• *"Lightning never strikes twice."* If you don't believe the story about the park ranger, ask the guy who owns the Empire State Building. It's hit by lightning thousands of times a year. And so are many mountain peaks and radio and television antennas. Whatever it is that attracts lightning to an object will attract it repeatedly.

A STORM IS BORN

A thundercloud is a giant electrical generator, cranking out thousands of megawatts of juice with each lightning bolt. It all starts when a cold front (high-pressure system) collides with a warm front (low-pressure system). The warm, moist air rises over the cold air, forming a cumulonimbus (thunder) cloud as the moisture in the warm air condenses into water particles in the form of raindrops, snow, hail, and ice crystals. These particles collide and pick up electrical charges as they are whipped around by violent updrafts and downdrafts in the cloud. The negatively charged particles collect in the bottom of the cloud and the positively charged particles in the top of the cloud, creating an enormous electrical potential between the two regions. Air is a poor conductor of electricity, so this potential can reach hundreds of millions of volts before the electrical energy is dissipated as lightning strikes within the cloud *(sheet lightning)* or from cloud to ground *(streak lightning).*

As the thundercloud scuds across the surface of the earth, the strong negative charge in the bottom of the cloud induces a positive charge in the normally negatively charged earth. When the electrical potential becomes great enough to overcome the insulating properties of the air between ground and cloud, there is a flash of lightning. (The positive charge created by the thundercloud can also make your hair crackle and stand on end and is the force behind St. Elmo's Fire, the eerie, dancing blue or green lights seen in a boat's rigging or on an airplane's wing before a storm.)

Contrary to what your eyeballs tell you, lightning doesn't move just from cloud to earth, but mostly from earth skyward. That giant, forked spark that you see is called the *leader stroke,* or "stepped ladder." It's a 30-million volt, 250,000-amp trailblazing stroke that moves relatively slowly toward the earth, creating a low-resistance pathway through the air. As it nears the ground, a *pilot stroke* rises to meet it. Then a powerful *return stroke* rockets up this low-resistance channel at half the speed of light. The flickering light you see during a thunderstorm is a rapid sequence of secondary leader and return strokes flashing between earth and cloud.

LIGHTNING MORPHOLOGY

Lightning can take odd forms. *Ribbon lightning* is streak lightning blown by the wind. *Pearl lightning* is a flash broken into segments. *Ball lightning* is an eerie luminescent ball, 1 inch to several inches in diameter, that can be downright weird. (In 1685, a "ball of fire" floated into a gun room aboard the Royal Navy ship *Coronation*. It knocked a boy overboard, rendered several men unconscious, scorched the ship's timbers, and broke several windows before dispersing itself on the deck.)

Thunder

Lightning is hot stuff. Hot enough to heat the air it passes through to about 50,000°F (27,760°C) (five times hotter than the surface of the sun) in a fraction of a second. The clap and rumble of thunder is *not* the sound of Henry Hudson's crew playing tenpins (as they like to say in the Hudson Valley), but is attributed to shock waves created by the explosively expanding air. (You can estimate the distance in miles to the flash by counting the number of seconds between lightning and thunder and dividing by 5.)

INJURIES

Mechanisms of Injury

Lightning can hit you in any of several ways. If you are caught out in the open during a lightning storm, you may be the victim of a *direct strike*. Wearing or carrying a metal object above shoulder level, such as a backpack, ice ax or rifle, makes you an inviting target for a lightning strike. A *contact injury* occurs when you're holding a tent pole or some other object that is struck by lightning. A *splash injury* (also called *side flash* or *spray current*) classically occurs when lightning, seeking the path of least resistance, jumps from a tree to a person seeking refuge near the tree. Or, it may jump from person to person in a group. Lightning striking the earth or a body of water causes an electric current to spread outward from the point of impact in concentric waves. This *ground current (step voltage, stride voltage)* can strike groups of hikers or swimmers. And you can be seriously injured by the *blast effect* of exploding/imploding air as lightning passes through it.

The "Flashover Effect"

Remember, a typical lightning bolt packs more punch than a cruise missile: 30 million volts and 250,000 amps of electrical energy. You'd think anyone struck by lightning would be turned into charcoal. But they aren't, thanks to the "flashover effect." Lightning contact with the body is so brief (a millisecond or less) that there is usually not enough time for it to burn an entrance hole in the skin and pass internally. Instead, the current flashes over the outside of the body, vaporizing sweat and blasting off clothing and shoes. (Household current, on the other hand, causes the victim to "freeze" to the circuit. The skin is broken down and electricity surges through the tissues, baking internal organs.)

Specific Injuries

Lightning strike may blow your socks off, yet cause amazingly minor injuries, such as transient blindness and deafness, confusion, muscle pain, and concussion. A heavier jolt might knock you out, crack a few bones, and paralyze your limbs. Or, it might "strike you dead."

Cardiopulmonary. Lightning acts like a massive cosmic countershock, triggering a prolonged contraction of the heart muscle, followed by cardiac standstill for a brief period. It also paralyzes the breathing center in the brain. Death is not instantaneous, though. The heart almost always resumes beating soon after the shock. But the brain takes longer to recover, and after going without oxygen for a few minutes, the heart goes into ventricular fibrillation, and the victim dies of this *secondary cardiac arrest* unless a rescuer gives her mouth-to-mouth ventilation.

Central Nervous System. A lightning strike to the head is like a Muhammad Ali punch. With brass knuckles. It can fracture your skull and scramble your brains, leaving you confused and amnesic for days. It can cause subdural and epidural hematomas (intracranial bleeding, see pages 41–42). It may knock you out, leave you stunned, confused, and amnesic, and it may even change your personality. Two out of three lightning victims have transient paralysis of the legs, and one-third will have paralyzed arms. Not surprisingly, lightning victims often develop a phobia of storms.

Burns. Flashover protects the skin from deep burns, but you may be scorched by a belt buckle, jewelry, coins, or keys superheated by the lightning.

Or the lightning may leave its calling card in the form of *feathering burns,* leaflike patterns where the skin has been imprinted by electron showers.

Circulation. Spasm of the blood vessels can cause the limbs to turn blue, mottled, and cold. Pulses in the arms and legs may be diminished.

Ears. The intense noise of thunder, which at ground zero approximates the sound of a battleship falling off a 50-story building, can cause temporary deafness. The shock wave or skull fracture may rupture your eardrums and cause vertigo and impaired balance.

Eyes. Lightning can cause a wide range of eye injuries, including transient or permanent blindness, corneal injuries, retinal detachment, bleeding into the front or back chamber of the eye, double vision, degeneration of the optic nerves, and loss of color vision. Cataracts are common and usually develop within a few days of injury. Lightning also can cause the pupils to become widely dilated and unresponsive to light. Fixed, dilated pupils are not a sign of death in a lightning victim.

Blast Effect. The explosive force of lightning may rupture the liver, spleen, or kidneys, or blow you off a horse or a mountain ledge, resulting in fractured ribs, skull, limbs, spine, or pelvis.

✚ Treatment

Recognizing Lightning Injury. Lightning strikes in the flash of an eye, and if you aren't on the scene when it happens, you may be unsure as to whether you are dealing with the victim of a seizure, stroke, heart attack, drug overdose, or foul play. If you come across a person lying unconscious in an open field with his clothes in shreds and bruises all over his body, you might logically conclude that he's been assaulted. But if he is unconscious or dazed, has burns in a feather- or leaflike pattern on his skin, blood draining from his ears, and his arms and legs are cold, blue, and mottled, you can safely assume that he's been struck by lightning.

First Response. *The Home Cookbook* in 1877 gave its readers this advice:

"*TO RESTORE FROM STROKE OF LIGHTNING. Shower with cold water for two hours; if the patient does not show signs of life, put salt in the water, and shower an hour longer.*"

Why don't you just skip that and remember the ABCs: *a*irway, *b*reathing, and *c*irculation (see page 4). If the victim isn't breathing and has no pulse, start CPR (see pages 8–10). If you are successful in restoring a heartbeat, continue breathing for the victim until he starts breathing on his own. (This might be several minutes or longer.) Then do a systematic search for other injuries, making sure that you keep his neck and back immobilized if you have reason to suspect spinal injury. Splint any fractures, attend to any wounds or burns, and treat him for hypothermia if he's been exposed to the elements for any length of time.

Group Therapy. Mass casualties are traditionally "triaged," or sorted, into three groups:

1. Those victims who are going to survive no matter what is done for them.
2. Those who are going to die no matter what is done for them.
3. Those who are going to die if something isn't done for them *right now.*

The first two groups are ignored until those in the last group are stabilized. But the rules change when you're dealing with a group of people who have been struck by lightning. Now, you "resuscitate the dead." People who are moaning and groaning are going to make it. Those in cardiac arrest have a good chance for survival if they are given CPR, particularly if you get to them before the heart goes into *secondary arrest* due to lack of oxygen. (Remember, if you are able to restore a heartbeat, prolonged artificial breathing may be necessary.) Then, go back to the ABCs as you evaluate and treat the other victims and prepare them for evacuation. Wounds, fractures and dislocations, burns, head injuries, and chest and abdominal injuries are treated in the usual ways (see Chapters 1–6). Ruptured eardrums don't require immediate treatment but do require eventual medical evaluation, as will many eye injuries (see Chapter 7). Cold, blue extremities are often a sign of shock or hypothermia, but in this setting they are more likely due to vascular spasm and should regain their normal color and temperature within a few hours. Naturally, if there are other signs of shock, treat the patient for shock (see pages 3–5). Paralysis after lightning strike normally also resolves within a few hours. If it doesn't, you'll have to assume that the victim has a brain or spinal cord injury and arrange for medical evacuation (see Chapter 5, pages 43–44, and Chapter 25).

OUT OF HARM'S WAY: AVOIDING LIGHTNING INJURY

Lightning is one of nature's great spectacles, but you don't want to become part of the show. Here's how to stay out of trouble during a thunderstorm:

- Seek refuge in a building or an all-metal vehicle.
- If you see St. Elmo's fire on nearby objects (or yourself), or feel your hair standing on end, hit the deck.
- Stay out of tents (tent poles can act as lightning rods).
- Put down guns or other metal objects, remove metal objects from your hair, take off hobnailed boots, and stay away from fences, power lines, and pipelines.
- If you are in a forest, wait out the storm in a low area under a thick growth of small trees.
- If you are in the open, stay away from single trees, cornstalks, and haystacks. Find a dry cave or a ditch and crouch down with your feet close together. Or lie curled up on the ground on a rubber or plastic raincoat.
- If you are with a group of people, spread out to avoid ground current and splashes.

If you are on the water in a small boat, the sound of thunder rolling across the bay may be the Heavenly Trumpeter calling you home to your maker if you don't act quickly. Your first move should be toward the ignition or the oars. Get under way and head for shore.

If you are offshore, look for a sailboat or a large cabin cruiser. You can pull alongside and ride out the storm under its cone of protection. If you are near shore, you can take refuge under a bridge or cliff. But stay inside the cabin if you have one or hunker down in the bottom of the boat. Keep your hands off the railings, windshield frame, radio antennas, stern light, fishing reels, outriggers, and downriggers. Anything metallic will attract lightning, so remove your jewelry and belt buckle and empty the change from your pockets. Pump the bilge and keep your feet out of the water. Lightning will take the path of least resistance through a boat and has been known to travel through water-filled hoses leading from the head to through-hull fittings and blow people off toilet seats. Stay out of the head. And stay out of the water. Groups of people in the water have been killed by ground current.

A sailboard is a lightning rod on a surfboard. If you can't get to shore quickly, just let the mast and sail go over and lie down on the board.

Aluminum is an excellent conductor of electricity, and an aluminum boat is a magnet for lightning. Sitting out a thunderstorm in an aluminum boat is like waiting out a forest fire in an ammunition dump. Not only are you vulnerable to a direct strike, but lightning striking the water anywhere within 100 yards can spread to your boat in the form of a lethal ground current.

Fiberglass, on the other hand, is such a poor conductor of electricity that it acts as an electrical insulator. But that doesn't make your fiberglass boat lightning-proof. That same quality can transform it into a giant capacitor. A *capacitor*, you may remember, is a device that stores electricity. It consists of a nonconductor separating conductors carrying opposite electric charges. A thundercloud passing overhead induces a positive charge in the people in the boat. This positive charge builds up until the electrical potential between people and water (ground, negatively charged) overcomes the resistance of the fiberglass, and a powerful current flows through the hull into the water, injuring or killing those on board.

Graphite and boron are electrical conductors, so fishing rods made of these materials can act as hand-held lightning rods. And so can a wet fiberglass rod. Most fishing lines are nonconductors, but water is a good conductor of electricity. Lightning hitting the water can flash up a wet line and shock the angler holding the rod. Reel in your line and get those sticks down the minute you see a thunderstorm approaching.

CHAPTER 12

DROWNING AND NEAR-DROWNING

"Lord, Lord! methought, what pain it was to drown:
What dreadful noise of waters in my ears!
What ugly sights of death within my eyes!
Methought I saw a thousand fearful wracks;
A thousand men that fishes gnaw upon."

—William Shakespeare, *Richard III*

Take it from me, drowning is a very unpleasant business. I fell into a well when I was a little shaver, and I'll never forget the few moments I spent in that murky water, thrashing about wildly, desperately grabbing for something to hang onto, sucking huge mouthfuls of water into my lungs before I blacked out. My Dad happened to come along, spotted my cowboy hat floating on the surface of the water, and pulled me out by the hair just as I was sinking out of reach. It was an experience I hope never to repeat.

About 9,000 people drown in the United States every year. Another 80,000 have near-misses, like mine. Drowning is the second-leading cause of accidental death in those under age 45. You can drown in a well, and you can drown in a puddle. A guy in Australia drowned in a wash bucket. And being a good swimmer won't always save you from a watery grave.

Let's define a few terms before we get in over our heads.

Immersion is the state of being in the water with your head out. *Submersion* is the state of being under the water, head and all. *Aspiration* is the inhalation of water or stomach contents into the lungs. *Drowning* is death by asphyxia following submersion. *Near-drowning* is at least temporary survival after being submersed.

PREDISPOSING FACTORS

Inability to swim is an obvious risk factor for drowning. Here are a few more:

- *Head and neck injury:* It is impossible to swim with a broken neck and paralyzed limbs. Head-first dives into shallow water and underwater obstructions are the number one cause of cervical spinal cord (neck) injuries. Look before you leap!
- *Alcohol and other drugs:* An Australian study of men who drowned showed that 64 percent had been drinking prior to the event. As little as two beers can slow your reaction time, dull your reflexes, and impair your judgment. Three or four beers will give you blurred or tunnel vision, decrease your coordination, and make you more susceptible to exhaustion, hypothermia, and cardiac arrest in cold water. So-called recreational drugs cloud your senses and impair your decision-making ability.
- *Hypothermia:* You can become hypothermic in any water that's cooler than 77°F (25°C) if you're in it long enough. Hypothermia saps your strength and stiffens your muscles. How are you going to climb back into a boat or up a muddy embankment if your muscles feel like Play Doh?
- *Seizures:* If you're epileptic, you know that a seizure can strike at any time. You'll be between the devil and the deep blue sea if you have a seizure while in the water.
- *Hyperventilation:* Remember how, when you were a kid, you used to try to knock your pal out by getting him to hyperventilate? If you hyperventilate before swimming under water, you can develop *shallow-water blackout.* Rapid breathing lowers the carbon dioxide content of the blood, removing the stimulus to breathe. As you continue to swim underwater, you use up oxygen. When the blood oxygen content gets low enough, the lightbulb goes out and you drown.
- *Gender:* Males dominate the drowning statistics. In boating-related drownings, male victims outnumber females 12 to 1.

THE PHYSIOLOGY OF DROWNING

The process of drowning is an action-packed series of events. Here's what happens:

1. First you panic. You kick, scream, and thrash about wildly. (The first thing they taught me when I became a lifeguard was how to approach

and subdue a drowning person. We mastered the half-Nelson before we
swam a stroke.)

2. All that to-do makes you too tired to keep your head above water, so
   you start holding your breath. (You also swallow lots of water, which distends your stomach and makes you vomit.)
3. When you can hold your breath no longer, you start gasping for air and
   inhale enough water to block your airway. This leads to a severe drop in
   blood oxygen content, and you pass out, breathe in more water, and suf-
   focate if you're not pulled from the water and resuscitated in time. When
   the brain goes without oxygen for more than four or five minutes, it's
   damaged irreversibly; and when the heart is deprived of oxygen for that
   length of time, it fibrillates. (Curiously, about 15 percent of drowning victims have such intense spasm of the vocal cords that they don't aspirate
   any water. This is called *dry drowning*. In the other 85 percent of drowning cases, the lungs are filled with water. This is called *wet drowning*.)

Freshwater Aspiration

Fresh water is *hypotonic* relative to *plasma,* the liquid component of blood: It
has a lower concentration of salts dissolved in it. When a few mouthfuls of
fresh water are aspirated, osmosis pulls some of the water across the inner
surface of the lungs and into the bloodstream, and then into the red blood
cells. This dilutes the blood and may stretch the red blood cells until they pop
(hemolysis).

Fresh water inactivates surfactant and washes it out of the lungs. *Surfactant* is a surface-tension–lowering substance that coats the inner surface of
the lung and prevents the small air cells in the lung from collapsing, in much
the same way that soap added to water decreases its surface tension and allows
you to blow bubbles. As these air cells collapse, the oxygen content of the blood
decreases and the lungs become stiff, increasing the work of breathing.

Seawater Aspiration

Seawater is salty, of course. So is the blood, but seawater contains a much
greater concentration of sodium, chloride, and other salts than does plasma,
and so is *hypertonic* relative to plasma. Rather than being drawn into the bloodstream, aspirated seawater draws plasma into the lungs, causing the air cells to
become saturated with water. The flow of plasma out of the bloodstream and
into the lungs causes a drop in blood pressure and a concentration of the blood.

Seawater doesn't inactivate surfactant, but it does wash it out of the air cells.

Brackish Water

Brackish water may contain any number of pollutants that can sear the lungs and cause an intense inflammatory pneumonia. It's also more likely to contain sand, seaweed, mud, and sewage. This material can be breathed in and obstruct the airway.

Fresh water and seawater cause different insults, but practically speaking, it doesn't make a drop of difference whether the submersion incident occurs in salt, fresh, or brackish water. The near-drowning victim is treated precisely the same, whether pulled out of the surf at Montauk, Long Island, or fished out of the Snake River in Idaho.

Immersion Syndrome

Jumping into icy water causes instant death, right? Well, sometimes. The shock of cold water on the skin causes a reflex gasp, which in turn causes you to inhale a lungful of water and drown. Or, it may cause a reflex slowing of the heartbeat that leads to cardiac arrest. But most people survive for up to an hour even in 32°F (0°C) water.

Cold-Water Drowning

There have been recent reports of children who were successfully resuscitated after being submerged in cold water for as long as 66 minutes. It was once thought that victims of cold-water submersion are protected by a primitive "diving reflex" that slows the heartbeat, closes down the airway, and shunts blood to the brain. Seals have such a reflex, but there is no evidence that humans do. It's now believed that these cold-water–submersion survivors underwent such severe and rapid cooling that they were in a "metabolic icebox" that protected their brains from permanent injury. Adults, having lower surface-to-mass ratios, cool too slowly to be protected in this way.

BASIC LIFESAVING

The first rule for any would-be rescuer is to not become a victim yourself. Panic can endow the drowning person with the power of Sampson. If you jump in the water and swim right out to him, he is liable to crawl right on top of you.

The safest approach to the person in distress in the water is to extend a long stick or pole out to him (see Figures 12-1 and 12-2). Let him grab the end of the stick and pull himself in. If a rope is handy, throw it to him, and pull him in.

If the victim is too far out to reach with a stick or rope, and you are trained in water rescue techniques, you are going to have to swim out and get him. Here is a review of the basic techniques:

Figure 12-1. Rescuing the near-drowning victim from the shore.

- If the victim is rational and cooperative, you can use the *tired swimmer's carry*. Approach him from the front, and tell him to put his hands on your shoulders. Then use the breast stroke to return to shore.
- If the victim is flailing wildly, use the *cross-chest carry* (see Figure 12-3). Swim to him underwater, turn him

Figure 12-2. Rescuing the near-drowning victim with a branch or log.

around so that he is facing away from you, and raise his head out of the water by lifting under his armpits. Next, place your hand under his jaw to keep his head out of the water, and allow his body to level off. Then, reach your arm around his chest and sidestroke to shore. If he panics, join your hands and just keep his face out of the water until he calms down. Or, escape by letting go of him and sinking down into the water.

✤ Treatment

What would you do if you pulled a near-drowning victim from the water? Roll her over a barrel? Throw her onto a horse and trot her around? Those were state-of-the-art resuscitation techniques in the seventeenth and eighteenth centuries. Nowadays, drainage procedures are considered useless and dangerous. Attention is focused instead on the ABCs (*a*irway, *b*reathing, and *c*irculation), stabilizing and protecting the cervical spine, placing the victim on her side or in a prone position so that she doesn't breathe in her stomach contents, and rewarming her if she is hypothermic.

If the victim is in cardiac arrest, start CPR (see pages 8–10) as soon as you get her on shore or into a boat. If the airway is blocked, perform the Heimlich maneuver (see pages 6–8) or remove mud and debris manually. Continue CPR until you revive the victim or emergency medical personnel take over. If you're in the wilderness, continue CPR until the victim has warmed to ambient temperature. Remember, the cold-water drowning victim is not dead until she's warm and dead.

Postimmersion Syndrome

Some near-drowning victims appear to be fine after they are pulled out of the water, but may develop severe shortness of breath minutes to hours after the incident. This is called *secondary drowning* or *postimmersion syndrome*. It probably represents the delayed effect of inactivation or washout of surfactant from the lungs, damage to the air cells, or an inflammatory response to chemicals in the water. Anyone who has been submersed for more than a minute or two should be evaluated medically and observed for onset of the postimmersion syndrome.

If you spend a lot of time on the water, you should consider taking a Red Cross lifesaving course. Armed with that, a CPR course, and a little common sense, you should do swimmingly.

Figure 12-3. The cross-chest carry.

A. Turn the victim and raise his head out of water by lifting on his hips.

B. Place a hand under victim's jaw to keep his head out of water and allow his body to level off.

C. Reach an arm around victim's chest and swim sidestroke to shore.

CHAPTER 13

SPIDER, SCORPION, AND INSECT BITES AND STINGS

"When I get sick of what men do, I have only to walk a few steps in another direction to see what spiders do."

—E. B. White

"This is the Black Widow, death."

—Robert Lowell, *Mr. Edwards and the Spider*

SPIDERS

I don't know about you, but I don't like spiders. Maybe it was that science fiction movie I saw as a kid—the one where giant spiders, ugly things with eight eyes and fur all over their bodies, terrorize a small town, eating the sheriff and a couple of his deputies before moving on to the grade school to scarf down a bunch of little kids.

Or maybe it was all those stories about the wicked black widow that prejudiced me against her kind. How one bite can kill you, and how she eats her spouse after mating. And the stories we used to hear about tarantulas made the black widow look like a harmless spinster.

No matter what your feelings about these creatures, you should know that there are about 50 species of poisonous spiders in the United States. The two most dangerous spiders found in the United States, the black widow and the brown recluse, hang out under stones, logs, and bark, in clumps of vegetation, fields, vineyards, woods, and in barns, sheds, outhouses, and other buildings.

Spiders are arachnids, a class (Arachnida) that includes scorpions, ticks, and mites. They live everywhere and are prodigious travelers, the hobos of the arachnid world. Up to 2 million may live in an acre of grassland, 265,000 in an acre of woodland.

Spiders have 2 major body segments, the cephalothorax and the abdomen; 8 legs; a pair of feelers; and a pair of jaws. At the end of each jaw is a hollow fang, which connects to a venom sac in the cephalothorax. Spider venom contains potent chemicals that paralyze and partially digest prey.

Spiders are meat eaters, dining mostly on other insects. The larger ones also feast on frogs, lizards, and fish. Most spiders are harmless to humans, but about a dozen of the thousands of species that make their homes in the United States can cause at least mild illness. The bites of some can be fatal.

The Black Widow Spider

Latrodectus mactans, the infamous black widow, is found throughout the United States and southern Canada. The dangerous female is the size (excluding the legs) of a thumbnail and has a shiny, coal-black body; a prominent, spherical stomach; and a characteristic red or orange hourglass marking on its undersurface (see Figure 13-1). The male is half the size of the female, too small to have a harmful bite.

Like venomous snakes, the black widow is not aggressive toward humans and attacks only when it or its web is threatened. Its venom is more potent than that of a cobra or coral snake but, happily, it doesn't inject much of it into its human victims.

After mating with and then eating her husband (when she can catch him), the female finds a dark corner, weaves a coarse web, and suspends her eggs in it. Although generally regarded as timid, black widows defend their eggs the way a grizzly mother defends her cubs. She can be downright nasty. In the days before indoor plumbing, half the reports of black widow spider bites involved people bitten on the genitalia while sitting in outhouses.

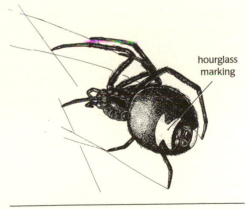

hourglass marking

Figure 13-1. *The black widow spider, showing the characteristic hourglass marking.*

✤ Signs and Symptoms

For all its fearsome reputation, the black widow spider bite is painless and invisible; you may not even realize that you've been bitten, and you may never develop any other symptoms either. More likely, however, 30 to 60 minutes later you'll start to feel as jumpy as a cat on a hot tin roof. Painful cramps in the area around the bite will spread up your arm or leg and then into your abdomen, limbs, and lower back. Sweat will pour out of you, and your temperature and blood pressure will head north. You'll look like you're in shock, with a weak, thready pulse; cold, clammy skin; shortness of breath; and slurred speech. You may develop excessive salivation, muscle twitching, fever, vomiting, and weakness; men may develop a prolonged penile erection. If you're bitten in the leg or genitals, your abdomen will become rigid as a board, and you may get taken off to the operating room for an operation you don't need. If you're bitten on the arm, you'll get terrific spasms of the chest muscles and pain that mimics a heart attack. And you may get a weird burning sensation on the soles of your feet, a splitting headache, dizziness, difficulty swallowing, nausea, vomiting, swelling of the face, and droopy eyelids that would make a bloodhound jealous.

That's the bad news. The good news is that black widow spider bites are rarely fatal. You may want to die at first, but after a few hours the cramps start to subside, and you'll be back to normal in two or three days.

✤ Treatment

First aid for the black widow bite victim consists of cleansing the bite wound and application of cold packs. Then you'd better head for the nearest hospital, where they can treat painful spasms with intravenous narcotics or sedatives and monitor your blood pressure. Antivenin is reserved for pregnant women and those with respiratory arrest, uncontrolled hypertension, or seizures. Hot baths may help as well once you're back at home. Cutting and suctioning *never* work.

Avoid this wrathful beast by wearing long-sleeved shirts and pants when you are in country known to be inhabited by black widows, and watch where you sit!

Brown Spiders

Loxosceles spiders, the brown recluse and its cousins, are much more of a threat to outdoor recreators than are black widows. There are more of them, both sexes bite, and their bites can cause *necrotic arachnidism:* gangrenous ulcers, systemic poisoning, and even death.

Identification. The brown recluse is a deceptively innocent-appearing, medium-size, fawn to dark-brown spider (see Figure 13-2). It has a characteristic violin-shaped figure on its back and is known as the "fiddle-back" spider. It ranges throughout the United States, but prefers hot, arid environments. True to its name, it remains secluded during the day, venturing out at night to hunt beetles, flies, and other spiders. During these nightly forays, it sometimes finds its way into bedding or clothing, thus setting the scene for a spider-human encounter of the worst kind!

✣ Signs and Symptoms

The bite of the brown spider may be virtually painless. More commonly, it causes a sharp, stinging pain that intensifies over a period of 6 to 8 hours, turning into a terrific ache as chemicals in the venom constrict the blood vessels in the area of the bite, shutting off blood flow to the skin and underlying fat. The skin around the bite swells and a large, violet blister develops. This blister becomes progressively darker over the next 24 to 72 hours and turns into a thick black scab. The scab sloughs off after a few weeks, leaving a deep ulcer.

Severe bites can be associated with fever, joint pain, rash, weakness, nausea, and vomiting. Children may have an especially severe reaction in which red blood cells and blood platelets are destroyed, resulting in anemia and a tendency to bleed.

✣ Treatment

Brown spider bites can't be effectively treated in the wild. The best thing to do is to apply cold packs to the bite, elevate and immobilize the bitten extremity, and head for a hospital.

Excision of the bite was once considered standard treatment for brown spider bites, but neither that nor cortisone injections have been shown to be of any value. The most promising approach appears to be a combination of antivenin (still experimental) injected directly into the bite, antibi-

violin marking

Figure 13-2. The brown recluse spider, showing the characteristic violin marking.

otics, and dapsone, a drug used in treating leprosy. Dapsone inhibits the influx of white blood cells into the area of the bite, and this in some unknown way counteracts the effects of the venom. Skin grafting is often needed to repair the necrotic ulcer.

✢ **Prevention**

Brown spiders can be controlled by cleaning up piles of wood and other debris and spraying sheds and outbuildings with a carbamate insecticide. The most practical advice for outdoorspeople is to shake out bedding and clothing in the morning.

Tarantulas

Bird spiders, funnel-web spiders, and trapdoor spiders are *tarantulas*—big, furry spiders that live long and move slowly. About 40 species of tarantulas are native to the United States. Their bites resemble bee stings and require nothing more than elevation, immobilization, and a couple of aspirins.

Wolf Spiders

Lycosidae are a family of hunting spiders that roam through fields looking for prey. Most wolf spiders in the United States cause a mild, stinging bite that requires nothing more than local wound care, ice, and elevation.

SCORPIONS

"My father hath chastised you with whips, but I will chastise you with scorpions."

—1 Kings 12:11

If any bug can rival the black widow's sinister reputation, it's the scorpion. This primitive arachnid stung more than 6,765 humans in 1991. It killed 75 Arizonans between 1929 and 1965, far more than were killed by rattlesnake bites.

Identification

Scorpions are easy to identify. They look like small lobsters, with an elongated abdominal segment that curves up over the body and ends in a *telson*, which contains a stinging apparatus.

Nocturnal animals, scorpions burrow in the sand or hide in fallen trees, under rocks and logs, in piles of wood or brush, or beneath houses and outbuildings during the day, and forage for insects, spiders, and other scorpions at night. Like their spider cousins, scorpions have poor vision. They rely instead on their sense of feel, stinging any moving object that touches or steps on them.

Scorpions hibernate in the winter and are most active May through August.

✤ Signs and Symptoms

Nonlethal scorpions—such as *Vejovis spinigeris, Hadrurus arizonensis,* and most species of the genus *Centruroides*—are denizens of the Sonoran desert in Arizona and New Mexico and rarely cause more than a mild sting. You may think you've been stung by a bee or wasp, and there may be a little redness at the sting site. These stings need only a cold pack and antihistamines.

Centruroides exilicauda

This is the only scorpion that causes severe toxicity in the United States. These guys are heavy hitters. They were responsible for 69 fatalities in Arizona between 1929 and 1954.

Called the "bark scorpion" because of its yellow to brown coloration, *Centruroides exilicauda* is about 3 inches long, has a knob at the base of its stinger, and may have dark stripes down its back. Its home is the Sonoran desert, but its range is spreading into southern California, Texas, and northern Mexico. *Centruroides* venom is *neurotoxic:* it causes prolonged hyperstimulation of the nervous system. Its stings can pack a wallop, but most serious envenomations occur in children, the elderly, and those with high blood pressure. Most adult envenomations aren't serious, causing only mild pain for a few hours. At first, you may feel nothing more than a pricking sensation; it leaves no bite mark (swelling or discoloration indicates that the sting was caused by a nonlethal species).

In more severe envenomations, pain intensifies over a period of a few minutes to an hour and the area becomes exquisitely sensitive to the touch. Tapping the sting site sends pain and tingling sensations shooting up the arm or leg. The victim becomes jumpy and jittery; children may flail about grotesquely, as though they are in pain, but they usually are not. (This hyperactivity has been described as "break-dancing in bed.") They may appear to be convulsing but are alert and can talk.

Other signs of severe scorpion envenomation include high blood pressure, headache, salivation, abdominal cramps and vomiting, muscle twitching, roving eye movements, temporary blindness, rapid pulse, heavy perspiration, and goose bumps.

Children sometimes develop wheezing and may have trouble breathing.

✤ Treatment

Mild stings can be treated with ice packs and aspirin or acetaminophen. If the victim starts to develop significant pain, he has a serious envenomation and needs to be brought to a hospital. Cold packs will help control the pain en route, but he may need intravenous medications to counteract the nervous system stimulating effects of the venom. An antivenin made from goat serum is available in Arizona but has not yet been approved by the FDA and is still considered experimental.

Don't let scorpions get your goat. Outdoors people can avoid these nasty critters by:

- Wearing shoes when walking outside at night.
- Shaking out shoes and clothing before dressing each morning, and sleeping bags before turning in at night.
- Keeping hands out of potential scorpion hideouts, especially woodpiles and under rocks, logs, and tree bark.

BLOOD-SUCKING FLYING INSECTS

"We all needed rest and refreshing sleep, but were denied either, for no sooner had we unpacked our animals than we were assailed by myriads of small black gnats and ravenous mosquitoes. The gnats were simply irresistible; one could not breathe without inhaling them; they buried themselves in one's flesh, burning like so many coals of fire; they got into every article of food, without, however, improving its flavor; they swam in the tea in such quantities that it became a nauseating puree of gnat, and in fact made life quite unendurable; while the mosquitoes stung and poisoned every exposed portion of our bodies. We anointed ourselves with mud, buried our heads in our blankets, and tried to snatch a little sleep . . . the gnats crawled down our backs, filled our hair and ears, eyes and noses; and . . . made us so utterly wretched that not one of us closed our eyes in slumber the whole night through."

—George Bayley, in his account of his 1883 ascent of Mt. Rainier, as quoted by E. H. Chase, in *Mountain Climber*

Mosquitoes

These winged vampires rely on an exquisite sense of smell to find a blood meal, and carbon dioxide on the skin or in the breath really perks up their taste buds. Some prefer to feed at night, others during the day, but most will bite at twilight. During the day they rest in cool, dark places. They breed in tidal marshes and flooded lowlands near lakes and rivers and find some humans tastier than others, for reasons unknown.

In the tropics, mosquitoes are feared as the carriers of such serious diseases as dengue, malaria, and yellow fever. In the United States, mosquitoes are just plain nuisances. Nevertheless, these whining, swarming hellions on wings can make life miserable for outdoor enthusiasts, as can their coastal cousins, the gnats.

The problem starts when a female mosquito, attracted by carbon dioxide and human sweat, alights on your skin and takes a meal. It drills that syringe-like nose under the skin and injects saliva that contains a substance that thins the blood in the area of the bite, a few proteins that can trigger an allergic reaction, and possibly a few microorganisms to boot.

❖ Signs and Symptoms

An itchy weal is the skin's first reaction to being drilled by Madame Mosquito. Within 12 to 24 hours, the area becomes red, swollen, and more itchy.

❖ Treatment

An ice pack will minimize the swelling and itching in the first few minutes after a mosquito bite. Calamine or Caladryl lotion will decrease redness and itching. More intense reactions may require diphenhydramine (e.g., Benadryl), 25 or 50 mg by mouth every 6 hours.

Blackflies

These humpbacked, human-hating bloodsuckers breed in fast-flowing streams and take over the woods in many northern areas early in the summer. They are day feeders and rely mostly on visual cues to find a blood meal. The adults prefer open, sunny areas, but they are attracted to dark, moving objects. They hate dark *places,* such as the insides of tents and vehicles. They seem to have a fascination for eyes, ears, nostrils, and whatever is under your clothing.

Most bites are on the upper body and leave large, bleeding puncture wounds. The bite then becomes red, swollen, and painful, and it may take weeks for the weeping, crusted sores to heal. Treatment consists of local wound care. Insect repellents and everyday clothing don't deter these hombres when they attack in droves.

Biting Midges

Midges, a.k.a. "punkies," "flying teeth," moose flies, sand flies, sand gnats, and no-see-ums, are ⅛-inch long hellions that attack in swarms, crawl through your scalp, and bite repetitively. They are particularly bad when the wind is calm, and they have an uncanny ability to find and attack people loading their boats onto their trailers after sunset.

Tabanids (horseflies, greenflies, deerflies, and yellow flies)

You may not even know these silent slashers are around until you feel a vicious bite and discover a large, bleeding hole in your skin. They are most active on, warm, overcast days, and rely on hideously large eyes to find targets.

Protecting Yourself

It's still okay to hate bugs. It may even be politically correct. I knew a man who allowed his pet rat to snuggle inside his shirt, and another who thought it was great fun to allow a python as long as my surf rod to wrap itself around his body in great, serpentine coils. But I've yet to meet anyone who would knowingly permit a measly insect to tread upon his or her person for more than 2 microseconds.

If you are beset by swarms of mosquitoes, blackflies, gnats, and other winged demons every time you try to wet a hook, you are not delusional. Biologists haven't discovered it yet, but I am convinced that all flying insects have a gene that programs them to attack two-legged creatures wearing baseball hats, fishing vests, and waders, especially when they are swinging long sticks back and forth over their shoulders. And I'm sure that one of these days scientists will announce the discovery of high-resolution radar organs in mosquitoes, gnats, and blackflies that enable them to detect (at great distances, even over the horizon) anglers standing in midstream changing their terminal tackle or attempting to untangle snarled lines.

In the last few decades we have harnessed the atom, explored the moon, and perfected monofilament fishing line. So why can't we put the kibosh on these little *#!/@*&s? The problem is that bugs have mastered the numbers game. There aren't any flying insects on the endangered species list. If you wipe out 99 of the 100 mosquitoes circling around inside your cabin or tent on a summer night, you have won the battle but lost the war. One female mosquito can produce 20 million progeny in a single season. You can't lick mosquitoes, flies, and gnats with overwhelming force, but you can outsmart them by taking a three-pronged approach to personal protection against flying insects based on avoidance, physical barriers, and chemical deterrents.

Avoidance. Bugs *always* have the home-field advantage when you are outdoors. Follow these rules to avoid confrontations:

- Steer clear of tall grasses, bushes, animal burrows, hollow trees and logs, caves, and other mosquito hangouts during the day.
- Stay indoors at dusk.
- Stay out of the woods altogether during the early part of the season in blackfly country.
- Use lights sparingly.
- Camp on high, dry, open ground. And keep a campfire going. The smoke will usually keep the mosquitoes away.
- Become familiar with the biting midges in your area, and try to time your outdoor activities to when they are lying low.

Physical Barriers. You won't find mosquito-proof clothing in your Eddie Bauer or L.L. Bean catalog, but you'll do fine with the threads you already own if you follow these guidelines:

- Wear loose-fitting, brightly colored clothing made of tightly woven fabric and pad it with leaves, grass, or bark. (Dark clothing is a real turn-on for mosquitoes and flies.)
- Wear long pants and a long-sleeved shirt with a T-shirt underneath.
- Protect your head and neck with a brightly colored, full-brimmed hat.
- Use a head net when the bugs are really swarming. If you don't have one, tie off the arms and neck of your undershirt and slip it over your head. Keep it off your scalp by padding your head with bark or leaves and cut slits for your eyes.

Chemical Deterrence. You have two trump cards in your battle against mosquitoes, flies, and gnats: DEET and permethrin. DEET, the active ingredient in most insect repellent formulations, is the most effective insect repellent. It repels mosquitoes, flies, and gnats and can be applied directly to skin, clothing, tents, screens, sleeping bags, and blankets (see below for fabrics that are sensitive to DEET). However, it can cause skin and eye irritation and has (rarely) been associated with brain damage in children. Here are some tips on using DEET-containing repellents:

- Use a repellent containing 30 percent DEET (10 percent DEET for children). Apply cream or lotion directly to all exposed skin but not near the eyes, mouth, nose, sunburned areas, cuts, or rashes.
- Spray repellent liberally on your clothing, especially where it fits tightly.
- Reapply as needed on hot or rainy days and after swimming.
- Wash the repellent off when you no longer need it.

- Don't use repellent near plastics, spandex, rayon, and acetate. DEET and its solvents can destroy items made from these materials.

DEET and the insecticide permethrin make a great one-two punch against flying insects. Studies conducted by the U.S. Army in Alaska showed that soldiers wearing DEET on their skin and clothing impregnated with permethrin were 99.9 percent protected against mosquitoes. Permethrin is safe and it adheres to clothing for months, even through many washings. It's available as a spray (Permanone, Duranon, Armor On-14, Permethrin Arthropod Repellent) or a solution (Perma-Kill 4 Week Tick Killer). To spray clothing with permethrin, lay the garment out and spray it front and back until the fabric is damp, then hang it up to dry. For longer protection, use the soaking technique. First, make up a solution by pouring 2 ounces of permethrin into a waterproof bag, adding 1½ cups of water, and shaking twice. Then, fold the garment lengthwise, roll it up, and tie the middle with a string. Place the garment in the bag, shake it twice, and let it soak for at least 2½ hours. Then remove it, untie the string, and hang it up until it dries.

Some people have found that a garlic capsule by mouth in the morning gives them near-total protection from both vampires *and* flying insects. But don't waste your time or money on light traps, sound devices, and thiamine pills. They don't work. Avon's Skin-So-Soft bath oil provides weak protection for an hour or so. Some plants, including allspice, bay, cedar, cinnamon, citronella, geranium, lavender, nutmeg, pennyroyal, peppermint, pine, thyme, and verbena, provide modest protection for up to two hours.

STINGING INSECTS

The average bee weighs about as much as a candle flame but packs the firepower of a miniature F-16. Instead of bomb racks, they have venom sacs attached to their stingers. The sting of a bee, wasp, hornet, yellow jacket, or ant (all members of the order Hymenoptera) means instant pain. It also may mean instant death if you are one of the many people who are allergic to bees.

Honeybees are kamikazes. Their barbed stingers and venom sacs remain embedded in the skin after stinging, and when they fly away, they are disemboweled, and soon die.

✤ Signs and Symptoms

If you disturb a nest, you're liable to be swarmed. The first bee on the scene releases *pheromones*, chemical signals that trigger aggressive behavior in other bees. One sting will cause pain, swelling, and redness. Multiple bee stings can cause massive swelling, vomiting, diarrhea, shortness of breath, shock, and collapse. One hundred to 200 stings can be fatal.

Allergic reactions to bees range in severity from simple hives, nausea, and dizziness to *anaphylaxis,* a severe allergic reaction that causes swelling of the face, lips and throat; wheezing; shock; and respiratory arrest. Most allergic reactions develop within a few minutes, although they may be delayed as long as six hours.

✤ Treatment

Ice placed over the sting site and elevation of the limb will suffice for the 99 percent of people who are not allergic to bees. "Sting sticks" containing a local anesthetic and antihistamine lotions may relieve some of the discomfort. A couple of aspirin or acetaminophen tablets will also help.

If you *are* allergic to bees, you'll need a shot of adrenaline and an antihistamine if you develop any sign of a severe reaction (wheezing, swelling of the face and throat, collapse). Kits are available (e.g., Ana-Kit, EpiPen) that have preloaded syringes of adrenaline and diphenhydramine tablets for emergencies. If you have had a severe bee sting reaction in the past, apply a light tourniquet just above the sting if it's on an arm or leg.

A bee stinger continues to pulsate and squeeze venom into the tissues, so it should be removed quickly. It doesn't matter how you remove it, just get it out of there.

✤ Prevention

- Don't leave food out in the open. Yellow jackets are attracted to meat, fruits, and fruit syrup. And keep an eye on open drinks: If you swallow a yellow jacket, it can sting you in the esophagus or in the nether regions of your gastrointestinal tract.
- Take great pains to avoid hymenopteran nests, or you will be in great pain. Honeybees favor rock crevices and hollow trees; you'll see wasp nests hanging from trees; yellow jackets nest underground in animal burrows and tree stumps; fire ants are found throughout the southern United States in mound nests in open, grassy areas.
- Stay out of the way of bees or other hymenopterans flying in a straight line. They may be making a "beeline" to their nest and may become aggressive if they think you are blocking their way.

- If you have an encounter with a bee, don't slap at it. That will just make it mad. Do the smart thing—run. Take refuge in a tent, building, vehicle, or in a dark, shady area.
- Be especially wary of bees on cloudy days. Like most of us, they are more irritable when the sky is gray and it's threatening to rain.
- Keep your shoes on when walking around in the woods.
- If you have a history of bee-sting allergy, take a bee-sting kit along with you into the wilderness and don't hesitate to use it.

CENTIPEDES

Centipedes are ubiquitous in the United States, but the giant desert centipede is the one you want to watch out for. This 6-inch monster uses his curved, hollow fangs to cause an intensely painful bite with localized swelling and redness over the sting site and inflammation of regional lymph glands. If he hangs on long enough to squirt an extra dollop of venom under your skin, the swelling and tenderness may persist for three weeks, and the skin around the fang marks may slough off.

Treatment consists of thorough washing of the bite with soap and water and application of an ice pack. Avoid centipede bites by checking out your shoes, clothing, and sleeping bag before use when in centipede country. Keep your fingers out of crevices and leave every stone unturned.

MILLIPEDES

Millipedes aren't endowed with fangs and venom. They fend off perceived attackers by showering them with a disagreeable chemical spray, after the fashion of skunks. If this stuff gets on your skin it can cause an irritating rash. If it gets in your eyes, it's worse than irritating. It'll make you shed buckets of tears, and your lids will clamp down like bear traps. It can cause swelling of the whites of the eyes, corneal ulcers, and even blindness. Skin exposure should be treated like a superficial burn: Wash the area with soap and water and apply antibiotic ointment. Anyone sprayed in the eyes with this millipede mist needs to have her eyes washed out with copious amounts of water and then be evaluated by a physician.

CHAPTER 14

SNAKE AND OTHER REPTILE BITES

"And the Lord God said unto the serpent, Because thou hast done this, thou
art cursed above all cattle, and above every beast of the field; upon thy
belly shall thy go, and dust shall thy eat all the days of thy life."

—*Genesis 3:14*

*T*he snake struck with the speed and ferocity of a cruise missile. Fred screamed
as the serpent buried its fangs in his thigh. A hit-and-run artist, it was nothing more than a blurred flash of copper slithering into the undergrowth by the
time he realized what had happened. He lay on the ground in agony, clutching
his throbbing leg, fighting back a wave of panic. He was alone in the Talladega National Forest in Alabama, hours away from the nearest hospital. He reached into
his pack for a knife.

Snakes have been getting people into trouble since the Garden of Eden. And
you don't have to go to Idaho to get snakebit. The limbless wonders inhabit virtually every state and call a wide range of terrains home, from desert and
swamps to mountains. Many can swim or climb trees.

Two families of venomous snakes are indigenous to the United States: the
Elapidae, which include the eastern and western coral snake, and the Crotali-
dae, or *pit vipers,* which include copperheads, cottonmouths (water moc-
casins), and rattlesnakes.

PIT VIPERS

Although the eastern coral snake is far deadlier, pit vipers have the country blanketed from coast to coast and are responsible for most of the snakebites reported in this country.

Identifying Marks—Poisonous-Snake Anatomy 101

You've got to be able to "get a make" on the snake that bites you, since treatment depends on the perpetrator's species. Pit vipers have four distinguishing characteristics (see Figure 14-1):

1. A heat-sensing *pit* between the eye and nostril on each side of the head. These pits can detect changes in temperature as slight as .00167°F (0.009°C). Crotalids use these heat-detecting organs to home in on prey like a heat-seeking missile.
2. Catlike vertical, *elliptical pupils.*
3. A *triangular head* that is distinct from the rest of the body.
4. A single row of *subcaudal* (under the tail) *scales.*

Pit vipers also have heavy bodies and upper fangs that fold back when they aren't biting (see Figure 14-2). And rattlesnakes have rattles, of course, which are thick, interlocking skin segments that accumulate as the snake sheds its skin from time to time. Pit vipers range in size from about a foot and a half *(pygmy rattlesnake)* to over 8 feet *(eastern and western diamondback rattlesnakes).*

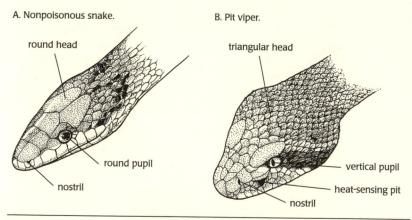

A. Nonpoisonous snake.

round head

round pupil

nostril

B. Pit viper.

triangular head

vertical pupil

heat-sensing pit

nostril

Figure 14-1.

Coral snakes are smaller (12 to 48 inches), skinnier snakes, with short, fixed fangs; alternating bands of red, black, yellow, or white encircling their bodies; black snouts; round pupils; and a double row of subcaudal scales.

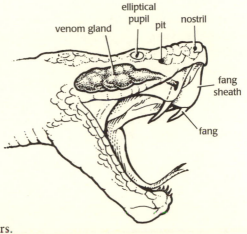

Figure 14-2. Pit viper identifying marks.

SNAKE PHYSIOLOGY 101

You may not have noticed, but snakes don't have ears. None that you can see, at any rate. But they do have inner ears and are very sensitive to ground vibrations. And their keen sense of smell derives from their forked tongues, which they use to pick up scents. But their poor vision makes them the Mr. Magoos of the reptile world.

Warm-blooded animals have internal thermostats (humans are set at 98.6°F/37°C). Snakes, being cold-blooded animals, don't have thermostats. Their body temperature fluctuates with the ambient temperature. But, like automobile engines, they have optimal running temperatures. Snakes hum along at 81°F to 90°F (27°C to 32°C). Below 46°F (8°C), they stop in their tracks, such as they are. And they roast when their temperature gets much above 108°F (42°C). So they sun themselves on rocks on cool days, feed at night during the warm season, and hibernate during the winter.

SNAKE EATING HABITS

Snakes are meat eaters, but they are not aggressive hunters. The rattlesnake's modus operandi is to use its natural camouflage to hide alongside a bunny trail or gopher burrow, wait patiently for a tasty morsel to come within

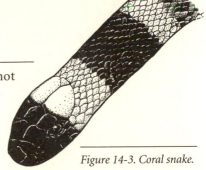

Figure 14-3. Coral snake.

striking distance, and then lunge at it like a fanged rocket. The snake uncoils its body and unhinges its jaws, brings its fangs forward, buries them deep in its prey's body, and injects a lethal dose of venom. The venom paralyzes and starts to digest the critter, who soon finds itself in the unenviable position of being swallowed whole by the snake.

Although their tastes normally run to rabbits or rats, mice, and other rodents, rattlesnakes will bite larger animals or humans when provoked. Most human bites occur in the southeastern states and the desert Southwest. And since snakes are most aggressive when they are emerging from or preparing for hibernation, more bites occur in the early summer and early fall.

THE LINE-UP

Here's a rogues' gallery of venomous American snakes:
- *Cottonmouth:* A semiaquatic snake found in lakes and swamps in the Northeast and in lakes, ponds, lagoons, and bayous in the Southeast. Its mouth has a distinctive white lining. It's a scrappy snake that can make you walk on water should you find yourself sharing a swimming hole with it.
- *Copperhead:* Inhabits meadows, mountains, abandoned buildings in the Northeast; swamps and uplands in the southeast and central U.S.; wooded hills in central Texas. Usually docile, but never trust a snake that can climb trees.
- *Timber rattlesnake:* Prefers wooded and mountainous areas in the Northeast and wooded rocky hills in the Southeast. Likes to soak up the rays on rocky ledges.
- *Pygmy rattlesnake:* Prefers swamps, marshes, lakes, and rivers in the Southeast and grasslands in southeastern Arizona, New Mexico, and southern Texas. A nasty little cuss, but its hiss is worse than its bite.
- *Eastern diamondback rattlesnake:* A big, mean hombre that hangs out in low coastal areas, dry pine woods, and scrub palmetto. It won't run from a fight. The biggest and most dangerous rattlesnake.
- *Eastern coral snake:* Found in grasslands, dry woods, and along streams in the southeastern states and Texas. Won't bite unless provoked, but then won't let go.
- *Western (Sonoran) coral snake:* A denizen of the Great Sonoran Desert of Arizona and New Mexico. Its potent venom can cause total paralysis.
- *Massasauga rattlesnake:* Inhabits prairies, dry wooded areas, woodpiles,

grasslands, hayfields, and cellars in the central states and prairies in Texas and Arizona. This is a reclusive snake that bites only if cornered.

- *Prairie rattlesnake:* Favors rock hills and grasslands—open mountain slopes in the central states, grasslands and hills in the southwestern states. A real snake in the grass.
- *Sidewinder:* They named a missile after this snake. Hangs out in sandy flats; dunes; and arid, rocky hillsides in southwestern and western deserts. Rests with its body buried in the sand. A real snake in the sand.
- *Western diamondback rattlesnake:* Found in open and cultivated areas, and near farm buildings in the Southwest and southwestern California. Aggressive, like its cousin, the eastern diamondback.
- *Northern Pacific rattlesnake:* Lives in semiarid areas to 11,000 feet in northern California, Oregon, and Washington.
- *Southern Pacific rattlesnake:* Hangs out in semiarid areas in southern California. A laid-back cousin of the Northern Pacific rattlesnake.

MODUS OPERANDI

Snakes don't hypnotize their prey, nor do they necessarily hiss or give a warning rattle before they attack. Nor do they have to be coiled to strike. They don't even have to be alive to strike. A primitive reflex enables a severed rattlesnake head to bite for 20 to 60 minutes after decapitation. A 17-year-old boy was envenomated when he impaled his wrist on the fangs of a dried snake head!

Bitter Poison

The potency of a snake's venom and the amount it injects depends on its age, size, the timing of its last meal (it takes three weeks to replenish the venom after a bite), time of year (venom is more concentrated when the snake emerges from hibernation in the spring), and the species. The eastern diamondback, for instance, can inject up to 800 mg of very potent venom, compared to the cottonmouth's 145 mg of moderately potent venom and the copperhead's 40 to 70 mg of mildly toxic venom. The eastern coral snake, on the other hand, only injects 2 to 6 mg of venom, but it gets a lot of bang for the bite. Its venom is 30 times as potent by volume as most rattlesnakes'.

Putting the Bite on You

Pit viper venom is a witch's brew of enzymes that destroy muscle and fat, oxidize amino acids, trigger the release of histamine from cells, cause small blood vessels to leak, rupture red blood cells, and disrupt the normal blood clotting mechanism. But not everyone who is bitten develops "envenomation syndrome." Around 20 percent of bites are *dry bites* (no venom is injected), and in another 10 percent the snake injects an insignificant amount of venom. If you're not in that happy 30 percent, you've got problems, depending on:

- *Your age and size:* Adults rarely die of snakebite, but children can have severe reactions. The bigger you are, the less vulnerable you are to snake poisoning.
- *Your health:* Snakebite is especially dangerous in old people, menstruating and pregnant women, and anyone with hypertension, peptic ulcers, diabetes, or bleeding disorders.
- *Location and depth of the bite:* Snakebites on the head, trunk, and arms are especially dangerous. Injection of venom directly into a blood vessel can put you into shock.
- *Duration of the bite:* Rattlesnakes bite and run. Coral snakes don't know when to let go.

✤ Signs and Symptoms

Pit viper bites don't hurt much at first. Just a little burning sensation, and you see a fang mark or two, with a little bleeding. But then enzymes in the venom start to liquify your connective tissues, allowing the venom to spread through the tissues. Other enzymes ravage muscle fibers and fat, destroy proteins, rupture cell walls, and lay waste to the landscape, like Sherman marching through Georgia. Within hours, your arm or leg swells up like a balloon and turns shades of blue and purple rarely seen on this planet. Blebs and blisters pop out all around the bite site. By this time the pain has become intense, you feel weak and nauseated, and you're sweating profusely. As the venom seeps into blood vessels, it ruptures red blood cells and screws up the clotting system. You bleed from every orifice: nose, mouth, rectum, and bladder. By now, several hours after the bite, you're in shock.

Coral Snake Bites

Coral snake bites are a different story. Their venom contains a neurotoxin similar to the curare that South American Indians used to dab their arrowheads in.

✤ Signs and Symptoms

The bite of the eastern coral snake is painless and produces little swelling and no blisters, discoloration, or necrosis. There may not even be any fang marks. All you feel is a little tingling and muscle twitching at the bite site. You may shrug it off, thinking the snake was nonvenomous. But the neurotoxin works its way through your bloodstream, attaches to your nerves, and starts to exert its grisly effects after a few hours. You may become euphoric and then get drowsy or nauseated. Later, you find it hard to swallow, and start drooling. Your vision becomes blurred, your eyelids droop, and then your arms and legs become weak and paralyzed. The gruesome process ends in asphyxiation. But don't lose sleep worrying about the coral snake. Only 40 percent of their bites cause serious envenomation, and fatalities are rare.

Western coral snakes rarely bite humans and, when they do, cause only mild neurological symptoms.

✤ Treatment

It's been said that the only thing you need in order to treat snakebite is car keys, so you can drive yourself to a hospital for proper treatment. Many of the traditional measures, such as tourniquets and incision and suctioning, are fraught with danger and are of questionable value. Ice doesn't seem to influence the spread of venom in tissues, and you don't need frostbite on top of snakebite. Pressure wraps, although they may delay spread of the venom for a while, do not really prevent swelling, discoloration, and clotting abnormalities and bleeding.

There are a few anecdotal reports of electric shock being used to treat bee stings and snakebites, but this dangerous technique has never been scientifically proven to increase survival.

The Extractor device (Sawyer Products, Safety Harbor, FL) may remove a significant amount of venom if used within 3 minutes after the bite and kept in place for 30 minutes. The Extractor consists of a syringe attached to a suction cup, which is placed over the bite wound. Pulling the plunger out creates negative pressure in the syringe, which pulls venom out of the wound.

These are the things you *should* do after being bitten by a snake:

1. Beat a hasty retreat out of the serpent's striking range (about the length of the snake). It's as anxious to leave the scene of the crime as you are. But if you don't back off, it may bite you again.
2. Keep cool. You can't act rationally if you're excited.
3. If you were bitten by a coral snake, apply a constricting band—but loosely, so that it barely indents the skin. A shoelace or strips of cloth will do the job.
4. Use the Sawyer Extractor if you have one.

5. Gently cleanse the wound and apply a sterile dressing. Splint a bitten upper extremity or simply place it in a sling and keep it at heart level or lower. Immobilizing the bitten part minimizes necrosis and delays spread of the venom into the bloodstream. The same logic dictates that you try not to move around too much.

6. Do *not* use pressure dressings, tourniquets, cold packs, electric shock, or attempt to incise the tissue and suck out the venom. These techniques do not work.

7. Have your buddies bring you to a hospital. You can walk to a car if it's less than a 20-minute walk. Otherwise, you should be carried out by litter, horse, or helicopter. If there's going to be a long wait for transportation, let the extremity hang down below heart level. If you are alone, start walking. You probably will be able to walk for several hours before severe envenomation symptoms start.

8. Bring the snake with you (if it's dead) so that it can be identified at the hospital.

✤ **Prevention**

Here are some tips:

- Stay out of snake country (swamps, caves, deserted mines, and buildings) and avoid rocky crevices and ledges.
- Watch where you step, sit, and reach. Be careful walking over rocks and fallen logs and don't reach into holes or bushes. Stay on clear paths when possible. Check your sleeping bag, clothing, and boots before using them.
- Dress for success. That means knee-high leather boots, long pants, and long-sleeved shirts.
- Take a friend with you into snake country.
- The night belongs to the snakes. Stay in camp at night.
- Let sleeping snakes lie. Don't handle a snake unless you're a herpetologist (if you don't know what the word means, you aren't one). Remember, even decapitated snakes can bite.

LEAPIN' LIZARDS

Only two species of venomous lizard are found in the United States: the Gila monster and its cousin, the Mexican beaded lizard. They are denizens of the Great Sonoran Desert and northwestern Mexico.

These lizards look like giant salamanders. They range in size from 11 to 16 inches; have large, flat heads; massive jaw muscles; short, stubby legs; and long, tubular tails. Their thick skin is a variegated mixture of gray, pink, orange, yellow, and black.

Just the sight of one of these miniature dragons crawling toward you over the sand might kill you. But these charmers also come armed with a venom apparatus consisting of venom glands and 9 or 10 grooved, lancelike teeth on each side of the lower jaw. Fortunately, the venom rarely causes life-threatening reactions in humans.

The Gila monster is a sluggish-appearing animal, but it sheds that mild image when it goes on the attack. It lunges at its victim, burying its teeth in its prey's flesh. Then it either drops off or starts chewing. If it elects to chew, you're in trouble. Its jaws are powerful, and you may have to use a crowbar to loosen its grip. (And they say that *ticks* are hard to remove!)

A Gila monster bite causes a severe, burning pain that may radiate up and down the limb, as well as a good amount of swelling, bleeding, and bluish discoloration in the bite area. You may break out in a cold sweat and feel lightheaded and nauseated.

✦ Treatment

Treatment is simple, once you've detached yourself from the beast. Copiously irrigate the wound with sterile water and then soak it in antiseptic solution for a few minutes. Make sure you remove any teeth that may have been left in the wound. Then apply a sterile dressing and elevate the part above heart level to minimize swelling. Soak the wound once or twice daily in an antiseptic solution and be on the lookout for infection. (And make sure your tetanus immunization is up-to-date.)

CHAPTER 15

PLANT DERMATITIS

"Out of this nettle, danger, we pluck this flower, safety."
　　—William Shakespeare, *Henry IV*

I t's a jungle out there! And I'm not talking about the birds and the beasts. They've learned from hard experience to keep their distance from us. I'm talking about the plant life. Those green things that lie passively about on the forest floor, poking and scratching at you as you walk by. Plants don't have the brains or the decency to get out of your way as an animal does. No respect for the primacy of humans. Try to clear them out of your way, and you'll get a hide full of stickers and thorns. Kick them into pulp, and you'll get smeared with sap that will turn your skin into pizza and your eyes into jam.

Don't let their names fool you. A rose by any other name is still poison ivy, oak, or sumac if it gives you a blistering, weeping rash. And daisies, dahlias, and snow-in-the-mountain are every bit as dangerous as their cousins the asthma plant, nose-burn, and crown-of-thorns.

Plants can harm you in one of three ways: by direct mechanical injury, by causing an irritant *dermatitis* (inflammation of the skin), or by causing an allergic contact dermatitis.

MECHANICAL INJURY

Any hiker who has ever fought his way through a blackberry patch knows about spines and thorns, bristles and briars. I shudder every time I think of those thorn apple shrubs bristling with spines as long and sharp as bayonets, and those prickle-studded vines strewn along the ground like barbed wire.

You can always pick out a partridge hunter. He's the guy who looks as though he has been mauled by a mountain lion, the one with those hideous scratch marks all over his legs, arms, and face. It's amazing he has any skin left at all after struggling through a no-man's-land teeming with the devil's walking stick and holly, juniper and choke cherry, blackthorn and prickly ash.

A thorn in the side is better than a thousand barbed hairs in your hand. Cacti and certain weeds and fruits have myriad fine hairs *(trichomes)* and barbed hairs *(glochids)* which can be almost impossible to remove once they get under your skin.

✤ Treatment

Spines, thorns, and bristles rarely cause serious injury. Clean up those scratches with soap and water and apply Burow's solution compresses to promote healing. Thorns that penetrate the skin should be removed as soon as possible, especially if the entrance wound is over a joint. In that case, you need to watch for signs of joint infection (pain, swelling, and warmth around the joint).

Thorns and bristles that break off under the skin can lead to fleshy growths called *foreign body granulomas.* A week or two after stumbling into thorn apple, you notice a firm, red patch on your arm or leg. Surgery may eventually be required to remove the thorn.

Removing cactus hairs can be like pulling needles out of a haystack. You can try to remove the spines individually with fine tweezers, but this can be an exercise in futility. It's easier just to apply a thin film of rubber cement or facial gel over the affected area, let it dry, and pull the hairs out en masse.

PRIMARY IRRITANTS

There are several groups of plants whose juices contain acids, detergents, and other chemicals that can cause skin irritation. This is not an allergic rash; anyone exposed to the juices of these plants will develop some degree of redness, burning, and itching, depending on the area of the body exposed to the plant. The skin is thick and hard on the palms and soles, and is resistant to irritation. The skin on the face, neck, chest, and tops of the hands and feet is thinner and more sensitive to these plants.

Crown-of-thorns, snow-on-the-mountain, candelabra cactus, milk buds, and other members of the spurge family have a milky white sap that causes a weepy, red, blistery rash. Marsh marigolds, anemones, buttercups, and other members of the buttercup family have a highly irritant oil in their sap that can cause a similar rash.

Nettles have stinging hairs on their leaves that poke into the skin and inject a stream of irritating chemicals that incite a small riot on the skin's surface, causing a hivelike reaction. The skin burns and itches intensely for about an hour and remains red for a variable period.

Contact with the mustard seed plant and radishes can lead to blisters.

✤ Treatment

Primary irritant dermatitis is short-lived and doesn't require much in the way of treatment. But make sure you wash the exposed area with soap and water to remove irritant chemicals. Later, you can apply cold Burow's solution compresses and take an antihistamine to control itching.

ALLERGIC PLANT DERMATITIS

Poison ivy and its cohorts in crime—poison oak and poison sumac—grow in every one of the lower 48 states. As a rule, poison ivy is found east of the Rockies, poison oak west of the Rockies, and poison sumac in the Southeast. Poison ivy is rarely found at elevations above 4,000 feet or in deserts or rain forests, but grows exuberantly along cool streams and lake shores. It often blankets hillsides that are bathed in sun, but is found only in isolated patches in cool, dry climates. It grows as a deciduous shrub up to 6 feet in height, or as a small tree or vine. Its shiny leaves are arranged in groups of three ("leaves of three, beware of me") and turn flaming red or reddish violet in late summer or early fall.

Figure 15-1. Poison ivy.

Susceptibility

You may have nothing to fear from poison ivy. Fifty percent of American adults are immune to it. Some people, perhaps 10 to 15 percent of the population, seem to have a natural tolerance to poison ivy. Another 10 to 15 percent are exquisitely sensitive to the plant, breaking out in an

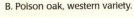
B. Poison oak, western variety.

A. Poison oak.

Figure 15-2.

intensely itchy, blistery red rash within a few hours of coming into contact with the sap. Another 35 percent are *subclinically sensitive:* they are resistant to poison ivy until middle age, when they suddenly break out in a severe rash after rubbing against the broken leaves or stems of the plant.

No one develops a poison ivy rash the first time she touches the plant. First, the immune system has to be sensitized to *urushiol,* the oil responsible for the reaction. Then, on subsequent exposures, the body recognizes the oil as a foreign substance and mounts a terrific inflammatory response in an effort to destroy it. Repeat exposure maintains the allergic state, but the severity of the allergic reaction tends to diminish with time. And a severe bout of poison ivy dermatitis can actually render a person immune to the oil for a period of time. This is called *hardening.*

Urushiol

Urushiol is a sticky, colorless oil that flows through the internal plumbing system of the poison ivy plant year-round. When the leaf or stem is broken, the oil is exposed to the air and oxidized, and turns black. (A black stain on the leaves or stem may be the only clue that you are looking at a poison ivy plant after the leaves fall off in the fall.)

Figure 15-3. Poison sumac.

The urushiol in poison ivy plants is only slightly different chemically from the urushiol in poison oak and poison sumac plants. If you are sensitive to one of these plants, you are sensitive to all of them. And you may also be sensitive to cashew nut shell oil, mango fruit peels, and Japanese lacquer, all of which contain oils that are chemically similar to urushiol.

✤ Signs and Symptoms

Here is what happens when poison ivy resin comes into contact with sensitized skin: The sap causes immediate primary irritation of the skin, the degree of burning and irritation depending on the amount of oil involved. Meanwhile, the resin quickly penetrates the skin and triggers an allergic reaction. It penetrates thin skin (eyelids, between the fingers and toes, the backs of the knees) most rapidly, and these areas may remain highly sensitive to urushiol for up to one year. Even minute amounts of the oil may trigger flare-ups weeks after the rash has healed.

Once the sap of the poison ivy plant touches your skin, you become an allergic time bomb. If the resin isn't washed off within 5 to 10 minutes, it's only a matter of hours (usually 24 to 72) before you break out in a rash. Any area that comes into contact with the resin will react, except the mucous membranes, such as the lips, mouth, and inside of the nose. (There's always the exception that proves the rule. A doctor in Washington reported recently that he developed poison oak urethritis [inflammation of the urethra] after clearing brush.)

The rash starts as red, swollen patches, with a few small fluid-filled blisters. As the reaction intensifies, the blisters become larger and then break down and weep. The whole area becomes covered with an oozing, scaling crust.

The poison ivy rash is one of the itchiest known, and it's almost impossible to resist the temptation to scratch it. But this introduces bacteria into the open sores, making secondary bacterial infection a common problem.

✤ Treatment

The poison ivy rash is self-limited. It usually resolves in 10 to 14 days, no matter what you do. But there are a few things you can do to ease the intense itching and promote healing.

The most powerful weapon against poison ivy dermatitis is cortisone, but only if it's given early in the course of the illness. A shot of cortisone can be curative if given in the first 24 hours. After that, oral prednisone can be given to tame the inflammation if the rash involves the face, hands, or genitals or is widespread and severe. Adults should take the prednisone on a declining-dose schedule every morning as follows:

      days 1 through 4: 80mg

      days 5 through 8: 60mg

      days 9 and 10: 40mg

      days 11 and 12: 20mg

      days 13 and 14: 10mg

Children should be given one-quarter to one-half the adult dose of prednisone. Make sure that you adhere to this schedule and don't discontinue the prednisone when you start feeling better after a few days. That could lead to a severe, prednisone-resistant flare-up.

If you are highly sensitive to poison ivy, ask your physician for a supply of prednisone to take along on wilderness treks.

You can take a more conservative approach to a mild rash that doesn't appear until several days after exposure:

- Cool compresses with Burow's solution relieve the itching and accelerate drying. Do this for 15 minutes 3 to 4 times a day.
- Calamine lotion also helps relieve itching and promotes drying. Apply a layer of it after each session with the cool compresses.
- If large areas of skin are involved, an oatmeal bath at home or back at the cabin will be helpful. Add a cup of oatmeal (I recommend Aveeno) to the tub and soak in it for 15 minutes 2 or 3 times a day.
- Aloe vera may aid skin healing. Apply the lotion to the rash twice a day.
- Don't pick at scabs. Soften crusts with moisturizing lotion.
- Antihistamines by mouth will take the edge off the itching, but antihistamine lotions don't help. Anesthetic sprays and lotions not only don't help, they may actually sensitize the skin and aggravate the rash. That can be like pouring gasoline on a fire.
- Hydrocortisone cream is probably helpful only when there is a flare-up after 10 to 14 days, when the rash has almost healed.

✤ Prevention

The obvious thing to do is to avoid the plant. And wear protective clothing, including plastic or rubber boots and gloves. But you can avoid the plant and still get poison ivy dermatitis. Active resin may remain on shoes and tools for years, and urushiol particles on burning poison ivy plants may float into the air on soot and be dispersed over a wide area.

If you are very sensitive to poison ivy, you may want to invest in a bottle of Stateogard Outdoor Cream, which your pharmacist can order for you. This is an organoclay barrier that confers about 95 percent protection to skin exposed to poison ivy. If you *do* come into contact with poison ivy, wash it off with soap and water immediately. (Water chemically inactivates urushiol.) If your tools or equipment become contaminated, wipe them with a rag soaked in gasoline, kerosene, or some other organic solvent.

A final note: Poison ivy is not contagious. You can't give it to another person, and you can't spread it to other parts of your body, unless you have urushiol on your hands.

CHAPTER 16

INFECTIOUS DIARRHEA AND FIELD WATER DISINFECTION

"He who drinks a tumbler of London water has literally in his stomach more animated beings than there are men, women, and children on the face of the globe."

—Sydney Smith, Letter to the Countess Gray, November 19, 1834

Sydney Smith could have been talking about the crystal-clear water from almost any wilderness stream in North America. Just because you can see clear to the bottom of the streambed doesn't mean the water is pure. Chances are, if you could put a drop or two under a microscope, you'd see the same microorganism that Anton van Leeuwenhoek, inventor of the microscope, first saw when he looked at his own stool in 1681: a funny-looking one-celled animal named *Giardia lamblia*. Drink that water without disinfecting it, or even brush your teeth with it, and you may be in for trouble. Within a week or so, your upper small intestine will be carpeted with millions of *Giardia*.

BEAVER FEVER

Giardia is not the only pathogenic microbe cruising the waters of the North American wilderness. It rubs shoulders, or cell walls, with a whole array of gastroenteritis-causing bacteria and viruses, including *Salmonella* and *Shigella* bacteria and the notorious Norwalk virus. But *Giardia* is the number-one waterborne bowel disrupter in the great outdoors. Humans are the major carriers of *Giardia* infection, but many animals carry it, too, and serve as reservoirs of infection. The farther you travel from civilization, the less you have to be concerned with waterborne bacteria and viruses, and the more you have to worry about *Giardia*.

You may find it hard to believe that a pristine stream high up in the High Sierra, the Rockies, or the Adirondacks could be fouled with disease-causing parasites, but most such streams are. Here's how it happens: *Giardia* is carried in the small intestine of infected humans, beavers, cows, sheep, and dogs in the mature *(trophozoite)* form. Periodically, these trophozoites roll up into hard balls, called cysts, divide into two, and pass out in the stool. An infected animal may shed millions of cysts each day. These cysts may lie around on the ground or in a lake or stream for two or three months before they are eaten by an unsuspecting animal or human. As the cysts pass through the stomach, they lose their thick outer wall and mature into the active trophozoite form. The trophozoites multiply manyfold, until the walls of the upper small intestine are blanketed with giardias. Through some still undefined mechanism, the giardias cause diarrhea, and the trophozoites are transformed into cysts and pass out in the stool to start the cycle again.

A beaver, deer, or other animal may become infected while foraging downstream from its usual habitat. When it returns to higher elevations, it will start shedding *Giardia* cysts in its stool. Some of these cysts will eventually be washed into rivulets and brooks, and then into larger streams, until the entire watershed is contaminated.

Mountain streams are prime beaver habitat, and beavers have taken the rap for several large, waterborne *Giardia* epidemics over the years. Dogs, cats, deer, sheep, cattle, and several species of fish, reptiles, and amphibians are also known to be chronic carriers of the disease. But people are chiefly to blame for the spread of *Giardia* to remote wilderness areas. "Backpacker's diarrhea" may be a more fitting sobriquet than "beaver fever."

✤ Signs and Symptoms

Drinking surface water in the wilderness is a roulette game. You may get real sick, you may not get sick at all, or you may only experience a prolonged spell of "acid indigestion," volcanic belching, bloating, flatulence, and diarrhea. But you've got to ask yourself, as you raise that tumbler of ice-cold mountain spring water to your parched, quivering lips, "Am I feeling lucky today?"

Your intestine can become coated with giardias without your realizing that you have become a home for wayward protozoa. You may suffer nothing more distressing than a vague rumbling in your belly and a few loose stools, and you may walk around unwittingly shedding *Giardia* cysts for the next few weeks or months. Or you may feel as though your stomach and intestines were turned inside out and thrown into a washing machine, on the "heavy soil" cycle. You'll start off with explosive, eruptive, camp-disruptive diarrhea. Your stomach will feel like a charcoal pit, and you'll find yourself worshipping at the porcelain throne, or its outdoor equivalent. You'll have foul, jet-propelled flatus; fever; a grinding ache in your bones; and plenty of room in your tent as your buddies hightail it to safety. After a few days, a calm will descend over the battlefield, and the belly pain, diarrhea, and flatulence will slowly taper off. That's what "beaver fever" can do to you.

✤ Treatment

It takes an average of nine days for swallowed *Giardia* cysts to sprout into trophozoites, attach to the gut wall, and start beating a tattoo on your GI tract. By that time, you may be back home. On the other hand, you may be back-packing in a remote area of the Bitterroot Range in Montana. Or you may be trout fishing on Kepimits Lake in western Labrador, your only link with civilization a float plane that won't be back until next week.

Here's what you do if the "GI blues" strike while you're still out in the woods: If *Giardia* is the likely culprit, the ideal treatment is 250 mg of metronidazole, 3 times a day for 7 to 10 days. This antibiotic eradicates *Giardia* from the GI tract in 90 to 95 percent of cases. But it's important that your stool be tested a week or two after treatment to make sure that you are no longer shedding *Giardia* cysts. (If you're venturing into areas where *Giardia* is endemic, especially the Rocky Mountain area, it wouldn't be a bad idea to bring a supply of metronidazole.)

The key to surviving diarrhea, whether it's caused by a virus, bacteria, or *Giardia,* is to avoid dehydration. Take frequent sips of water, juice, weak tea, or other clear liquids. If your fluid losses are large, you'll need to take in 4 or 5 quarts of fluid every 24 hours. Some foods, such as milk and milk products, caffeine, alcohol, high-fiber foods, and fatty foods will go through you like the Cannonball Express. But staples such as bananas, cereals, lentils, and potatoes are good sources of calories and nutrients and do not aggravate diarrhea.

You can also mix a batch of the oral rehydration solution recommended by the Center for Disease Control. They suggest that you alternately drink the following mixtures:

> glass #1: 8 ounces fruit juice, ½ teaspoon honey or corn syrup, and a
> pinch of salt
> glass #2: 8 ounces treated water and ¼ teaspoon baking soda

If you are dehydrated, try to drink 8 ounces of solution every 30 to 60 minutes (up to 1.5 ounces per pound of body weight in the first 4 to 6 hours, depending on how dehydrated you are).

If, after a few hours of vomiting and diarrhea, you notice that your lips have become parched and your urine dark, and your skin starts to take on the look and feel of parchment paper, then you are well on your way to dehydration. You're running a fluid deficit: There's more going out than coming in. At this point you may benefit from Pepto-Bismol, Donnagel, Imodium, paregoric, codeine, Tylenol No. 3, or Lomotil. These are all antidiarrheals or *antimotility agents.*

The use of antidiarrheals is controversial. They diminish the force of intestinal contractions and decrease the frequency of bowel movements, relieving you of pain and diarrhea. But theoretically, the *Giardia,* or whatever is causing your diarrhea, is going to sit in your intestinal tract for a longer period of time, irritating your bowels. On the other hand, if you're losing fluid at an alarming rate, an antidiarrheal may do more good than harm. Be warned: If you continue to have severe diarrhea (more than 10 stools a day), persistent vomiting, fever, and blood and mucus in your stool, you need to be evacuated to a hospital (see Chapter 25). Blood and mucus are not characteristic of giardiasis, and suggest the possibility of *colitis* (inflammation of the colon), *Salmonella,* or some other bacterial infection, especially if you have fever and chills.

Prevention

Giardia and the other microbes that cause infectious diarrhea are transmitted by the fecal-oral route. Control their spread by observing these rules of personal hygiene in the wild:
- Bury human waste 12 inches deep and at least 100 yards from the nearest water.
- Do not defecate within 40 yards of a lake shore or stream runoff.
- Wash your hands after each bowel movement.
- Do not prepare food if you have diarrhea.
- Rinse cooking utensils and dishes in chlorinated water.

WATER DISINFECTION

The only sure cure for giardiasis is to stay away from surface water when you're in the wilderness. But you can have your water and drink it too, *if* you disinfect it first.

The aim in disinfecting water is to remove or destroy harmful microorganisms. What you want is potable water, water that's safe to drink. It may have a few microorganisms in it, but not any more than your body can easily fight off.

You can disinfect water using physical or chemical methods.

Physical Methods

Whatever method you choose to disinfect water, the process will be more effective if you start with the clearest water available. Cloudy, muddy water is a suspension of silt and clay particles and organic debris that may be contaminated with bacteria and parasitic cysts. You can rely on *sedimentation* to separate out the bigger particles simply by allowing the water to sit for an hour or more. These large particles will settle on the bottom of the container, and you can decant the clear water into another container.

Small particles and chemicals will remain suspended in the decanted water, but you can precipitate them out. Add a three-finger pinch (⅛ to ¼ teaspoon) of alum (aluminum sulfate) per gallon of water, stir for 5 minutes, and allow the suspension to settle for an hour before you decant it or pour it through a coffee filter or fine-weave cloth. Then disinfect the water using heat or chemical means.

If you don't have alum, you can use baking powder (3 ounces per 5 gallons of water), baking soda (1 ounce per 5 gallons of water), charcoal from a wood fire (2 pounds of charcoal per 5 gallons of water), or fine white ash from a wood fire (2 ounces per 5 gallons of water).

Mechanical water *filters* consist of a screen with pore sizes as small as 0.2 micron and an activated charcoal element. Micropore filters will remove most bacteria, but not viruses, so the water will have to be either boiled or chemically treated before it is used.

Granular activated charcoal removes bad tastes and odors from water by adsorbing dissolved chemicals. It adsorbs some, but by no means all, viruses and bacteria, so it cannot be relied upon to disinfect water. It's probably most useful for removing chlorine and iodine from water after chemical disinfection.

Heat

If you're not in a hurry, the simplest way to disinfect water is to boil it. *Giardia* cysts are killed immediately in boiling water, and so are most other microorganisms, even at high altitudes.

If you melt snow or ice for drinking water, bring it to a boil just as you would any other water. Chances are, it's just as contaminated as the surface water in the area.

Chemical Disinfection

Chemical warfare was outlawed by the Geneva Convention. But *Giardia,* viruses, and bacteria are still fair game. They are all killed by chemical disinfection with *halogens* (iodine or chlorine). Halogens oxidize the essential cell structures of microorganisms when they are in contact with them in high enough concentration for a sufficient period of time.

Contact time and concentration of halogen are inversely related. The greater the concentration of halogen, the less time is necessary to destroy microorganisms. Conversely, the longer the contact time, the lower the concentration of halogen necessary to disinfect the water. For example, if you double the concentration of halogen, the water will be disinfected in half the time. Or you can halve the concentration of halogen if you simply double the contact time.

The third factor influencing the disinfection reaction is water temperature. When disinfecting cold water, either the contact time or the concentration of halogen has to be doubled to ensure disinfection.

Halogens in high concentrations impart a bad taste to water. The taste of halogen-treated water can be improved by
- Using less halogen and increasing the contact time.
- Filtering the water with granular activated charcoal after contact time.
- Adding flavoring to the water after contact time.
- Using a zinc brush (Cl-Out), or adding ascorbic acid (vitamin C) crystals or powder or sodium thiosulfate granules to disinfected water.
- Using heat or filters to disinfect the water.

DISINFECTION TECHNIQUES AND HALOGEN DOSES*
(All doses added to 1 quart water: dose/contact time)

IODINATION TECHNIQUES	AMOUNT FOR 4 PPM (parts per million)	AMOUNT FOR 8 PPM (parts per million)

Iodine tabs
  tetraglycine hydroperiodide
  EDWGT (emergency drinking water germicidal tablet)
  Potable Aqua
  Globaline
	½ tab	1 tab

2% iodine solution (tincture)	0.2 ml (milliliters) 5 gtts (gtts=drops)	0.4 ml (milliliters) 10 gtts (gtts=drops)
10% povidone-iodine solution	0.35 ml 8 gtts	0.70 ml 16 gtts
Saturated iodine crystals in water (commercial name: Polar Pure)	13 ml	26 ml
Saturated iodine crystals in alcohol	0.1 ml amount for 5 ppm	0.2 ml amount for 10 ppm
Halazone tabs mono-dichloraminobenzoic acid	2 tabs	4 tabs
household bleach 5% Sodium hypochlorite	0.1 ml 2 gtts	0.2 ml 4 gtts

CONCENTRATION OF HALOGEN	CONTACT TIME IN MINUTES AT VARIOUS WATER TEMPERATURES		
	5°C	15°C	30°C
2 ppm	240	180	60
4 ppm	180	60	45
8 ppm	60	30	15

Note: Recent data indicate that very cold water requires prolonged contact time with iodine or chlorine to kill Giardia cysts. These contact times in cold water have been extended from the usual recommendations to account for this and for the uncertainty of residual concentration.
*From the Wilderness Medical Society Practice Guidelines for Wilderness Emergency Care, 1995

Table 16-1. Disinfection Techniques and Halogen Doses*

CHAPTER 17

MOTION SICKNESS

"The only cure for seasickness is to sit on the shady side of an old brick church in the country."

—English sailor's proverb

B*art looked out over the windswept lake and tried to think of something other than the gathering storm in his stomach. He had long since forgotten about salmon. But then, Tom had warned him about Lake Champlain's volatility. When they had left the dock that morning the lake was smooth as glass. Now it looked like the typhoon scene from* The Caine Mutiny*; 5-foot seas were battering the 27-foot fishing boat, causing it to roll and pitch like a drunken sailor. He ducked into the cuddy cabin and lay down for a while. But that just made him feel worse. He wished he had had the sense to put on one of those patches Tom was wearing behind his ear. His salmon-fishing trip was ruined by seasickness!*

Motion sickness is the pits. And we are all susceptible to it. We've all got a limit to the amount of spinning and turning, dipping, and lurching our stomachs can take before we head for the rail or reach for the airsickness bag. The saltiest Key West, Montauk, and Lake Michigan charter captains have days when the sea is so rough their stomachs flop around like boated salmon. I spent so much time on the water as a boy growing up on Long Island Sound, my parents had to scrape the barnacles off me each fall. I fancied myself a real sea dog, too wise in the ways of the sea to get seasick. But I met my match the summer I went to sea as an ordinary seaman on an oil tanker. A hurricane crossed our path as we steamed past the Outer Banks of North Carolina. My stomach felt as though it were wrapped around the propeller shaft, and I turned a shade of green rarely seen on this planet before the bosun gave me his cure for seasickness: stewed tomatoes, eaten cold with saltines.

Stewed tomatoes cured *my* seasickness. But they may not help *yours*. Besides, medical science in recent years has come up with a number of remedies that are a lot easier to tote around than canned tomatoes. And prevention is the best cure yet, but to prevent motion sickness you need to understand what causes it.

A BALANCING ACT

Motion sickness is an information processing problem. The body has three systems that process raw information about body movement and position and give us a sense of body orientation in space, better known as "balance"—sort of like the way gyroscopes keep rockets upright as they hurtle into space. These are: the *visual system;* the system of *body position sensors* (specialized nerve cells in the skin, muscles, and joints that send information to the brain regarding body position); and the *vestibular system.* The latter consists of three semicircular canals and two small bones *(otoliths)* in each inner ear, as well as their connections to the brain. The semicircular canals sense angular acceleration (spinning motion), while the otoliths sense linear acceleration (straight-ahead motion) as well as gravitational forces. Normally, these three systems work in harmony to keep you on an even keel. The problem comes when you're on a small boat or in a moving car or airplane and you get conflicting information from these different systems. Your eyes may tell you that you're standing or sitting still. (And you are, but the vehicle you're in isn't. It's rocking and rolling, bumping and lurching, or bobbing like a cork.) But those position sensors in your skin, muscles, and joints feel you tensing up, leaning over, bending your legs, moving every which way in an effort to keep your balance as you stand on deck or walk down the airplane's aisle. Meanwhile, your vestibular system is sending a stream of messages to your brain about the different up-and-down, back-and-forth, and spinning movements that you are being subjected to. This is a lot of information, and much of it is contradictory. Your brain doesn't know what to make of all this, so it does the only thing it can do. It orders your stomach to vomit.

Prevention

What distinguishes us from the lower animals is our ability to learn. Our brains are able to assimilate information and use that information to adapt to the environment. If you spend a few days at sea or on the road, your brain learns how to handle all that contradictory information the way a teenager handles algebra: It ignores it. That's great, but if you're planning an offshore tuna-fishing trip next week, you probably don't have the time or wherewithal to spend a few days beforehand getting your sea legs.

Nor is that necessary. There are several tricks you can use to ward off motion sickness. Here are a few that have stood the test of time:

- Keep your eyes on the horizon or any stationary object, such as a distant landmark or the shoreline. This gives your brain a fixed point to focus on, enabling it to tune out most of the other signals coming in from the body position sensors and the vestibular system. Sit in a semireclined position with your head motionless and eyes straight ahead. Bart, the would-be salmon fisherman, made the cardinal error of lying down in the cabin. He had no fixed points of reference in there, and his seasickness worsened.
- If you are on a boat, sit in the center, where there is less movement. If you are in an airplane, sit over the wing. In a car, sit in the front seat or get out of the car and lie on the ground with your eyes open.
- Eat stewed tomatoes and saltines before setting out. Or have a cola drink, or whatever you have heard works. If you believe it's going to help, it probably will. I can think of no scientific reason why a full stomach should help, but the placebo effect can be very powerful against this malady in which anxiety and stress play such large roles. Most medical authorities recommend a liquid diet starting a few hours before the trip, with no solids at all until you are back on terra firma. Do what seems to work for *you*.
- Eat a few gingersnaps or drink some ginger ale or ginger tea. Ginger relieves nausea and calms the stomach and intestines. You can buy capsules of powdered ginger root at your health food store. For seasickness I recommend two 500 mg capsules before you venture on stormy seas, or one 250 mg capsule 4 times a day.
- Avoid alcohol. It dulls your reflexes and prolongs motion sickness.
- Acupressure bands (e.g., Sea-Band) have many disciples among boaters. These bands reportedly prevent motion sickness by exerting pressure on

the Neiguan (P6) point on both wrists. There is some scientific support for their effectiveness in controlling nausea and vomiting.

MEDICATIONS

"Seasickness, when a man has it beaten, leaves him feeling wonderfuly fit."
—James Brendan Connolly, SEA-BORNE *Thirty Years Avoyaging*

People have been casting about, looking for a magic potion against motion sickness since the first cave dwellers set out in a dugout canoe. Almost any concoction you can imagine, everything from creosote to mixtures of horseradish and red herrings, has been swallowed in hopes that it would stave off motion sickness. Most of these rotgut combinations don't work, of course. But now, at last, there *is* a magic potion. Well, not a potion, exactly. More like a pill, or a patch.

There are a number of medications you can take before or during your trip to prevent or treat motion sickness. These medications fall into two broad categories: antihistamines and scopolamine. Both antihistamines and scopolamine are thought to prevent motion sickness by inhibiting the flow of nerve impulses from the vestibular system to the brain. Both are effective, but they have different dosages and side effects. Here are the most commonly used preparations:

- Meclizine (Antivert, Bonine). A nonprescription antihistamine that needs to be taken only once every 24 hours, starting 1 hour before embarkation. It causes moderate drowsiness and dry mouth, as do all antihistamines.
- Dimenhydrinate (Dramamine). The old standby. An over-the-counter antihistamine that is relatively cheap, but it must be taken every 4 hours and causes considerable drowsiness. One advantage is that it comes in liquid form for children.
- Promethazine (Phenergan). This prescription antihistamine is effective in preventing *and* treating motion sickness, but it makes some people very drowsy.
- Scopolamine (Transderm Scop). The latest and (perhaps) greatest. Scopolamine was used in tablet form for years, but caused serious side effects. Now it is available as an ear patch that slowly releases minute quantities of the drug at a steady rate over a period of three days. You

stick a patch on the skin behind your ear 4 hours before your trip and forget about motion sickness for the next 72 hours. It may give you a dry mouth, a dilated pupil on the side where you are wearing the patch, or blurred vision. (Some people who have worn a series of scopolamine patches over a period of days have developed a withdrawal syndrome 48 hours after removing the patch. This consists of nausea, dizziness, sweating, numbness, and other strange feelings in the hands and feet, and difficulty concentrating.)

Transderm Scop is an expensive prescription drug, but it is convenient and effective, and the side effects are rarely a problem.

Remember: all these remedies can cause drowsiness that can impair your ability to operate a boat or a car. This drowsiness is greatly magnified when these remedies are combined with other depressant drugs or alcohol.

CHAPTER 18

RABIES, LYME DISEASE, AND OTHER INFECTIONS

"Some little bug is going to find you some day,
  Some little bug will creep behind you some day."

  —Roy Atwell

RABIES

Rabies. Now there's a word that'll prick up your ears. Make your heart beat a little faster, put a little cotton wool on the roof of your mouth, make you squirm a little. It's become a metaphor for the suffering of the damned. Derived from the Latin word *rabere*, "to rave," it always summons up in my mind the image of a rabid, foaming-at-the-mouth Glenn Ford in that old movie, stalking the streets of a small western town, sending the terrified townspeople running into their houses, where they watch in abject horror as he drops to the dirt and dies in a series of grotesque, jerking spasms.

How Rabies Is Spread

A dangerous myth persists that rabies is a disease primarily of domestic dogs. In Africa, it is. But over the last two decades the incidence of rabies in domestic animals in the United States has declined dramatically, while there has been an upsurge in rabies among wild animals, especially skunks, bats, foxes, raccoons, and bobcats. Skunks, raccoons, and bats account for 85 percent of rabies cases in this country. Wolves, bobcats, coyotes, beavers, groundhogs, weasels, woodchucks, cats, horses, and cows can also transmit the disease. Animals *not* associated with rabies include rodents (rats, mice, squirrels, prairie dogs, gerbils, hamsters, and chipmunks), lagomorphs (rabbits and

143

hares), birds, and reptiles. While there have been only one or two cases of rabies reported in humans in the United States over each of the last few years, the risk of infection is rising as an increasing number of people hike, camp, hunt, and fish in progressively shrinking wildlands.

The rabies virus is deadly efficient. It takes over its host's body to replicate itself and then drives the animal into a raging fury so that it attacks another animal, where it repeats the cycle. But the diseased animal doesn't have to bite to transmit rabies. All that's required is that the infected saliva come into contact with fresh, open wounds or mucous membranes, such as the lips or inner surfaces of the eyelids. There have been several human rabies cases in which the victim was not even aware of being exposed to a rabid animal. Several years ago two spelunkers died of rabies shortly after visiting a bat cave in Texas. Airborne transmission of the virus was suspected after rabies virus was isolated from the air in the cave.

✤ Signs and Symptoms

Here's what happens when an animal (or a person) is bitten by a rabid animal: The rabies virus travels up the peripheral nerves to the brain and spinal cord, and then back down the nerves, spreading throughout the body. When the virus is shed in the saliva, the animal becomes infectious. The incubation period can be anywhere from 9 days to more than a year. The usual range is 20 days in bites to the face, to 60 days in bites on the leg.

Following the bite, there is a *prodrome* (set of promonitory symptoms) consisting of fatigue, loss of appetite, headache, fever, cough, sore throat, abdominal pain, nausea, vomiting, and diarrhea. (Sounds like the flu, doesn't it?) After 2 to 10 days, nervous system symptoms appear. The victim complains of anxiety, irritability, insomnia, depression, disorientation, hallucinations, stiff neck, double vision, muscle twitching, and sensitivity to light, and she may have seizures. *Furious rabies* follows: The victim will engage in biting, running around aimlessly, and other forms of bizarre behavior. The muscles of the face and throat go into painful spasms whenever she attempts to eat or drink. The mere thought of water will induce these spasms, and she drools to avoid swallowing. Sometimes the mere sight of water is enough to trigger the spasms. This is the well-known *hydrophobia*. Fanning or blowing air in her face has the same effect *(aerophobia)*. After several hours or days, the rabies lays waste to the nervous system, and the victim becomes paralyzed, lapses into coma, and dies.

There have been only three reported cases of recovery from human rabies. In each case, the victim had received preexposure and/or postexposure *prophylaxis* (preventive measures) and intensive medical care.

You might think, "I don't have to worry about rabies; I wouldn't think of exposing myself to a rabid animal." But here's the hook: Classic rabies (foaming at the mouth, unprovoked attacks) is seldom seen in this country. The virus may be excreted in the saliva for a few days before the animal manifests any of the commonly recognized symptoms of rabies. And a rabid animal will attack *without provocation,* even if it doesn't look particularly dangerous.

✦ Prevention

Here's what to do if your *dog* is exposed to rabies: If the animal has been vaccinated against rabies, it should receive a rabies booster shot and be observed for 90 days. If it has *not* been vaccinated, it should be destroyed. (If you are unwilling to do this, the animal *must* be held in strict isolation for six months and receive the rabies vaccine one month before being released.)

All animal exposures should be reported to the local health department. When possible, the suspected wild animal should be destroyed and the head removed, refrigerated or frozen, and delivered to a veterinarian or health department, where the brain will be examined for microscopic evidence of rabies. When *you* are exposed to rabies, destroy the animal that infected you and bring the head in for testing. If the animal escapes, check with the local health department. They will make a decision as to whether you should receive postexposure prophylaxis based on a consideration of such factors as the species of animal involved, nature of the exposure (*unprovoked* attacks are highly suggestive of rabies), and whether the animal is available for testing. If the animal is a dog or cat, it should be confined and observed for 10 days. If the animal is a stray, it should be destroyed and tested for rabies.

If you are bitten by a rabid animal, you're in trouble. But you won't die like a mad dog unless you ignore the bite. The first thing you should do is wash the wound thoroughly with lots of soap and warm water. Detergents kill the virus, and water flushes it from the wound. You'll need a tetanus booster if it's been more than five years since your last one, and antibiotics to prevent bacterial infection might be a good idea. The sooner you wash the wound, the better. And scrub it up well. This is your only chance to prevent the virus from getting inside those peripheral nerves and traveling up to your brain. *You'll have almost no chance of developing rabies if the wound is cleaned within 3 hours.*

There is some good news about rabies. The old series of painful abdominal injections has been replaced by a new vaccine, human diploid cell vaccine (HDCV), which is administered in a series of five shots in the arm or buttock. This vaccine stimulates the body's immune system to produce *antibodies* (proteins produced by the body to destroy foreign invaders, including viruses) to the rabies virus. The shot is virtually painless and is 100 percent effective in preventing rabies when given *before* the exposure. For prophylaxis *after* exposure, HDCV is always given in conjunction with human rabies immune globulin (HRIG), a serum that contains rabies antibodies. A small amount of HRIG is injected directly into the bite and an equal amount injected into the arm or buttock. Both HDCV and HRIG should be given within 24 hours of the exposure.

You have a much better chance of picking the winning lottery ticket than getting rabies. But if you do get rabies, your ticket is punched.

LYME DISEASE AND OTHER TICK-RELATED DISORDERS

Ticks are the commandos of the insect world. The roughest, meanest ticks go on search-and-destroy missions against hunters, anglers, and backpackers. This is their modus operandi: They load up on bacteria and viruses, climb 2 or 3 feet up into a bush, and wait there patiently for their quarry. When an unsuspecting human or animal comes along and brushes against the plant, the tick is catapulted onto its next meal. But it doesn't just eat and run. It drills its syringelike proboscis deep into the skin, gorges itself on blood for a few hours, and injects a slew of disease-causing microorganisms into the bloodstream. The tick's repertoire includes the following:

Lyme Disease

Lyme disease wasn't even discovered until 1975, and now it is the most commonly reported vector-borne disease in the United States (a vector is a carrier of an infective agent). It's caused by infection with *Borrelia burgdorferi,* a close cousin to the whip-tailed bacteria that causes syphilis. The Northeast, Upper Midwest, and California are Lyme disease hotspots, but it has been reported in most of the lower 48 states.

Lyme disease is transmitted by *Ixodes* ticks: the deer tick in the Northeast and Midwest and the western black-legged tick in California and Oregon. Tick larvae are infected when they feed on deer mice, a reservoir for *Borrelia,* and harbor the Lyme bacteria in their midgut over the winter. In the spring, the larvae transform into nymphs, and the bacteria migrate into the tick's salivary glands. The nymph takes a blood meal on a mouse, deer, dog, or human the following spring or summer and injects *Borrelia* into its unsuspecting host. The nymph is tiny (about the size of a poppy seed); 70 percent of Lyme disease patients cannot recall a tick bite.

The bacteria then spread outwardly from the bite, causing a large, round, red rash with a clear center. This marks the first of three stages of Lyme disease infection. Fever and tender lymph glands are also common during this stage. You may feel as though you have the flu.

After a few days or weeks, the rash fades and the Lyme bacteria spread by way of the bloodstream to other parts of the body, including the heart and brain. Symptoms of this second stage include severe headache, rash, irregular heartbeat, and bone and joint pain. Sixty percent of those who are not treated go on to a third stage marked by arthritis of the knee, shoulder, elbow, and other joints.

Lyme disease can be treated very effectively with antibiotics. But it can be hard to diagnose, and many cases go untreated until they reach the second or third stage. Good enough reason to concentrate on preventing tick bites. Wear long-sleeved shirts and long pants when you venture into grassy woodlands during tick season (May through August) and tuck your pants into your socks. You can spray DEET onto your skin and clothing to repel ticks, or just spray your clothing with a repellent containing permethrin (for more on use of various repellents, see pages 111–112). Check yourself carefully at least twice a day for ticks. They prefer warm, dark areas, such as the scalp and thighs, so wear light-colored clothing and check these areas extra carefully.

The tick probably has to be attached to the skin for at least 24 hours before it injects Lyme disease bacteria, so prompt removal may prevent infection. Here's the best way to detach the rascal: Grasp its head with a pair of fine tweezers and apply steady pressure until the tick is out. Be careful not to crush it, or the bite wound will become contaminated with its body juices. Then wash the wound with soap and water and apply antibiotic ointment.

Rocky Mountain Spotted Fever (RMSF)

RMSF does cause a fever, and its victims do break out in spots, but it's by no means restricted to the Rocky Mountain area. In fact, it has been reported in all of the continental United States except Maine and Alaska, and is most common in the Middle Atlantic states. The culprit is a *rickettsial* bacterium that hitches a ride with the wood tick, dog tick, and the lone star tick. The rickettsia (a microorganism carried as a parasite) will get under your skin through the tick's proboscis, but it can also access the bloodstream via abrasions and cuts exposed to tick feces or when the tick is crushed between the fingers in the process of removal. Ninety-five percent of cases occur between April and September, when ticks are most active and feeding on the blood of dogs, ground squirrels, rabbits, and bear.

RMSF is like a super flu. You start out with a cranium-crunching headache and then go through the chills and fever, fire and ice routine, muscle aches, and gut-wrenching nausea and vomiting. After a while, your eyes become sensitive to light and then you get round, pink spots on your wrists, ankles, palms, and soles. Untreated, RMSF will run its course in about two weeks and carries a mortality rate of 20 to 30 percent. With antibiotics, this figure drops significantly.

Colorado Tick Fever

This is a viral illness transmitted by wood ticks throughout the mountainous areas of the western United States and Canada. It's like a mild form of Rocky Mountain spotted fever without the spots. No treatment is necessary, which is a good thing, since none is available.

Tick Paralysis

Some western strains of wood tick secrete a neurotoxin in their saliva that causes paralysis. Five or six days after being bitten by a female tick, you will start to feel restless and irritable, and develop tingling in your hands and feet. Over the next day or two you will develop paralysis that starts in the legs and works its way up into your arms. You will have severe generalized weakness that may compromise your ability to swallow, talk, and even breathe. Recovery is complete within 48 hours of removing the tick.

OTHER WILDERNESS INFECTIONS

Jack was burning up. The fever had struck out of nowhere, it seemed, and sent a surge of napalm through his veins. Sweat poured out of him in buckets, lacquering his skin and drenching his clothing. He reached down and gingerly touched the tender mat of glands in his groin, wondering if they were in some way connected to the fever.

Jack didn't get the answer to that question until some days later, after he'd staggered out of the woods and driven himself to a hospital. He was shocked when the doctor informed him of his diagnosis: plague.

Jack wasn't lost in a time warp. Now, in the late twentieth century, backpackers and outdoors enthusiasts in many parts of the United States are at risk for contracting plague and a number of other exotic infectious diseases. In many wilderness areas rabbits, squirrels, deer, foxes, bear, and other game animals are reservoirs of plague, tularemia, leptospirosis, and various tick-borne illnesses (see descriptions below). An apparently healthy animal can carry some mighty virulent microorganisms in its digestive or urinary tract or in the fleas and other parasites that infest its skin. Anyone who is exposed to such an animal is susceptible to a variety of infectious diseases that are unheard of in urban areas. All of these infections are highly treatable, but they are more easily prevented. The key: "know your enemy." Let's take a look at this rogues' gallery of wilderness infections.

Plague

Plague, the infamous "Black Death" that ravaged Europe in the Dark Ages and Asia in the early twentieth century, continues to smolder in many places around the world, including the southwestern United States. It's a fixture in parts of Arizona, New Mexico, California, Colorado, Utah, Oregon, and Nevada, where it bounces back and forth between wild rodents and their fleas. Deer mice, voles, prairie dogs, chipmunks, ground squirrels, wood rats, rabbits, hares, and marmots all fall plague to plague. Meat-eating animals can get it either by eating one of these infected animals or by being bitten by one of their fleas.

Human plague usually follows the bite of rodent fleas but can also be transmitted by ticks and body lice or directly through cuts and abrasions during the process of skinning and dressing infected rabbits. One man got plague after skinning an infected coyote; two others got it after skinning infected bobcats.

Plague bacilli are the marines of the bacterial world. They storm ashore onto an arm or leg and establish a beachhead on the skin. After setting up a local infection, they send armored columns up the lymph channels and overrun the lymph nodes in the groin or armpit, which become swollen and matted together into a tender mass called a *bubo (bubonic plague)*. From the lymph nodes, assault teams ride the bloodstream to other organs.

In the Dark Ages, plague was synonymous with death, but modern antibiotics make short work of this ancient marauder. Nowadays the infection rarely advances beyond the bubo stage. And you can prevent plague entirely by avoiding contact with susceptible rodents and their fleas; by dousing your dogs liberally with flea powder when in high-risk areas of the West and Southwest; by destroying rodents around lodges or cabins in such endemic areas (but make sure you kill their fleas first, or you'll be their next host); and by taking prophylactic antibiotics when visiting these areas. A plague vaccine is available and may be a good idea if you live in the rural Southwest.

Tularemia

Plague is tough, but tularemia is no slouch either. This infection comes on like gangbusters, starting with a thermometer-bursting fever and a bone-rattling chill. It's often mistaken for plague, and it causes many of the same symptoms, including skin infections and swollen, tender lymph nodes.

The bad guy here is *Francisella tularensis,* a bacterium transmitted to humans mainly by ticks (dog tick, wood tick, lone star tick), deerflies, mosquitoes, and other blood-sucking insects that have taken a blood meal on infected cottontail rabbits, hares, beavers, squirrels, deer, sheep, and other mammals. "Frankie" usually works his way into your blood, if not your heart, through the skin or mucous membranes. He can pass through the skin or the eyes when you skin or dress infected animals, especially rabbits, or through the bite or scratch of an infected cat, dog, fox, coyote, or skunk. You can also get tularemia by ingesting food or water contaminated with feces or urine from infected animals or fish. Airborne *Francisella* will settle in your lungs and cause pneumonia.

Tularemia is not rare. Several hundred cases are reported each year in the United States. Here's how to avoid becoming a statistic: Wear rubber gloves when skinning rabbits, squirrels, deer, and other mammals, especially in tularemia hotspots such as Arkansas, Missouri, Oklahoma, Texas, and Utah. Cover your clothing and exposed skin with insect repellent, and remove ticks promptly.

Francisella has been recovered from wilderness streams, which is another good reason to disinfect spring, stream, or lake water. And even if you like your game cooked rare, you might want to consider leaving it on the fire a little longer.

Leptospirosis

Leptospira interrogans, the bacterium that causes leptospirosis, is easier to get than it is to spell. Leptospirosis is the common cold of animals, infecting virtually every domestic and wild species the world over. It has been reported in every section of the United States, and up to 50 percent of opossums, foxes, skunks, and raccoons are infected at any given time. What's tricky about this disease is that many infected animals don't become sick, and they traipse around in the woods shedding the bacteria in their urine for years. Dogs, notorious for this, shed leptospires even after being immunized.

Leptospires are close cousins of the syphilis bacterium. But leptospirosis is *not* a venereal disease. It's worse than that. This hombre gets into your muscles and makes you feel as though you have been stretched on the rack. And your head feels as though it has been dribbled like a basketball. Then the fun begins. Fever and chills like fire and ice. More headaches and muscle aches. The GI tract checks in with nausea and vomiting, gobs of leptospire-infected mucus clog your lungs, causing pneumonia, and you become delirious. After a few days your eyes turn red and your skin may turn yellow. The leptospires often invade the central nervous system and cause meningitis and other nervous system disorders.

Leptospirosis is not a common disease, but it's a nasty one, with a mortality rate between 3 and 6 percent. Antibiotics are very effective if started within four days.

The good news about leptospirosis is that you can't get it from the bite of an infected animal. The bad news is, you can get it almost any other way you can imagine. Trappers and hunters may contract leptospirosis by handling diseased animals. But you're more likely to get it by ingesting food or water contaminated by the urine of infected animals. You can even get leptospirosis by swimming or wading in contaminated water. The leptospires enter the body through abraded skin, or through the eyes, nose, and mouth. So the key to prevention is to keep food out of the reach of animals, disinfect all drinking water, and wear rubber gloves when skinning animals, especially if you have open sores or cuts on your hands.

CHAPTER 19

HIGH-ALTITUDE ILLNESS

"Because it is there."

—George Leigh Mallory, when asked why he wanted to climb Mount Everest

George Leigh Mallory was an English mountain climber who disappeared near the summit of Mount Everest in 1929. His fate remains a mystery. He may have become blinded by the snow and toppled off an icy precipice to his death. He may have died of hypothermia. Or he may have succumbed to high-altitude illness.

You don't have to go to the Himalayas to get high-altitude illness. Most people who rapidly ascend above 8,000 feet develop one or more symptoms of acute mountain sickness. This and the other forms of high-altitude illness can make any high-country venture not only unpleasant, but downright dangerous as well.

Here's the problem: Oxygen is the fuel that drives your metabolic machinery. But the machinery starts to sputter when you climb higher than 4,900 feet above sea level and the air gets thinner. As the barometric pressure drops with increasing altitude, oxygen molecules spread out; there are fewer of them in each breath you take. The oxygen content of the blood drops, so less oxygen is delivered to the tissues.

The body adapts to altitude by:
• Increasing the rate and depth of breathing.
• Increasing the heart rate and the volume of blood that the heart pumps.

- Loosening the chemical bond between oxygen and hemoglobin, so that more oxygen is released to the tissues.

Because there is less oxygen in each lungful of air that you breathe, your ability to perform muscular work or exercise progressively diminishes as you ascend to higher altitudes. You have to breathe harder just to satisfy your body's resting requirements for oxygen. Breathing itself becomes a chore. And you develop *periodic breathing*—waxing and waning cycles of heavy and light breathing interspersed with intervals of no breathing.

The increased work of breathing and periodic breathing wreak havoc on the sleep cycle. Difficulty falling asleep, frequent awakening, and bizarre dreams are common at altitude. Thus the skier's adage, "ski high, sleep low."

ACUTE MOUNTAIN SICKNESS

"Then the slope steepened and the first effects of altitude and unfitness overcame me. Already I had climbed 6,000 feet or more that day. . . . Once, after stopping to rest, it was a struggle to force myself on again. A hundred steps before I stop again, I resolved; if I keep going like that, it will not be long. But I felt sick, and no sooner did I realize it than I wanted to vomit. I stopped again. I thought it would leave me weak and managed fifty more steps; leaned on my axe, panted and managed another fifty. Then I changed my mind; I was slowing down, getting nowhere, and vomiting could do no harm. Afterwards I took glucose and felt better temporarily."

—B. M. Annette, "Solo," in *Peaks, Passes and Glaciers*, edited by Walt Unsworth

No one knows what the exact incidence of acute mountain sickness is at any given altitude. Between 12 and 47 percent of people who ascend to heights of 6,000 to 9,800 feet, and up to 55 percent of those who climb to higher elevations, will get it. If you are going to get acute mountain sickness, you'll know within a few hours of ascending to altitude. Whether or not you get it depends on how high you ascend, how quickly you make the ascent, how much you exert yourself during and after the ascent, how long you stay at high altitude, and your own individual susceptibility to mountain sickness. Like seasickness, some people seem to be relatively "immune" to mountain sickness. And, just as your body gets used to a heaving deck, you can "acclimatize" to altitudes up to about 17,000 feet.

Insufficient oxygen is the cause of acute mountain sickness, but it's the body's reaction to this deficiency of oxygen that causes the symptoms. Much remains to be learned about this complex disorder, but researchers have shown that insufficient breathing for the conditions, fluid retention, the shift of fluids into the cells, increase in pressure on the brain, and the accumulation of water in the lungs all contribute to the development of acute mountain sickness. Of these, the buildup of pressure on the brain is probably the most important factor.

✤ Symptoms

Mild mountain sickness is like a hangover. It starts with a throbbing headache that is worse at night and on awakening and is aggravated by strenuous exercise, coughing, or bending over. Lassitude, loss of appetite, nausea and vomiting, irritability, and shortness of breath, especially during exertion, follow in short order. You may wake up feeling short of breath at frequent intervals during the night, and develop a dry cough.

✤ Treatment

You can stay put, and the symptoms of mild mountain sickness will resolve in one to three days. (Do not go up until your symptoms go down.) Or you can descend 1,000 feet and get better quickly. Supplemental oxygen (at a flow rate of 1 liter/minute) helps, if you have it. Limiting your movements also helps. Aspirin, ibuprofen, or acetaminophen will usually relieve the headache of acute mountain sickness.

Promethazine (Phenergan) can be given as a 25 mg suppository every 8 hours to control nausea. And salt restriction counteracts the body's tendency to retain fluids at altitude.

Acetazolamide (Diamox) increases respiratory drive and has a number of other effects on body processes. It accelerates acclimatization to high altitude and can be used both to prevent and treat acute mountain sickness.

Dexamethasone (Decadron), a cortisone preparation, is also effective in treating acute mountain sickness (see below under "Prevention").

The *Gamow bag* is a plastic bag, large enough to accommodate one or two people, that serves as a sort of "recompression chamber" when it is inflated to higher than ambient atmospheric pressure.

When the victim of mountain sickness starts to stagger, refuses to eat or drink, insists on being left alone, and becomes progressively more confused, disoriented, and lethargic, he is suffering from *severe mountain sickness* and needs to be led back down the mountain right away.

✤ Prevention

Here are a few tips on how to avoid mountain sickness. Keep them in mind the next time you go up the hill, unless you own a space suit:

- *Stage your ascent.* Allow yourself time to acclimatize to the thin air at altitude. The key is where you sleep. Your respiratory drive is diminished at night, so that is when your blood oxygen levels fall to their lowest levels. Your first camp should be at 8,000 feet or lower, with subsequent camps at intervals of 1,000 to 2,000 feet. Or, you can spend two nights at the same altitude for every 2,000-foot ascent, starting at 10,000 feet. Climb higher during the day and return to a lower elevation to sleep ("climb high, sleep low").
- *Avoid alcohol,* at least during the first two nights at altitude.
- *Stay well hydrated.* You lose more fluids at high altitudes. If you are not putting out lots of clear urine, you need to drink more fluids.
- *Avoid strenuous exercise* until you are acclimatized. Mild exercise probably aids acclimatization.
- *Eat a high-carbohydrate diet* (greater than 70 percent carbohydrates), starting a day or two before your climb. This will reduce the symptoms of acute mountain sickness by one-third.
- *Take preventive medication:*

  Acetazolamide—Acetazolamide increases ventilation and blood oxygen content, and will prevent acute mountain sickness in most cases. If you are forced to climb rapidly to a sleeping altitude greater than 9,000 feet, start taking acetazolamide, 125 mg twice a day, the day you start your ascent. You should also take it if you have a history of acute mountain sickness. WARNING: Do not use acetazolamide if you are pregnant or allergic to sulfa.

  Dexamethasone—If you cannot take acetazolamide, or are forced to ascend rapidly to very high altitude (14,000 feet), take dexamethasone, 4 mg by mouth every 6 hours, starting 2 to 4 hours before beginning your ascent.

HIGH-ALTITUDE CEREBRAL EDEMA (HACE)

Pressure on the brain causes the headache of acute mountain sickness. When that pressure becomes high enough, sufficient blood can no longer flow into the brain, and the victim is said to be suffering from *high-altitude cerebral edema* (swelling of the brain). One of the most reliable signs of HACE is loss of coordination. The victim can't hold on to a tool or implement, nor can he walk in a straight line. He may complain of headache and nausea and may halluci-nate or throw a fit. He becomes lethargic, progressively more confused and dis-oriented, and slips into a stupor or a coma.

HACE is treated by immediate descent to a lower elevation, and oxygen, dexamethasone, and the Gamow bag, if they are available. HACE is just an extension of acute mountain sickness, so prevention is the same.

HIGH-ALTITUDE PULMONARY EDEMA (HAPE)

After a rapid ascent to high altitude, the blood vessels supplying the lungs sometimes become "leaky," and the lungs become engorged with fluid. This is called *high-altitude pulmonary edema*. It is much more common in young men and usually develops within the first two to four days after ascending to alti-tude, often during the second night.

The first signs of HAPE are fatigue, shortness of breath on exertion, weak-ness, and a dry cough. Severe HAPE is marked by profound weakness, bluish discoloration of the lips and nails, shortness of breath at rest, rapid pulse and breathing rate, a gurgling in the chest, and a cough productive of pink, frothy phlegm.

HAPE is the most common cause of death at high altitude, so it must be recognized while it is still in the mild stage and treated by heading down the hill pronto. A descent of 2,000 to 4,000 feet may be lifesaving. Give acetazo-lamide, 250 mg every 6 hours in mild cases; in severe cases, administer nifedip-ine, 20 mg sublingually or chewed and swallowed immediately, and 20 mg by mouth every 6 hours thereafter. Oxygen, minimizing movement, the Gamow bag, and keeping warm also help.

Measures that help to prevent acute mountain sickness also help to pre-vent HAPE. Nifedipine, 20 mg by mouth every 8 hours while ascending and for 3 additional days at altitude, is an effective prophylactic drug. However, it has many side effects and should be used only when gradual ascent has failed or in individuals with a history of HAPE.

HIGH-ALTITUDE FLATUS EXPULSION (HAFE)

Just as oxygen molecules spread out as atmospheric pressure diminishes, so do intestinal gas molecules. The result is increased intestinal gas and flatus. HAFE has more serious social than medical implications. Immediate descent may be face-saving.

CHAPTER 20

DENTAL EMERGENCIES

"The man with toothache thinks everyone happy whose teeth are sound."

—George Bernard Shaw, *Man & Superman*

W e take our teeth for granted, until they start to hurt. Then, they are more precious than diamonds. And the intensity of a toothache always seems to vary directly with the distance to a dentist. Consequently, you can expect your worst toothaches, and other dental emergencies, to occur when you are in the wilderness, several days from the trailhead.

Dental emergencies in the wild take many forms. Toothache, lost fillings, bleeding, and broken dentures are just a few of the dental dilemmas that may confront you on the trail. Some of these problems can be prevented by a pre-emptive visit to your dentist before you set out into the wild. Other problems can't be anticipated. But you can practice crude, and trip-saving, dentistry in the wild if you have a dental first aid kit. You can purchase a kit, or make up your own. It should include the following:

eugenol (oil of cloves)	vanilla extract
tea bags	zinc oxide powder
cotton pellets	cotton rolls
2" × 2" cotton gauze	temporary filling material (e.g., Cavit; IRM)
dental mirror	dental wax
small cotton pliers	toothpicks
electrical tape	pen light
dental broach	#11 scalpel

Here is a look at some of the dental emergencies you are most likely to run into in the wilderness.

TOOTHACHE

Teeth are more than little ivory slabs that sit in your mouth and grind food. They are living structures, with a central cavity, called the *pulp,* that contains blood vessels and nerves that supply the outer hard layers of the tooth, the *dentin* and *enamel.* The part of the tooth that extends above the gums *(gingivae)* is called the *crown.* The tapering portion that fits into the socket in the jaw is called the *root.*

The tooth and all its supporting structures are richly supplied with nerve endings. Toothache can be caused by:

Pulpitis

Pulpitis is inflammation of the soft, gelatinous material in the pulp of the tooth. It announces itself with moderate to severe pain, which arises spontaneously or only after the tooth is exposed to heat, cold, or sweets. The pain is generalized, and you may not be able to localize it to any one tooth. You may not even be sure whether it is coming from a top or bottom tooth. But you'll have no doubt which side of your mouth the pain is on. The tooth won't be sensitive to direct pressure, but you can ascertain precisely which tooth is the culprit by applying an ice cube or cold food to each of the teeth on the painful side until you localize the source of the pain.

Most often, pulpitis is secondary to a cavity or a missing filling. Both should be obvious, and both are treatable. First, dry the tooth with a piece of gauze and use a toothpick or a cotton pellet held with cotton pliers to remove as much of the carious material as possible. Then, apply eugenol or vanilla extract to the tooth to deaden the pain. You can make a temporary filling by mixing a small amount of zinc oxide powder with a few drops of eugenol to form a paste. Use a toothpick or the cotton pliers to apply the paste to the tooth. Or you can use Cavit, a premixed filling material. Squeeze a little onto your finger, roll it into a small cone, and apply it to the tooth. Bite it into place and use a toothpick to shape it. This is only a temporary filling, and you will have to repeat this procedure every few days until you can get to a dentist. Darvocet N-100, one every 4 to 6 hours, may be necessary to relieve nagging toothache.

Periapical Periodontitis

Periapical periodontitis is inflammation of the supporting structures near the root of the tooth. It causes a constant, throbbing pain, and the tooth is sensitive to pressure. The absence of swelling over the base of the tooth is what distinguishes periapical periodontitis from infection. It can be caused by trauma or by the leakage of necrotic material from decaying pulp. Minor swelling at the base of the tooth pushes it out a little, so chewing becomes painful. Emergency treatment consists of analgesics, a soft diet, and placing a wad of gauze on the unaffected side to take some of the pressure off the affected tooth.

Myofascial Pain-Dysfunction Syndrome (MPD)

This is one of those "vicious-cycle" disorders. Stress causes muscle tension, which incites spasm of the muscles in the back of the neck and the muscles used in chewing around the jaw, which produces pain, which leads to more stress, which perpetuates the cycle by causing increased muscle tension. An unexpected encounter with a grizzly bear or other tense situations on the trail can cause you to grind or clench your teeth, which can cause an exacerbation of a chronic MPD problem. An acute flare-up will give you pain over the jaw (especially in the area right in front of the ear), a headache, and pain on chewing such foods as granola and smoked meat. Treatment consists of a soft diet, warm compresses over the tender muscles, and analgesics, such as ibuprofen.

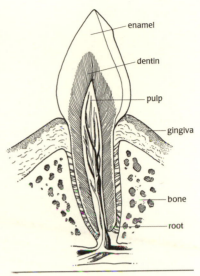

Figure 20-1. Cross section of a tooth.

INFECTIONS

Acute Apical Abscess

An *acute apical abscess* is caused when bacteria from a cavity spread into the pulp and then through the apex of the tooth into the tooth socket. The usual symptoms are swelling and pain on the cheek side of the jaw. Although apical abscesses are usually preceded by toothache, it often subsides, and the tooth may not be sensitive to pressure, heat, or cold. The ideal treatment is drainage of the abscess, but that may have to wait until you return home, unless there is a dentist or qualified physician in your party. Warm compresses and antibiotics (Pen VK, 500 mg every 12 hours) will help keep the infection under control in the meanwhile. And a soft diet and analgesics help.

Periodontal Abscess

A *periodontal abscess* is a collection of pus between the tooth and the gingiva, usually due to food particle entrapment. The tooth will be sensitive to pressure but not to heat or cold. And the gingiva will be swollen and tender along the gum line. Treatment consists of numbing the affected area with eugenol or vanilla extract, and then probing along the gum line with a blunt instrument to remove food particles and break up the abscess. Dental flossing, warm salt-water rinses, and 500 mg of Pen VK every 12 hours also help.

Pericoronitis

Pericoronitis is an infection of the gingiva where it covers an emerging wisdom tooth, usually one of the bottom two. It can cause pain on opening the mouth and can mimic strep throat. Repeated biting on the flap of gingiva covering the tooth causes it to swell and become infected. Use eugenol or vanilla extract to numb the area and then remove the flap using a #11 scalpel. Control bleeding by having the patient bite down on a piece of gauze or a wet tea bag for a few minutes (tannic acid in the tea inhibits bleeding). Then have her rinse with warm salt water every 2 hours, and give her 500 mg of penicillin v potassium every 12 hours.

Deep Infections

Apical abscesses can spread into the face and neck, causing diffuse neck and facial swelling and difficulty swallowing or breathing. These are dangerous, life-threatening infections. Start the patient on Pen VK, guard his airway, and evacuate him to a hospital (see Chapter 25).

DENTAL TRAUMA

Fractured Tooth

If there is no bleeding from the tooth, then the pulp is intact, and no emergency treatment is necessary. If the fracture extends down into the root, remove the loose fragment.

If you see a small amount of blood in the center of the tooth, the pulp is exposed. The tooth will die if it is not attended by a dentist within 48 hours. Meanwhile, you can apply a few drops of eugenol and cap the tooth with Cavit or IRM (intermediate restorative material, a soothing anti-inflammatory dressing).

Loose Teeth

If the tooth is loose but in good position, or looks as though it has been pushed in, leave it alone. If it is out of position, use your fingers to reposition it. Then splint it with 3M's Express Putty; after mixing the putty base and catalyst, you have 2 minutes to mold the material over the loose tooth and the adjoining tooth on each side. Or you can apply dental wax around the tooth to hold it in place.

If the tooth has been knocked out, it should be replaced within 30 minutes or it will probably die. Pick it up by the crown, gently rinse it off, and put it back into the socket. Use dental wax to hold it in place, and give the patient penicillin v potassium, 500 mg every 12 hours, for a week.

Lost Crown

Find the crown and rinse it off. Apply a few drops of eugenol to the crown and reposition it onto the tooth. If you get a comfortable fit, remove the crown, apply a little Cavit or IRM, and put it back into your mouth. Bite it into place, and use a toothpick to remove excess filling material. If you can't get a comfortable fit, apply eugenol to the tooth and cover it with dental wax. Save the crown.

Broken Denture

Dry the denture, and then apply a strip of electrical tape to the side of the denture facing the tongue.

CHAPTER 21

FOOT CARE IN THE WILD

"It's a hell of a lot more important to keep your feet clean than it is to brush your teeth! You do not walk on your teeth! You use your feet all the time to get at the enemy. Keep your feet clean."

—General George Patton

Corns, calluses, blisters, athlete's foot, and ingrown toenails are just a few of the foot disorders that can make life thoroughly miserable for a hiker. Let's take a look at some of these problems.

BLISTERS

Blisters made the headlines on July 7, 1924, when President Coolidge's 16-year-old son, Calvin Junior, died of an overwhelming infection that started in a blister on his toe. He had gotten the blister a few days earlier while playing tennis on the South Lawn of the White House. Infection set in, and bacteria spread into his bloodstream. There were no antibiotics in those days, and doctors weren't able to check the infection. He died of "an acute case of septic poisoning." And you could, too, if you get a blister in the deep woods and don't treat it properly.

Most blisters are caused by new or poorly fitting boots. They usually develop over the toes, the front of the foot, and the heel, because the skin in these areas is thick and tough and bound down to the underlying bone. As your foot slides back and forth inside your boot, shearing forces produce small clefts within the skin. Fluid then flows into these clefts and, voilà, you have a blister.

If your boots are too loose in the instep, you will get "downhill blisters" on your toes and the front of your feet as your foot slides forward while hiking downhill. You may get "uphill blisters" on the heel or over the Achilles tendon while climbing steep trails.

You can always count on your feet getting hot and moist when you walk the ridges on a warm spring or fall day, and a hot, slightly moist foot is a blister waiting to happen. A thin layer of moisture causes your socks to adhere more tightly to your skin and increases friction within the skin. When your feet are soaked or dry, there is less friction between socks and feet, and less risk of blistering.

Walking on blistered feet is about as much fun as walking barefoot across a bed of hot coals. One well-placed blister can severely reduce your mobility and put a real crimp in your hiking style. A neglected or improperly treated blister can become ulcerated and infected and spawn a rapidly spreading skin infection called *cellulitis*, or even *sepsis*, the "blood poisoning" that killed Calvin Coolidge, Jr.

✤ Treament

Your aims in treating a blister should be to keep your foot comfortable, promote rapid healing, and prevent infection. Here are my recommendations for treating blisters in the wilderness:

- A "hotspot" is a red, tender area, a blister in the making. Never ignore a hotspot: Cover it immediately with a bandage; a piece of smooth, thin tape; or a hydrogel dressing, such as Spenco 2nd Skin.
- If the roof of the blister is torn, use scissors and tweezers to remove all the dead skin, and treat the wound as an abrasion. Cleanse it with dilute hydrogen peroxide, antiseptic solution, or soapy water, and cover it with antibiotic ointment and a bandage twice daily until it heals.
- If the roof of the blister is nearly intact, don't remove it. It serves as a comfortable, infection-resistant biological dressing, and the blister will heal faster if its roof reattaches to its base. Cleanse the blister as described above and then

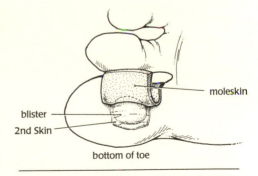

Figure 21-1. Cleanse blister with soap and water, then apply 2nd Skin and a layer of moleskin.

apply a layer of antibiotic ointment and cover it with a bandage, or a strip of tape, if that's all you have. If you have a hydrogel dressing in your medical kit, strip the cellophane off both sides of an appropriate-size piece, apply it to the blister, and cover with the adhesive knit bandage provided. Moisten the hydrogel dressing through the bandage several times a day and leave it in place until the blister heals. If you don't have a hydrogel dressing, cover the blister with gauze or felt; secure it with thin, smooth tape or moleskin; and apply a layer of petrolatum or silicone over the tape or moleskin to decrease friction. (The tape or moleskin will adhere better if you first apply benzoin to the skin around the blister.) Check the wound in 3 days. Remove any dead skin and reapply the bandage for 3 more days.

- If the blister is intact, drain it so that the roof can reattach to the underlying skin. First, cleanse the area with Betadine, Hibiclens, rubbing alcohol, or soap and water. Then, puncture the edge of the blister with a sterile hypodermic needle or a pin that has been sterilized in rubbing alcohol, or held in an open flame until the tip is red-hot. Gently press on the blister to express the fluid, then apply antibiotic ointment and a bandage. Puncture the blister 3 times within the first 24 hours, or once 24 to 36 hours after the blister forms.

- If the blister starts to drain cloudy fluid or pus, the surrounding skin becomes red, swollen, and tender, or you see red streaks extending up your foot, infection has set in. *Never take a foot infection lightly!* Stay off your feet, keep the infected foot elevated above heart level, and soak it in warm, soapy water every 4 hours. Start taking cefadroxil, 500 mg every 12 hours. If the infection doesn't start to resolve within 24 to 36 hours, head home and see a physician *immediately,* especially if you develop fever or chills.

✤ Prevention

An ounce of prevention is worth a pound of cure, and the best way to prevent blisters is by reducing friction between your boots and your feet. Here's how:

- Make sure your boots fit well. Shop for a new pair in the afternoon, when your feet are slightly swollen, and wear the socks that you plan to wear with the boots. Walk around in them for a few minutes to see if they are comfortable, and make sure that there is a thumb's width of space between the tip of the longest toe and the end of the boot.

- Break in new shoes gradually by wearing them for a couple of hours the first day, then an additional hour each day thereafter until they are supple and fit your feet perfectly. If there are any loose or tight areas in either boot after you have worn them for a few days, you can work the leather to make it more supple or apply a shoe insert or pad to tighten loose areas.
- Wear a combination of socks that will limit moisture and friction (see below).
- Foot powder absorbs moisture and reduces friction by keeping your feet dry. Apply it liberally at least twice a day. *Drysol* (20% aluminum chloride hexahydrate) and other antiperspirants inhibit sweating. If you don't have an antiperspirant in your pack, boil a couple of tea bags in a pint of water for 15 minutes, add the tea to 2 quarts of cool water, and soak your feet in the solution for 20 minutes every night. Tannic acid in the tea will keep your feet dry and smelling like roses.
- Keep blister-prone areas covered with tape, moleskin, or petrolatum, and apply benzoin or alum powder to these areas to toughen the skin.
- Toughen up your feet and tune up your muscles and cardiovascular system a few weeks before your wilderness trek by taking progressively longer hikes in the boots you plan to wear during your sojourn in the wild.

CALLUSES

Tight-fitting shoes or deformed feet or toes can produce *calluses*—thickening of the tough layer of dead cells on the surface of the skin. Calluses are protective, but when they become too thick, blisters will develop at their edges. The best remedy is to keep them trimmed with a callus file. When calluses return, apply a pad or adhesive tape over prominent bones where calluses form. If the problem is a crooked heel, a heel cup may be the answer; it spreads the force of heel strike over a wide area of skin. The last resort is a new pair of boots.

CORNS

Have you ever had painful little volcano-shaped craters between your fourth and fifth toes? These are *corns*, a type of callus. They are painful because the skin at the bottom of these craters is perpetually bathed in perspiration, which causes it to become very thin and sensitive to pressure. These calluses are usually secondary to a prominence on the outer surface of the fourth toe. The best treatment is to wear wider boots. A wisp of cotton between the toes soaks up the perspiration and decreases pressure on the skin. Corn pads are good, too.

INGROWN TOENAILS

Tight boots can also cause ingrown toenails. The thick, rigid edge of the nail of the big toe digs into the adjoining skin, producing redness, irritation, swelling, and "weeping" as the inflamed skin secretes fluid. There are a number of ways to deal with ingrown toenails. First, cut a "V" in the middle of the nail to make it more flexible. Then fold a small sheet of aluminum foil until it's the size of a match head and insert it under the corner of the nail where it's digging into the skin. Place a wisp of cotton along the nail to keep the area dry, and keep the foot elevated as much as possible. If these conservative measures don't work, or infection develops, see your doctor.

ATHLETE'S FOOT

After hiking for a day or two, your feet can get downright grungy with accumulated sweat. The heat and moisture inside your boots encourage growth of *Trichophyton,* the fungus that causes athlete's foot. Scaling, red, intensely itchy areas, with vesicles and fissuring between the toes, are characteristic of this condition (which is *not* easily transmitted from person to person, contrary to popular belief). The key to prevention and cure is to eliminate heat and perspiration. Wear shoes and light cotton socks that allow for adequate ventilation. Wash and gently dry the feet every day, if possible, and apply tolnaftate (e.g., Tinactin) liquid to infected areas twice daily. Sprinkle an antifungal powder containing tolnaftate or undecylenic acid (e.g., Breezee Mist Foot Powder) between the toes and into the socks every morning. The powder will soak up moisture and destroy the fungus before it can establish a toehold on your feet.

SOCK IT TO ME

When you're packing your gear, don't just reach blindly into your drawer for a pair of socks to wear with your boots. Grab several pairs, including some thin, 100 percent acrylic socks to wear as an inner layer, thicker cotton or wool socks (depending on the season) to wear as an outer layer, or some of the new "double-layered" socks. When you wear two or three pairs of socks, movement occurs mostly between the layers of socks, rather than between your sock and skin. Acrylic socks hold their shape and wear better than cotton socks, dry quickly, and wick moisture away from the skin. They are also thinner over the top of the foot, which allows for better air circulation. If you have bunions or hammer toes, wear socks with extra cushioning in the toes. And always wear socks that fit well. They should be higher than your boot tops and loose enough that they don't bunch up or wrinkle, but not so tight that they pinch your toes. And always carry extra socks in case your feet get wet.

CHAPTER 22

ABDOMINAL PAIN AND OTHER GASTROINTESTINAL EMERGENCIES

"It's this damned belly that gives a man his worst troubles!"

—Homer, *The Odyssey*

A GASTROINTESTINAL ROAD MAP

The GI system will remain a dark mystery to you unless you take a moment to study Figure 22-1.

Here's what happened to your breakfast this morning: After chewing and swallowing your food, it passed down your esophagus and into your stomach. There, it was mixed with digestive juices and then propelled down into the *duodenum* (upper small intestine) where most of the food was digested and absorbed. The fat in your bacon and eggs then stimulated the gallbladder to contract and secrete *bile* into the small

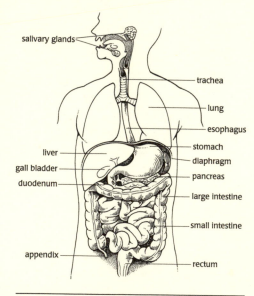

Figure 22-1. The digestive system.

intestine. (Bile, which helps to emulsify and absorb fats, is manufactured in the liver and stored in the gallbladder.) At the same time the lining of the small intestine and the *pancreas* (the big digestive gland situated behind the stomach) released a mixture of enzymes that helped to digest fat, carbohydrates, and proteins. After these enzymes worked their magic, what remained of your breakfast was pushed along into the large intestine *(colon)*. There, water and salt were absorbed into the bloodstream and the end product of the digestive process, feces, was stored pending your next bowel movement.

ABDOMINAL PAIN

Making a correct and timely diagnosis in a patient with abdominal pain is rarely easy. The diagnosis remains obscure in 40 percent of people presenting to the hospital with acute abdominal pain; 30 percent are misdiagnosed. If your partner develops a bellyache when you are three days from the trailhead, you don't have to make a precise diagnosis. But you *do* have to decide whether she is well enough to ride it out in the woods or so sick that she needs to be taken to a hospital.

There is never an easy solution to the abdominal-pain puzzle, but the information in the following sections will help you to make at least a provisional diagnosis in most cases.

Things That Can Cause Abdominal Pain
Problems Inside the Abdomen

- *Blockage of hollow organs:* The intestine, the gallbladder and its duct, and the *ureters* (the tubes connecting the kidneys to the bladder) can, and frequently do, become blocked. When they do, the result is colicky pain and (usually) nausea and vomiting.
- *Peritoneal inflammation:* The *peritoneum* is the thin membrane that lines the abdominal cavity. When blood, urine, digestive juices, or bacteria spill onto the peritoneum from a diseased or injured abdominal organ, it becomes inflamed. Appendicitis and cholecystitis (see under "Gallbladder Attack") often lead to peritoneal inflammation.
- *Vascular problems:* A tear in the aorta in the chest *(aortic dissection)* or a leaking abdominal *aortic aneurysm* (stretching and weakening of the wall of the aorta) can cause terrific abdominal pain. A blood clot in the major artery to the intestines *(mesenteric thrombosis)* will cause pain and shock as the bowel dies.

Problems Outside the Abdomen

- *Chest problems:* Pneumonia, pneumothorax (collapsed lung), *pulmonary embolus* (blood clot in the lung), esophageal spasm, and heart attack can all cause pain in the abdomen.
- *Abdominal wall strain or injury.*
- *Pelvic problems:* Ectopic pregnancies (pregnancies in which gestation occurs outside of the uterus), ovarian cysts, and pelvic infections can be perceived as abdominal pain.
- *Metabolic problems:* Uncontrolled diabetes, spider and scorpion bites, and heavy-metal poisoning can cause abdominal pain.

Symptom Groups

Abdominal pain may be the patient's only symptom, or he may also have vomiting, rigidity of the abdominal muscles, or abdominal collapse or bloating. Here are the most common symptom groups, and the most likely causes of each:

- *Abdominal pain only:* Pain is the only symptom early in the course of many conditions, including appendicitis, large-bowel obstruction, kidney stone, and gallbladder attack.
- *Central abdominal pain:* Simple intestinal colic, early appendicitis, early small-bowel obstruction, pancreatitis, early mesenteric thrombosis, and heart attack.
- *Severe central abdominal pain and shock:* Pancreatitis, mesenteric thrombosis, heart attack, ruptured aortic aneurysm, ruptured spleen, or ruptured ectopic pregnancy.
- *Pain, vomiting, and distension (no rigidity):* Intestinal obstruction.
- *Abdominal pain, constipation, distension:* Large-bowel obstruction.

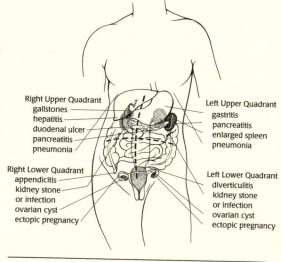

Right Upper Quadrant
gallstones
hepatitis
duodenal ulcer
pancreatitis
pneumonia

Left Upper Quadrant
gastritis
pancreatitis
enlarged spleen
pneumonia

Right Lower Quadrant
appendicitis
kidney stone
or infection
ovarian cyst
ectopic pregnancy

Left Lower Quadrant
diverticulitis
kidney stone
or infection
ovarian cyst
ectopic pregnancy

Figure 22-2. Common causes of abdominal pain.

- *Severe abdominal pain, collapse, and rigidity:* Perforation of the stomach or duodenum by a peptic ulcer; rarely, perforation of the gallbladder or appendix.
- *Right upper-quadrant pain and rigidity:* Gallbladder attack.
- *Right lower-quadrant pain and rigidity:* Appendicitis, kidney infection, ovarian cyst, or tubal pregnancy or infection.
- *Left lower-quadrant pain and rigidity:* Diverticulitis (see "Diverticulitis," pages 173–174), kidney infection, ovarian cyst, or tubal pregnancy or infection.

Appendicitis

The appendix is that little wormlike thing that hangs down from the *cecum* (the first part of the colon). When the appendix gets plugged up for any reason, bacterial infection sets in. This is called *appendicitis.* If an appendectomy is not performed within 24 to 48 hours or so, the appendix becomes gangrenous and ruptures, spreading infection into the peritoneal cavity. The result is *peritonitis* (inflammation of the peritoneum, or abdominal lining), a dangerous condition.

✤ **Signs and Symptoms**

The symptoms almost always appear in this order.
1. Pain (upper or midabdominal first, then moving to the right lower quadrant.
2. Nausea, vomiting, and loss of appetite.
3. Tenderness in the right lower quadrant.
4. Rigidity of the abdominal muscles over the appendix.*
5. Distension in the right lower quadrant.*
6. Fever (low grade).
7. Constipation.
   Often, but not always.

✤ **Treatment**

When the worm turns, it must come out. Take the patient to the nearest surgeon (see Chapter 25).

Gallbladder Attack

Gallstones cause inflammation or obstruction of the gallbladder, leading to:
- *Gallstone (biliary) colic:* This begins with sudden, agonizing, pain in the upper midabdomen or right upper quadrant when a gallstone plugs the

cystic duct. The pain radiates to the right shoulder blade, and the patient usually vomits and breaks out in a cold sweat. The attack, which is often preceded by a fatty meal, subsides when the stone passes into the bile duct after 1 to 4 hours.

- *Acute cholecystitis (inflamed gallbladder):* If the gallbladder is unable to rid itself of the stone, it becomes inflamed and bacterial infection sets in. The right upper-quadrant pain is aggravated by breathing, coughing, or pressure over the area. There will be a low-grade fever, slight elevation of the pulse, and nausea. Look for *Murphy's sign:* place your fingertips under the right lower ribs, and ask the patient to take a deep breath. If he stops in midinspiration when the tender gallbladder touches your fingers, he probably has acute cholecystitis.

✤ Treatment

Avoid fatty foods. Acute cholecystitis is a surgical emergency.

Peptic Ulcer Disease

Every time you eat or drink, your stomach releases gastric juice containing hydrochloric acid, one of the most corrosive acids known. Normally, the *mucosal barrier* protects the lining of the stomach and duodenum against stomach acid. However, alcohol, coffee (even decaffeinated), cola, cigarette smoking, or aspirin, ibuprofen, and similar drugs can weaken the mucosal barrier and lead to the formation of ulcers. A peptic ulcer takes one of two forms: duodenenal ulcer (occuring on the *duodenum,* or the first section of the small intestine) or gastric ulcer (occuring in the stomach).

✤ Symptoms

Peptic ulcers cause burning pain in the pit of the stomach, immediately following eating in the case of a gastric ulcer, and two hours after eating when the ulcer is in the duodenum. A duodenal ulcer may also wake the patient in the middle of the night. If the ulcer erodes a blood vessel in the stomach or duodenal lining, the patient may vomit coffee-ground material and have tarry, black stools.

✤ Treatment

- Eat frequent, small meals.
- Avoid coffee, tea, alcohol, and cigarettes, as well as aspirin, ibuprofen, and other arthritis medications.

- For duodenal ulcers, take an ounce of antacid 1 hour and 3 hours after meals and at bedtime.
- Take Pepcid, 20 mg twice a day.

Intestinal Obstruction

An intestinal obstruction interrupts the normal movement of food through the intestinal tract. *Small-bowel obstruction* is usually caused by *adhesions* (scar tissue) from previous abdominal surgery or by the bowel becoming incarcerated in a *hernia* (see "Intestinal Hernia," page 174). *Large-bowel obstruction* can be caused by *fecal impaction* (hard stool in the rectum), by tumors, diverticulitis, or by an abnormal twisting of a segment of the colon (*volvulus*).

Here's why intestinal obstructions are bad: When the intestine becomes blocked, the bowel distends with fluid and gas and loses its ability to absorb water and nutrients. The patient starts to vomit and becomes severely dehydrated. The outcome will be fatal if the obstruction is not relieved.

✢ **Signs and Symptoms**

Pain is usually severe from the onset of the obstruction and is felt in the midline in the upper, mid-, or lower abdomen, depending on where the obstruction is. The pain is cramping in nature and comes in waves. The patient becomes restless and nauseated; vomiting starts early in small bowel obstruction, later in large bowel obstruction. In the latter, the vomit is feculent. There may be one small bowel movement after the onset of the obstruction. The abdomen becomes progressively more distended as gas and fluid accumulate upstream of the obstruction, but it doesn't become rigid and tender unless the blood supply to the intestine is blocked as well. In that case, you'll see all the signs of shock if the obstruction is not relieved within several hours: dilated pupils; cool, wet, pale skin; feeble pulse; and scant, dark urine.

✢ **Treatment**

The patient needs to be hospitalized for evaluation and possible surgery (see Chapter 25).

Diverticulitis

Most middle-aged and elderly people have numerous little outpouchings, called *diverticula,* in weak areas of the colon. When stool blocks the opening of a diverticulum, bacterial infection sets in, causing *diverticulitis* as the diverticulum and the area around it become inflamed. The infection may be limited to a small abscess in the colon, or it may spread into the abdominal cavity, causing peritonitis.

✤ Signs and Symptoms

Steady discomfort in the left, lower abdomen is the most common symptom. The pain is made worse by defecation, and the patient may have *tenesmus* (painful, ineffective straining at stool), low-grade fever, abdominal tenderness, and rectal bleeding. If the infection perforates the colon, bacteria spread throughout the abdominal cavity, causing peritonitis, *sepsis* (spread of bacterial toxins in the bloodstream), and shock. A large abscess may form and burrow into surrounding organs, and the colon may become obstructed.

✤ Treatment

Mild cases of diverticulitis, with no sign of perforation of the colon, may respond well to bed rest, a liquid diet, stool softeners (e.g., Senokot-S), and an antibiotic, such as amoxicillin, 500 mg every 8 hours for 7 to 10 days, or tetracycline, 500 mg every 6 hours for the same time period. The patient needs to be hospitalized if his pain and fever increase or his general condition deteriorates. Rectal bleeding can be massive but is usually transient. If the patient develops peritonitis, bowel obstruction, or a large, spreading abscess, surgery may be required.

INTESTINAL HERNIA

An *intestinal hernia* is the protrusion of a loop or knuckle of bowel through an abnormal opening, usually in the groin. Most hernias are asymptomatic, but a groin hernia may cause a dragging sensation. The patient may be aware of a lump in the groin, but he is able to push it back into the abdominal cavity *(reducible hernia)*. If the hernia becomes acutely *incarcerated* ("stuck" outside the abdominal cavity), he won't be able to reduce it. It will be painful and tender and accompanied by nausea and vomiting if the intestine becomes obstructed. If the blood supply to the incarcerated bowel is compromised, the hernia is said to be *strangulated*. The patient will become quite ill and exhibit all the signs and symptoms of bowel obstruction.

✤ Treatment

You can attempt to reduce an acute incarcerated hernia, but if there is a question as to its duration, don't manipulate it. Pushing gangrenous bowel back into the abdomen could be fatal.

First, place the patient on his back. Place a warm compress over the hernia for a few minutes to relieve swelling and relax the abdominal muscles, then gently try to push it back into the abdominal cavity. If you can't reduce it, or if it is tender, give up the attempt and take the patient to a hospital (see Chapter 25).

HEMORRHOIDS

A *hemorrhoid* is a varicose vein in the anus. They are very common, especially in pregnant women and in people with chronic constipation or cirrhosis of the liver. Bright red blood on the stool or toilet paper may be your only clue to the presence of an *internal hemorrhoid*. If it *prolapses* (passes out of the anal canal), however, it may become infected or *thrombosed* (clotted), become very painful, and bleed profusely after defecation. *External hemorrhoids* are a real pain in the derriere when they enlarge and become thrombosed. They turn blue and become firm and tender.

✤ Treatment

If you have access to appropriate facilities, warm *sitz baths* (hot baths taken in the sitting position) for at least 15 minutes 3 times a day are the mainstay of treatment. After bathing, gently but thoroughly dry the area. If the thrombosed hemorrhoid has been there for more than 48 hours and is not tense or exceptionally intolerable, warm sitz baths and a bulk laxative, such as Metamucil, may do the trick. If the thrombosis is of recent vintage, i.e., less than 48 hours, and is very painful, surgery may be indicated to give immediate relief. If you are a long distance from medical help and the patient is incapacitated, she may beg you to excise the clot. Here is the technique: Have the patient assume the prone position and anesthetize the skin over the hemorrhoid with ice. Then, using a No. 10 scalpel, make an elliptical incision in the skin over the hemorrhoid and remove the clot with a forceps. Tuck the corner of a small piece of gauze in the wound to control bleeding, and then apply a pressure dressing over it. Remove the dressing and gauze when the patient takes her first sitz bath 8 to 12 hours later. If bleeding, pain, or uncontrollable itching become a problem, she needs to see a physician.

Anal Fissures

An anal fissure is a small, painful tear of the anal canal that develops during the passage of a large, hard stool, or after prolonged diarrhea. It typically causes painful, bright red rectal bleeding during and right after defecation. Most often, the fissure can be seen in the midline at the 12 o'clock position, and there will also be a *sentinel pile* nearby. This is not a hemorrhoid, but rather localized swelling of the tissue around the fissure.

✤ Treatment

Take a hot sitz bath 3 or 4 times a day and after each bowel movement. Clean the area thoroughly after each bowel movement to prevent infection, and include plenty of bran in your diet to prevent a *stricture* (constricting scar) from forming.

Diarrhea

The effects of diarrhea range from discomfort to life-threatening dehydration. Diarrhea, which can be caused by bacteria, virus, or, most commonly, the pathogenic microbe *Giardia lamblia,* is discussed in detail in Chapter 16, Infectious Diarrhea and Field Water Disinfection (page 131).

CHAPTER 23

PEDIATRICS

"Eat no green apples or you'll droop,
Be careful not to get the croup,
Avoid the chicken-pox and such
and don't fall out of windows much."

—Edward Anthony, *Advice to Children*

Children aren't micro-adults. Keep these differences in mind when tending an ill or injured child:

- *Anatomy:* Children have a greater surface/mass ratio than adults and have proportionately larger heads. These anatomic differences make them more susceptible to the adverse effects of exposure to sun and cold.
- *Bones:* Fractures in children heal quickly and remodel wonderfully. Their relatively soft, elastic bones often break on one side only *(greenstick fracture)* or wrinkle or buckle on the surface *(torus fracture)*. Trauma to a joint, especially the wrist, knee, or ankle, is much more likely to injure the weak growth plate near the ends of the long bones than the much stronger ligaments that support the joints.
- *Vital signs:* Children normally have higher pulse and respiratory rates and lower blood pressure than adults.
- *Heat regulation:* Kids are not as efficient as adults at controlling body temperature and are more susceptible to heat illness and hypothermia.
- *Infection:* Children have more frequent and more serious infections than adults.

Age	Weight (kg)	Weight (lbs)	Pulse	Respirations	Blood Pressure
1	10	22	120	20–30	n/a
2–3	12–14	26–31	115		80 + (age in years × 2)
4–5	16–18	35–40	100		
6–8	20–26	44–57	100	12–25	
10–12	32–42	70–92	75		
over 14	>50	>110	70	12–18	

Table 23-1. Age-Specific Vital Signs

FEVER

The normal temperature range is different for each individual, but averages around 98.6°F (37°C) orally. (Rectal temperatures are about 1° higher.) An individual's temperature will normally fluctuate in a 2° range depending on the time of day, ambient temperature, activity level, and other factors. A fever is a body temperature above the usual normal range, associated with a resetting of the body thermostat by a *pyrogen,* a chemical released by bacteria, viruses, white blood cells, or other body tissues. When the pyrogen bumps up the body thermostat, the patient naturally feels chilled. She will start to shiver, the blood vessels in her skin will constrict to conserve heat, and she'll put on additional clothing. All these things cause an increase in body temperature, or fever.

Significance of Fever

Infants (3 to 24 months). In infants, fevers are often caused by serious underlying infection. Such an infection may be associated with *bacteremia,* or seeding of the blood with bacteria. Lethargy, irritability, and poor feeding are all suggestive of serious infection. Inconsolable crying and increased irritability when handled may be signs of meningitis (see "Meningitis," page 185), and cough or a respiratory rate over 40 may signal the presence of pneumonia. Alertness, responsiveness to stimulation, consolability, and playfulness are all favorable signs.

Children Over 24 Months. A child over age two can often tell you what's bothering her. She's less likely to have bacteremia, but more likely to have strep throat.

✤ Treatment

> *"Dr. Bigelow's formula was, that fevers are self-limiting; afterwards that all disease is so; therefore there is no use in treatment."*
>
> —Ralph Waldo Emerson, *Journal*

A fever is not inherently harmful. However, the child will probably feel more comfortable if you lower her temperature with the following procedures:

1. Take off all or most of her clothing to increase heat loss by radiation. Resist the urge to bundle her up; extra clothing and blankets will only insulate her and drive her temperature even higher.
2. Increase her evaporative heat loss by giving her fluids and sponging her with tepid water. Rub her skin to dilate the subcutaneous blood vessels; this will facilitate transfer of heat from the body core to the periphery.
3. Administer acetaminophen or aspirin, 10 to 15 mg per kilogram of body weight, every 4 hours. Ibuprofen is a more potent and longer-acting *antipyretic* (fever-reducing agent). Give 5 mg/kg every 6 hours for temperatures below 102.5°F (39°C), 10 mg/kg every 6 hours for temperatures above 102.5°F (39°C). If you do not know your child's weight, refer to Table 23-2. Note that 1 kg = 2.2 lbs.

Age	Weight (kg)	Weight (lbs)
Term infant	3.5 (birth weight)	7.7 (birth weight)
6 months	7 (or 2 × birth weight)	15.4 (or 2 × birth weight)
1 year	10 (or 3 × birth weight)	23 (or 3 × birth weight)
4 years	17 (or ¼ adult weight of 70 kg)	38.2 (or ¼ adult weight of 154 lbs)
10 years	35 (or ½ adult weight)	77 (or ½ adult weight)

Table 23-2. Body Weight Estimation Guidelines

4. If you have reason to believe she has a bacterial infection (middle-ear infection, strep throat, urinary-tract infection, etc.) administer an appropriate antibiotic as described under "Common Childhood Infections" below.

Febrile Seizures

A *febrile seizure* is defined by the National Consensus Development Conference of Febrile Seizure as "an event in infancy or childhood usually occurring between three months and five years of age, associated with fever but without evidence of intracranial infection or defined cause." It is a generalized seizure that comes on during the onset of illness, usually when the temperature rises rapidly, and lasts 10 to 20 minutes. Febrile seizures are frightening but benign. The problem lies in distinguishing between a febrile seizure and infection of the central nervous system, such as meningitis. A child under six months of age with seizures and fever needs emergency medical evaluation (for evacuation procedures, see Chapter 25). An older child who has had febrile seizures before, and has no signs of meningitis (see "Meningitis," page 185) will require only good nursing care.

COMMON CHILDHOOD INFECTIONS

Otitis Media (Middle-Ear Infection)

Otitis media is inflammation of the middle ear, including the eardrum. You can't see the drum without an otoscope, but the symptoms of otitis media include pain, irritability, pulling on the ears, fever, drainage from the ear, and loss of hearing. It can be caused by a virus, but most often is secondary to bacterial infection, often following in the wake of a cold.

✛ Treatment

Give amoxicillin, 30 to 40 mg/kg/day in 3 divided doses. For immediate pain relief, instill Auralgan in the affected ear until the canal is filled, and then moisten a cotton plug with the solution and insert it into the opening of the canal. Auralgan contains dehydrated glycerine, which reduces congestion and inflammation of the eardrum, and benzocaine and antipyrine, which exert an anesthetic action. Repeat every 2 hours as needed.

Otitis Externa (Swimmer's Ear)

Otitis externa is inflammation of the outer surface of the eardrum, the ear canal, and the *auricle* (ear flap), usually caused by infection. High temperature and humidity, hyperhydration (prolonged exposure to water) and maceration (softening by soaking) of the skin of the ear canal, insufficient ear wax, and trauma are all precipitating factors. The child will complain of itching or a sense of fullness in the affected ear, and the ear canal will be swollen and tender. There may be a cheesy discharge, and manipulation of the ear will elicit an immediate and vocal protest. The lymph nodes around the ear will be swollen and tender.

✤ Treatment

1. Irrigate the ear canal with sterile water until it is clear and then dry the ear by having the child stand in a breeze.
2. Instill a few drops of 2% acetic acid (Otic Domeboro, Vosol, or Orlex) or Cortisporin otic suspension 4 times a day.
3. Don't allow the child to swim until the infection is resolved, and instill a few drops of acetic acid in both ears after he showers.
4. Give oral analgesics as needed.
5. If he doesn't respond to these measures in 48 hours, he should be seen by a physician.

Sore Throat

Sore throats can be caused by viruses or by streptococci and other bacteria. Strep is the only one you really have to be wary of, because it can cause severe infection and rheumatic fever if not treated. The peak months are January through May; strep throat is rarely seen in kids under the age of 3. The child will suddenly develop a sore throat and fever, and her throat and tonsils will be very red. There may be a grayish white patch on the tonsils, the lymph nodes in the front of the neck will be swollen and tender, and she may complain of headache, nausea, and abdominal pain as well as sore throat. If she also has a cough and runny nose, she probably has a viral infection.

✤ Treatment

Give penicillin v potassium, 250 mg 3 times a day for 10 days. (Give erythromycin in the same dosage if child is allergic to penicillin.) Simple analgesics and throat spray or lozenges help too.

Conjunctivitis

Conjunctivitis is inflammation of the *conjunctiva*, the clear membrane that covers the inside of the eyelids and the whites of the eyes. It can be caused by viral or bacterial infection, chemical exposure (e.g., soap, sunscreen), mechanical irritation, or allergies. Bacterial infection ("pink eye") causes intense itching, redness, thick, yellow-green drainage, and sensitivity to light. Visual acuity will not be affected, however. (If there is swelling and tenderness around the eye, decreased movement of the eyeball, and fever, you may be dealing with a far more serious *orbital* [in the eye socket] or *periorbital* [around the socket] infection.)

❖ **Treatment**

Irrigate the eye with water or saline until it is clear. Then, instill 1 sulfacetamide 10% drop in each eye every 2 hours (when the child is awake) for 5 to 7 days. WARNING! Pink eye is contagious. Wash your hands after instilling eyedrops.

Impetigo

Impetigo is a superficial skin infection with either strep or staph bacteria. The bacteria gain access to the deeper layers of the skin through small scratches or abrasions or through insect bites and then release toxic chemicals that facilitate their spread. It's most commonly seen in kids under age 6 and may occur sporadically or in epidemics. It starts as a red bump that evolves into a small, honey-colored blister and finally a crusted, coin-size lesion. You may see crusts anywhere on the body, but they are especially common between the upper lip and the nose. The lesions can spread widely and occasionally cause a kidney disease called *glomerulonephritis*.

❖ **Treatment**

- Give erythromycin or dicloxacillin, 50 mg/kg/day in 4 divided doses.
- Wash the skin with soap and water 2 or 3 times a day.

RESPIRATORY PROBLEMS

Pneumonia

Pneumonia can be hard to diagnose in a young child. He may have *apneic spells* (stop breathing), fever, poor feeding, grunting, lethargy, or vomiting and diarrhea. The most common sign is increased respiratory rate, and you may notice that he is struggling to breathe (flaring nostrils, use of the muscles around the chest to assist breathing). A school-age child will usually have a cough, fever, and rapid breathing and will complain of sharp chest pain.

❖ **Treatment**

- Make sure the child remains well hydrated.
- Antibiotics will help if he has a bacterial pneumonia (rapid onset, high fever). Give a young child amoxicillin, 40 mg/kg/day in 3 divided doses. Older children should receive erythromycin, 50 mg/kg/day in 4 divided doses.
- If there is no significant improvement in 24 hours, the child may require hospitalization.

Croup

Croup is a viral infection of the larynx, trachea, and bronchi in children 6 months to 3 years of age. Typically, the child has had a cold for two or three days, with a gradually increasing cough that turns into a very harsh, barking cough. The child may appear to be in respiratory distress, with shortness of breath and *stridor* (harsh, high-pitched breathing sounds). She will be anxious and hoarse, her fingers and toes may be blue, and the muscles between her ribs and surrounding her rib cage will retract when she breathes.

✤ **Treatment**

Usually, all that is necessary is reassurance and adequate hydration. Bringing her out into the cold night air may effect a dramatic, although perhaps temporary, cure.

Epiglottitis

Epiglottitis is a dangerous bacterial infection of the *epiglottis,* the trap door that protects the upper trachea. The child will experience the gradual onset of fever, sore throat, drooling, stridor (harsh, high-pitched breathing sounds), and painful swallowing over a period of hours. He will breathe very quietly and will talk in a whisper. Unlike the child with croup, he does not cough. He will be very anxious and will want to sit up with his chin forward and his neck slightly extended.

✤ **Treatment**

The airway in a child with epiglottitis can become obstructed at any moment. Don't attempt to look at his throat or lay him down. Stay by his side and reassure him while someone arranges emergency evacuation (see Chapter 25).

GASTROENTERITIS

Gastroenteritis is inflammation of the stomach and intestines that leads to vomiting and diarrhea. It can lead to severe dehydration in a small child. Use Table 23-3 to estimate the severity of her dehydration.

Viral gastroenteritis will often cause headache, fever, chills, and diffuse aches and pains in addition to vomiting and diarrhea. Giardiasis (infection with the protozoan parasite *Giardia lamblia*) causes greasy, foul-smelling stools and furious belching, and bacterial diarrheas usually cause blood in the stools as well as fever. It is self-limited. (See also Chapter 16.)

| | DEGREE OF DEHYDRATION | | |
SIGN	MILD	MODERATE	SEVERE
skin turgor*	normal	decreased	skin tents
tears	slightly decreased	absent	absent
mouth	dry	very dry	parched
fontanelle**	normal	depressed	sunken
urine volume	slightly decreased	decreased	scant
pulse	slightly increased	increased	rapid, weak
blood pressure	normal	slightly decreased	decreased
mental state	irritable	lethargic	unresponsive

*Fluid content, tested by pinching. Normally, the skin will immediately return to its normal shape.
**The fontanelle is the soft area on the top of an infant's scalp

Table 23-3. Criteria for Estimating Degree of Dehydration

✢ Treatment

Gastroenteritis is usually self-limited; if you can replace the fluids as fast as they are lost, the child will do fine. If she is dehydrated, give her 60 to 90 cc/kg of oral rehydration solution (e.g., Rehydralyte or Pedialyte-RS) over about 4 hours and repeat until she no longer appears dehydrated. (These solutions are high in sodium and contain about 2 percent glucose, which facilitates water and sodium absorption. Soft drinks, juices, and sherbets contain excessive sugar and can aggravate diarrhea. You can make your own oral rehydration solution by combining 1 teaspoon of salt and 1 cup of rice cereal with 1 quart of drinking water.) Then give maintenance fluids (e.g., Pedialyte, Lytren, Gatorade) ad lib to replace fluid lost through vomiting or diarrhea, up to 150 cc/kg/day. You can also give Jell-O water (1 package of flavored Jell-O in a quart of water), or flat, room-temperature ginger ale to kids over age 2. Start giving starchy foods, such as bananas, rice, toast, and applesauce, after the child is rehydrated. Seek a medical opinion if the vomiting and diarrhea haven't improved after 24 hours or have not resolved in 3 to 4 days, or if there is bile in the vomit or blood in the stool.

Loperamide (Imodium) dramatically safely decreases the duration of diarrhea when given in 4 times the recommended dose (0.8 mg/kg/day). Pepto-Bismol is safe and effective but has to be given in large doses (100 mg/kg/day).

MENINGITIS

Meningitis is a bacterial infection of the *meninges* (the membranes that invest the brain and spinal cord). Bacteria can spread to the meninges in the bloodstream or from an ear infection. It is uncommon, but it can devastate a young child.

✢ **Signs and Symptoms**

An infant with meningitis may or may not have a fever, vomiting, diminished appetite, *petechiae* (pinpoint, round, purplish spots in the skin), and bulging of the fontanelle. She may be lethargic or irritable and inconsolable. Older children may complain of headache, stiff neck, and back pain. They may go into shock from overwhelming infection.

✢ **Treatment**

Arrange for immediate evacuation to a hospital (see Chapter 25).

CHAPTER 24

WILDERNESS SURVIVAL

"This is the law of the Yukon, that only the
   strong shall thrive;
That surely the weak shall perish, and only the fit
   survive.
Dissolute, damned and despairful, crippled and
   palsied and slain,
This is the ~~Will of the~~ Yukon—Lo, how she
   makes it plain!"

   —Robert William Service, "The Law of the Yukon"

I n 1971, trapper Ron Woodcock became lost in the British Columbia wilderness. He trudged through the woods for two months, subsisting on game and vegetation, until he found an abandoned telegraph line, which he followed to a settlement. Merchant seaman Poon Lim survived 133 days on a raft in the Atlantic Ocean during World War II. When your world is an inhospitable wilderness or a raft bobbing on the sea, your needs are stripped to the basics: oxygen, water, enough heat to maintain a core temperature of around 99°F (37.2°C), and sufficient food to keep the metabolic furnace running.

If the spirit is willing, a human being will find a way to survive under the most adverse conditions. While Poon Lim was drifting across the Atlantic, German soldiers on the Eastern Front sought refuge from the brutal cold inside the bellies of disemboweled horses. Greenland Eskimos sometimes crawl inside their dogs to keep warm and don't hesitate to eat them when it's a matter of survival. Shipwrecked sailors have been known to take sustenance from every manner of flying and crawling beast, from roaches to rats to snakes. Members of an Uruguayan rugby team that crashed high in the Andes Mountains of Chile some years ago survived by resorting to cannibalism.

Everyone who has spent much time in the wilderness has a survival tale. Whether a skier disabled by a broken ankle, an angler adrift on the open water after the engine conked out, or a kayaker marooned on a frozen bay in a snow squall—all know the stark terror of being stranded in a forbidding environment armed with nothing more than the gear in their pack and their wits.

COLD-WEATHER SURVIVAL

In Chapter 8 we looked at the ways in which the body attempts to maintain a core temperature within the narrow limits of 95° to 100°F (35° to 37.8°C). Heat can be generated quickly by any form of muscular exercise. And metabolic heat production can be increased by eating food with a high *SDA* (specific dynamic action); this is the increase in the body's basal metabolic rate that results from eating various kinds of foods. Proteins have the highest SDA, but carbohydrates are metabolized more easily than fats and proteins and heat the body more rapidly. It is important to eat frequently, at least every 2 hours, when outside in cold weather. Alcohol and tobacco, which predispose to hypothermia and frostbite, should be banished from the trail.

Shelter

No matter how warmly you are dressed, you can't survive outside indefinitely in the cold. Eventually, you'll need to find or construct a shelter.

The key to preserving body heat is to eliminate the windchill factor by finding a windbreak of some kind. You can ride out a snow squall in the mouth of a cave, in a tree hollow, under a cliff overhang, in a lean-to, or on the lee side of a large rock or tree (a "tree well"). You can be reasonably comfortable in such a shelter if you build a fire and amplify its heat by building a barrier wall of logs or stones on its far side to reflect the fire's radiant energy back onto you. (But make sure that there are no snow-laden branches overhead. The snow will inevitably end up on the fire.)

"A light breath of air blew from the south, nipping the exposed portions of their bodies and driving the frost, in needles of fire, through fur and flesh to the bones. So, when the fire had grown lusty and thawed a damp circle in the snow about it, Sitka Charley forced his reluctant comrades to lend a hand in pitching a fly. It was a primitive affair, merely a blanket stretched parallel with the fire and to windward of it, at an angle of perhaps forty-five degrees. This shut out the chill and threw the heat backward and down upon

those who were to huddle in its shelter. Then a layer of green spruce boughs were spread, that their bodies might not come in contact with the snow."
—Jack London, *The Wisdom of the Trail*

You can enhance any shelter by building a windbreak of snowblocks or boughs about 2 to 3 feet high and 2 to 3 feet to windward of the shelter. If the windbreak is placed much farther away from the shelter, drifting snow will bury it.

Building a Snow Cave. Snow is one of the best insulating materials, which makes it a good construction material for a temporary shelter. You can build a *snow cave* by burrowing mole-fashion into the side of a snowbank. Slant the entrance tunnel upward, and excavate just enough snow to create a space large enough to kneel and stretch out in a sleeping bag. The sleeping platform should be elevated 18 inches off the floor and covered with boughs for insulation. Drill a ventilation hole through the roof and one in the snowblock used as a door. If you keep the cave small, you can heat it a few degrees with a candle.

Building a Snow Trench. Digging a snow cave can be a time-consuming process, and you'll be drenched with sweat by the time you are done. The

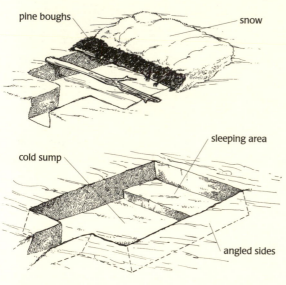

sweat will accelerate evaporative heat loss from your body, and that's obviously counterproductive. A *snow trench* may be a better idea. It's easier to build and doesn't require as much snow. You can construct an emergency shelter for two people in 20 minutes. Use a ski or pot to scoop out a pit 3 feet deep, 4 feet wide, and 8 feet long at the surface. Then, undermine the edges so that the trench is 8 feet wide and 10 feet long at the

Figure 24-1. Building a snow trench with a bed platform.

bottom. Lay skis, ski poles, or long branches width-wise across the top of the trench, cover this frame with a tarp or evergreen boughs, and pile snow or rocks on the tarp or boughs to hold them in place. If you leave one end of the trench open, you can build a fire at that end. If you have a camp stove, you can completely enclose the top of the trench, leaving only a narrow entrance and a 6-inch ventilation hole at one end. Whichever way you do it, don't let the temperature inside get above freezing, or your shelter will melt and you'll have to contend with water in your sleeping bag.

Starting a Fire

All outdoorspeople pride themselves on being expert fire starters, but starting a fire in a raging blizzard is no mean feat. Here's one surefire technique: Gather some of the small, dead lower branches from evergreen trees, as well as a few pieces of birch bark, dry leaves or grasses, plant stems, or other tinder. Clear a space on the ground, out of the wind, and arrange the twigs as a lean-to across a log, or in wigwam-fashion. (If you can't find dry twigs, whittle a pile of shavings off a stick.) Ignite the tinder, and apply kindling as the fire grows. Split soft woods ignite most easily and make the best kindling.

Add fuel slowly so that you don't smother the fire. After you get a good, hot fire going with soft woods, switch to hardwood fuel. It burns slowly and leaves lasting coals. Keep the fire small to conserve wood, and maintain a healthy supply of fuel by collecting several times more than you think you will need.

Starting a Fire Without Matches. You can try rubbing two sticks together, but there are easier ways to start a fire:

- Use the lens of a camera, binoculars, telescopic sight, or flashlight to focus sunlight on a pile of tinder.
- Use your knife or any piece of hard steel to strike sparks on a piece of flint, quartz, or pyrite. You can use charred rags, bird down, pulverized bark, or dry moss for tinder.
- Attach wires to the positive and negative ends of two C or D batteries in tandem and scratch the ends together to create a spark.

Food

"It is next to impossible to starve in a wilderness."

—George Leopard Herter

If you ever get lost in the deep woods, you'll have some anxious moments wondering where your next meal will come from. Not to worry. There are several tons of wholesome, nutritious food in every acre of forestland. All you have to do is go out and find it.

Now, you have to be in a certain frame of mind to down a meal of birch bark, roasted grubs, broiled beaver tails, and dandelion coffee. But you can be sure that fasting for a day or two will help you to acquire a taste for these and even more exotic items. The prospect of starvation will put a keen edge on your appetite and make you wonderfully receptive to culinary experimentation.

Everyone who hikes, camps, hunts, or fishes in the wilderness ought to know how to live off the land. This basic survival skill will give you a sense of self-reliance and will allow you to spice up your diet during prolonged sojourns in the wilderness. Supplementing prepackaged meals with food you gather in the wild will lighten your pack and add more nutrients to your diet as well. Dandelion greens have twice as much vitamin A as spinach, and young pokeweed shoots contain three times as much vitamin C as oranges.

Plants. Wild plants are usually the most abundant and most available food source in the wilderness, but you can't just start grazing. You need to know how to identify edible plants, where to find them, and which parts of the plants are most nutritious. You can acquire this knowledge through field guides, such as *The Wild Food Trailguide* by Alan Hall (Henry Holt, 1976), or by asking a friend who is knowledgeable about plants to tutor you.

Nuts are your best bet in a survival situation. They are high in proteins, fats, and carbohydrates and provide more calories, ounce-for-ounce, than any other food. You'll get more energy from a handful of hazelnuts or walnuts than you would from a lean sirloin steak! Hickory nuts, butternuts, chestnuts, acorns, beechnuts, and the seeds or nuts of pinecones are edible also. (Acorns are bitter and have to be roasted or boiled and leached.)

Here is a sampling of the common edible plants of the United States:

ROOTS AND TUBERS

> Wild onion (boil or eat raw)
> Wild and sweet potato (bake, roast, or broil)
> Nut grass (Chufa; eat fresh or boil)
> Solomon's seal (boil or roast)
> Pasture brake (roast the roots; remove the woolly covering of unrolled
>   fronds and cook like asparagus)

Arrowhead (bake, fry, roast, or boil)

Wild potato (raw or cooked, any way)

Cattail (eat fresh or bake or roast the roots; eat young stems raw or after boiling; boil immature flower spikes and eat like corn on the cob)

Wild rice (chew lower stem and roots; dry, then parch the seeds, remove the husks, and cook like rice)

FRUITS AND BERRIES

Juneberries, currants and gooseberries, blueberries and huckleberries, strawberries, blackberries, dewberries, and raspberries, elderberries, persimmon, hackberries, hawthorn, mulberries, cranberries, pawpaw, and grapes (eat raw, cook, or preserve by drying)

LEAVES, STEMS, AND SHOOTS

Purslane (young leaves and stems raw or boiled)

Dandelion (white leaves and top of the root excellent in salads; boil the leaves, changing the water at least twice to remove bitter taste)

Plantain (boil)

Burdock (peel leafstalks and eat raw; use young leaves in salads or boil in two changes of water and use as potherb)

Sorrel (chew on leaves to quench thirst, or use in salad; boiled leaves make tasty potherb)

Goosefoot (pigweed, lamb's quarters; leaves make excellent potherb; boil, mash, then grind up seeds into flour; eat as cereal after boiling and mashing)

BARK

The bark of poplars, birches, willows, Scotch pine, and lodgepole pine is edible. Remove the dark outer bark, which contains excessive tannin, and strip off the white innermost bark. Eat it raw or roast it.

How Can I Be *Really* Sure It's Safe to Eat? Before eating any mystery plant, subject it to the following edibility test:

1. Rub the leaf, sap, or juice of the plant on your inner wrist and wait 15 minutes. If you develop redness, swelling, blisters, or itching, the plant is a contact poison. Don't eat it.

2. Boil the plant for 30 to 60 minutes, changing the water twice, then chew a small piece of it. If it tastes bitter, hot, or soapy, the plant is poisonous. If not, spit out the pulp and swallow the juice.
3. If you haven't gotten sick after 8 hours, eat a teaspoonful of the plant. If you feel well 8 hours later, eat a cupful. If you still feel okay, go ahead and eat all you want.

Liquid Sustenance. You're going to need a beverage to wash down all that bark and roots. You can brew a delicious pot of tea by steeping the leaves of these plants in hot water: mint, blackberry, wintergreen, cassina, coltsfoot, Labrador tea, persimmon, raspberry, rose, or sweet goldenrod (leaves); birch, spruce, and hemlock (bark); and sassafras (roots). Or roast and grind dandelion and chicory roots, beechnuts, or cleavers fruits to make full-flavored (although caffeine-free) coffee. If you carry a gimlet in your pack in the early spring, you can tap into a birch tree and drain off some sap. Drink it right out of the tap; boil it down to make sugar, or add sugar or honey; boil it for an hour, let cool, and add yeast to make birch beer.

Animals. If you get tired of eating leaves, bark, and roots, it may be time to check out the animal kingdom for a meal. Keep in mind that life is more abundant and more concentrated in and near water. If you don't have a spinning rod with you, you can improvise. Use the inner bark of trees or unraveled fabric to make line; pins, wire, thorns, or fish bones to make hooks; and buttons, shiny metal, or small bits of cloth to make lures. You can fashion a spear out of a sapling, tie a T-shirt across a circular frame to make a scoop net, or catch fish with your hands by reaching under the undercut bank of a small stream.

Look for *frogs* along the banks of streams, lakes, and ponds, and spear them, club them, or catch them with hook and line. You can eat the entire frog, but the skin can be poisonous, so skin it first. *Newts* and *salamanders* are edible also. You'll find them wherever you find frogs, as well as under rotten logs and in damp woods. *Toads* are not edible.

Harvest *shellfish* by feeling with your hands or feet along the sandy or muddy bottoms of streams. All mollusks are edible, but steam them first to destroy bacteria, viruses, and parasites.

Freshwater *crustaceans* (prawns, shrimp, lobsters, and crabs) are edible but should be cooked first.

Lizards, snakes, and turtles are edible. So are alligators. Good luck.

If you like potato chips, tortilla chips, and other crunchy snack food, you'll love *insects*. They are very nourishing and are easy to find. Look under stones, under the bark of dead trees, and in rotten logs for grubs. They, as well as ants, grasshoppers, locusts, crickets, and termites, can be eaten raw or fried, boiled, or roasted. On the other hand, you may want to slip them by your buddies by disguising them in a stew.

Look in glades, the edges of woods, on animal trails, and near streams and riverbanks for small mammals and birds. You can use hanging or fixed snares, deadfalls, or bird lime to trap them. Turtle or bird eggs can be boiled, poached, or fried.

Water

Do you realize that you've been lugging around 40 liters (42.2 quarts) of water most of your life? That's how much water there is in the average, 70-kg (155-lb) person's body. Each of your 100 trillion cells is a miniature ocean, and virtually every tissue in your body is bathed in a saltwater solution. You can survive without food for weeks, but you can only make it a few days without water. When you go without food for a while, your body is able to mobilize energy stored as fat and sugar compounds in the muscles and liver. It can even convert muscle and other tissues into energy if the situation gets desperate enough.

But humans can't store water in humps the way camels do. Water that is absorbed through the intestine goes immediately into the cells, the extracellular fluid, the blood plasma, or one of the other body fluids. Each day approximately 1,400 ml (47 oz) of water is lost in the urine, 100 ml (3.4 oz) in the sweat, 300 ml (10.2 oz) in the stool, and 700 ml (23.7 oz) by evaporation through the lungs or skin. In order to keep from getting dehydrated, you need a constant supply of water, 2,400 ml (80 oz) a day on average. Six hundred ml (20 oz) of water is produced by the metabolism of food, so you need to drink a minimum of 1,800 ml (60 oz). In a hot climate or during vigorous exercise, your water requirements increase dramatically. After about 36 hours at a high altitude, your kidneys start working overtime, so you should drink at least 3 or 4 liters (or quarts) of water a day when you are above 8,000 feet.

Don't let thirst be your guide to your water requirements. The thirst center in your brain isn't stimulated until your cells become dehydrated. Keep ahead of the game by drinking liberally whenever you have the opportunity. And keep your canteen full.

Avoid eating snow. It takes too much of your body's energy to melt, and you don't know what fungi or bacteria are on it. Be especially wary of pink or stale snow. If you are going to melt snow on a fire or stove, or on a dark sheet in the sun, you'll get more water out of hard, packed snow or ice than freshly fallen powder snow.

Drinking urine or seawater is taboo. Seawater has three to four times the concentration of salts as body fluids, and even small amounts of it can cause dangerous elevations of sodium, potassium, and magnesium in the blood. Urine is loaded with metabolic waste products and will poison you.

Solar Still. If you have a plastic sheet, you can make a solar still and reprocess urine or water from vegetation. Scoop out a hole 2 feet deep by 3 feet across and put a clean container in the center of the hole. Pull up some grass or other vegetation and scatter it around the bottom of the hole, or put a bottle filled with urine in the hole. Then stretch the plastic sheet across the hole, securing it with logs or rocks, and place a small rock on the sheet directly over the pail. Water from the grass or urine will condense on the under-surface of the plastic sheet and roll down to the center and into the container.

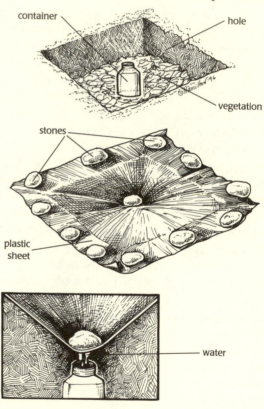

Vegetation Still. Take a large bag (a clear one, preferably) and fill it with vegetation. Then inflate the bag, tie off the top, and place the bag in the sun. After a few hours, water from the vegetation will condense and collect in the bottom of the bag.

Figure 24-2. Building a solar still.

You can obtain at least a little water by squeezing any freshwater fish and many plants. Small streams that run at right angles to the drainage system can be considered relatively safe to drink from. But boil the water first to be safe.

DESERT SURVIVAL

A third of the world's land surface is covered by desert. Half of this is the cold desert of the polar regions. The other half is hot, arid wasteland populated only by a few plant and animal species specially adapted to this harsh environment.

Deserts are not only hot by day (a thermometer-bursting 136.4°F [58°C] in the shade at Al-Aziziyah, Libya, on September 13, 1922), but surprisingly cool at night. Sand and rocks warm up quickly during the day but release their heat quickly at night. Nor is there much moisture in the desert air to retain heat, so the mercury can plummet 35 to 45 Fahrenheit degrees (19 to 25 Celsius degrees) after sunset.

The desert floor can get hot enough (185°F/85°C) to burn your shod feet. But there are other things going on that will keep you hopping—like flash floods, dust storms, and rattlesnakes. Not to mention the sharp rocks and thorns strewn along the ground. And sunburn is an omnipresent danger.

When it comes to desert attire, you can tear a page from the Bedouin's book. Their light-colored, loose-flowing robes protect them from sunburn and allow for adequate ventilation, while insulating them from the chill night air. Cotton is the material of choice in the desert. Its low insulating value and high wicking action allow for rapid heat dissipation and sweat evaporation in hot weather. A sunscreen with SPF 15 or greater, good-quality sunglasses, and a wide-brimmed hat with a foreign legion–style flap in the back will complete your protection against sunburn and sun glare. (If you don't have a hat, you can fashion an Arab burnoose out of a T-shirt or a piece of cloth.)

Shelter

You won't survive long without water in the desert, so if your canteen runs dry, you'll have to strictly conserve body fluids. Lay low during the day and travel at night when it's cool and you are less likely to sweat. The hottest place in the desert is the top few inches of the ground and the air for a foot or so over the ground. If you scoop away a layer of sand, you'll find the ground surprisingly cool. You can look for a rock overhang or use a plastic sheet or tarp to rig up a sunscreen. Or you can look for a natural shelter or stay in your stranded vehicle. But don't bed down in an arroyo or gully unless you want to get washed away in a flash flood.

Food

There's food all around you in the desert, but you have to look for it. Any crawling, leaping, or flying creature is fair game, including snakes, insects, rats, and lizards. Most vegetation is edible, including cactus fruits, wild cherries, wild currants, wild celery, piñon nuts, the soft parts of grass stalks, and seeds.

Water

All roads lead to water in the desert. At least, all animal trails do. Watch which way the critters are heading at dawn and dusk, and follow them. You won't go wrong. But beware of any pool that doesn't have animal tracks and droppings.

You can collect dew from leaves, flowers, or any cold surface. The flowers and fruits of plants, especially the fruit of the saguaro cactus, are loaded with water after a rainfall. After a heavy rainfall, look for water in the hollows of rock formations. And look for springs at the foot of cliffs or in gullies. Or try digging for water in the outer bends of dry streambeds.

CHAPTER 25

WILDERNESS EVACUATION TECHNIQUES

"Lewis had stretchers improvised from clothing and poles, giving orders to the bearers: 'We will take these men back, eight men to a stretcher so that no one will be worn out. No stretcher is to be put to the ground without orders from me. Any man who drops a stretcher will be shot.'"

—Burke Davis, *Marine! The Life of Lt. General Lewis B. "Chesty" Puller*

Jim knew they were in trouble even before Dan broke his ankle. They had spent the morning climbing in the high country near Yellowstone Park, but a furious early season snowstorm swept into the area at midday, and high winds and poor visibility forced them to call it quits and head back to camp. They had hiked only a few hundred yards down the trail when Dan lost his footing on a snow-slicked rock and went airborne. He came down with all of his weight on his right ankle, and his lower tibia snapped with a loud "crack"—a sound Jim mistook for a breaking pine bough until he looked up and saw Dan writhing in the snow. His partner's right ankle was grotesquely deformed, and a blood stain was spreading across his pant leg.

Jim set and splinted Dan's fractured ankle, then paused to consider his options. It would be dark in a couple of hours, and the drifting snow had almost obliterated the trail. Dan needed urgent medical attention, but the trailhead was a five-hour hike down the mountain in good conditions. There was no way he could carry him that far on his back in a snowstorm. Heck, he'd be lucky if he could lug him the 2 miles back to camp before dark!

What would you do if you were in Jim's position? Would you make a heroic effort to carry Dan out of the wilderness in a blizzard? Would you try to get him back to camp? Or would you find shelter, settle in for the night, and reassess the situation in the morning?

In this scenario, the last option is the most prudent one, although an argument could be made for carrying your injured buddy back to camp if you felt up to the task and were familiar with one-rescuer evacuation techniques. Any attempt to carry him out of the woods that afternoon would end in tragedy.

There is no formula that will tell you precisely what to do in every situation, but you can use the following guidelines to map out a strategy for dealing with any wilderness evacuation problem:

- Anyone with a minor injury, or an upper-extremity injury, should be able to walk back to camp or to the trailhead under her own power.
- Most people with leg or foot injuries can be carried out. Anyone with multiple fractures or spinal, chest, or abdominal injuries may need to be evacuated by helicopter.
- A very strong, fit person may be able to carry an injured adult on his back for a mile or two, but two or more people will be needed for longer transports, especially over rugged terrain.
- Never leave an unconscious, confused, or otherwise helpless person unattended.
- In remote, mountainous areas, self-evacuation is often faster than sending a messenger and waiting for help to arrive.
- Never set out on an evacuation at night or in severe weather.
- Don't create additional victims by placing yourself or others in a dangerous position during a medical evacuation.

If you elect to send for help, dispatch the fittest member of the group with a map showing your location, trails, and natural landmarks; the best route to the trailhead; and a note specifying the number of victims, their ages, the nature of their injuries, their condition, treatment given, supplies needed, and the urgency of the situation. Then erect a shelter and mark it so that it will be easily visible to rescuers. Smoke can be seen from the ground or air, and a large X laid out with sticks or stones in an open field or meadow will signal aircraft that you need medical assistance.

Generally, the wisest course is to wait with the victim while someone goes for help, but impending bad weather, inadequate clothing or shelter, dwindling food and water supplies, or worsening of the victim's condition may force your hand.

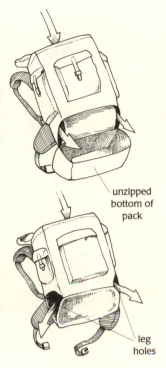

unzipped
bottom of
pack

leg
holes

ONE-RESCUER CARRIES

Carrying your buddy out of the woods will seem like the Twelve Labors of Hercules if you don't go about it the right way. After you have stabilized the victim as well as you can (see Chapter 1), you'll need to devise a way to convey him out of the woods. If you are the lone rescuer, you can use one of these one-rescuer carries:

- *The backpack carry:* Cut leg holes in the bottom of a large backpack, have the injured man or woman climb into it, then hoist it onto your back. (See Figure 25-1.)
- *Rope seat:* Pass a long, 1-inch-diameter rope or strap over the victim's head and pull the ends under his armpits and across his chest. Then lift him onto your back piggyback-fashion and pull the rope ends over your shoulders, under your arms, back between his legs, and

Figure 25-1. The backpack carry.

1-inch-
diameter rope

Figure 25-2. The rope seat.

then around his upper thighs. Take up the slack and tie the ends across your waist. (See Figure 25-2.)

- *Split-coil carry:* Coil a lengthy piece of rope and fix it at one point with a knot. Divide the coiled rope into two equal loops, and have the victim step into the loops and pull them up snug against her crotch with the fixed segment in front. Then have her stand on a stump or rock while you back up to her, place your arms through the free ends of the loops, and hoist her onto your back. (See Figure 25-3.)

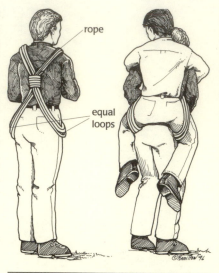

Figure 25-3. The split-coil carry.

TWO-RESCUER CARRIES

- *The four-hand seat:* The rescuers stand facing one another and form a seat for the victim by interlocking hands as follows: Each rescuer grasps her right wrist with her left hand, and then grasps the other rescuer's left wrist with her right hand palm-down.

- *The pole carry:* This technique requires two heavy backpacks or rucksacks and rescuers of near equal stature. First, find a sturdy, 5- to 6-foot-long tree limb and trim off the branches. Next, don your backpacks, stand side-by-side, and pass each end of the tree limb behind the pack and rest it on the hipbelt. Pad

Figure 25-4. The pole carry.

the limb and have the victim sit on it and drape his arms around you and the other rescuer for support. (See Figure 25-4, page 200.)

- *The coiled-rope seat:* Stand shoulder-to-shoulder with your fellow rescuer, pass a large coiled rope around your necks, and let it hang down in front of you. The victim then sits on the rope and drapes her arms around your shoulders.

LITTERS

Single- or two-rescuer techniques are appropriate for people with relatively minor injuries or illnesses. But you will have to use a litter to evacuate anyone who is unconscious or has difficulty breathing, a serious chest or abdominal injury, or fractures of the pelvis, hip, or femur. (If you suspect the victim has suffered a spinal injury, it may be best not to move him. You will have to evaluate the situation very carefully before attempting an evacuation; consider the severity of associated injuries, the weather, the number of rescuers in your party, and the availability of outside help. See Chapter 5, Head and Neck Injuries, for more information on checking for spinal injuries.)

When improvising a litter from available materials, any of the following may prove useful:

cord
vines
string
fishing line
twine
strips of cloth

You will need at least 6 rescuers to carry a patient and litter a short distance, and 12 or more for an evacuation over a greater distance. These litters are serviceable and easy to construct:

- *The pole litter:* Select two straight tree limbs or poles about 7 feet in length and lay them on the ground about 18 inches apart. Tie

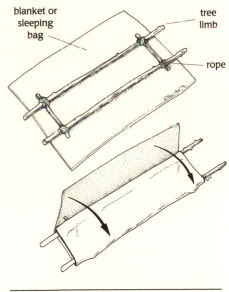

Figure 25-5. The sleeping bag litter.

cross supports to the limbs at 10- to 12- inch intervals.

- *The sleeping bag litter:* Spread a sleeping bag (or a blanket or tarp) on the ground and align the poles or tree limbs on it lengthwise, about 15 inches apart. Lash cross supports across the poles about 6 inches apart, and then fold the sides of the bag over the poles. The victim's weight will keep the bag from slipping between the poles. (See Figure 25-5.)
- *The pole-and-rope litter:* Make a frame as described for the sleeping bag litter and then tie one end of a rope to one corner of the frame. Loop the rope around one pole 8 to 10 times, leaving enough slack in each loop so that it can be pulled to the midpoint between the two poles, and tie it to the other corner. Repeat the process on the other side, but this time pass the free end of the rope through the loops you just created so that they interlock. When you are done, pull the rope taut to create a firm rope mattress. (See Figure 25-6.)

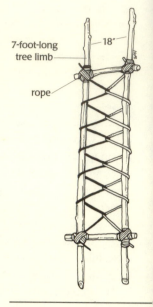

7-foot-long tree limb

18″

rope

Figure 25-6. The pole-and-rope

Before you start out, pad the litter so that the injured person doesn't get bedso Give her something to eat and drink and offer her an analgesic. Make sure that she i cured to the litter and insulated against the cold. Check her condition whenever stop to rest, and make sure that her bandages haven't soaked through and her sp haven't loosened. Do whatever you can to buck up her spirits.

WILDERNESS MEDICAL KIT

"Bayley carried a small bottle of spirits for healing, sustaining and fortifying uses, in case of encounters with triangular headed snakes, bears, Indians, mountain rams, noxious night airs, snow storms, etc.; and in case of vertigo and difficult breathing at great heights, together with broken bones, flesh wounds, skin erosions, abrasions, contusions. For in prudence, is it not well to realize that 'something might happen,' and well to have a helpful spirit—a guardian angel in a bottle ever near?"

—John Muir, from the account, printed in the San Francisco *Daily Evening Bulletin*, of his 1875 ascent of Mount Whitney

What's the first thing you look at every morning, after you stumble sleepy-eyed into the bathroom? Your mug in the mirror. And what's behind that grisly visage? Why, the medicine cabinet, of course. It's right in front of your face, conveniently situated so that you don't forget to take your medicines. But what do you do when you're camped out on the banks of the Snake River in Idaho or bivouacked on some Rocky Mountain peak? Do you pack all your medicines in a neatly organized satchel, or do you just throw it all into an old sock?

It seems that you never need half that stuff in your medicine cabinet until you're out in the woods somewhere, 50 miles of bad road between you and the nearest drugstore. Then you'd trade your sleeping bag for a bottle of calamine lotion for that poison ivy rash or a couple of aspirins for that headache. And you'd pay a king's ransom for a bottle of Imodium to ease those stomach cramps and diarrhea.

It would be nice if you could just pull that medicine cabinet out of the wall and throw it in the back of the truck along with the rest of your gear. But it would be easier to make up a medical kit, a sort of portable medicine cabinet, containing all the medical supplies you will need for emergencies in the field. I'm not talking about a Mobile Army Service Hospital, but a kit that you can tote around in a tackle box or a small canvas satchel. And you can make up a smaller kit-within-a-kit to stick in your fishing vest or your back pocket when you go afield.

The key to putting together a useful kit is organization. If you just go out to the drugstore, buy the items I have listed, and cram them all into an old sack, you might as well call it Pandora's box. Let's stay organized by grouping the supplies as follows:

WOUND CARE MATERIALS

bar soap
antiseptic solution, 4 oz bottle
antibiotic ointment, 1 oz tube
12 Adaptic dressings, 3" × 3"
24 sterile dressing pads, 4" × 4"
4 Kerlix or Kling roll bandages, 4" × 5 yd
4 Surgipads, 8" × 10", or ABD pads, 8" × 8"
1 roll waterproof adhesive tape, 1" × 5 yd
8 Bioclusive or Tegaderm transparent dressings, 2" × 3" or 3" × 3"
Spenco 2nd Skin
50 bandage strips (Band-Aids), 1" × 3"
Surgical staples (Precise Vista, 3M)
10 skin-closure strips, ¼" × 3" (Steri-Strips by 3M;
    Coverstrip Closures by Beiersdorf)
10 skin-closure strips, ½" × 3"
compound benzoin tincture, 2 oz
4 sterile eye pads
1% silver sulfadiazine cream (Silvadene), 8 oz jar
latex surgical gloves, 4 pairs
face mask, 1
silver nitrate sticks, 3

Bar soap (e.g., Dial, Ivory) is fine for daily cleansing of abrasions and superficial burns.

Antiseptic solution. Povidone-iodine 7.5% (Betadine), benzalkonium chloride, and chlorhexidine (Hibiclens) are three good ones.

Antibiotic ointment (e.g., Neosporin, Bacitracin). Apply a small amount to a wound before covering it with a dressing.

Adaptic pads. These are nonadherent mesh dressings that prevent the bandage from sticking to the wound.

Sterile dressing pads. Four-ply pads with a wicking action that absorbs blood and other fluids from wounds. Good for cleaning wounds as well.

Kling and Kerlix roll bandages. Stretchy gauze rolls for bandaging and securing splints.

Surgipads, ABD pads. You can use these big, bulky bandages to apply pressure to large, bleeding wounds and to cover burns.

Bioclusive or Tegaderm transparent dressings. Space-age technology in a wound dressing, they seal out water and dust but not air. Ideal dressing for blisters, abrasions, and small cuts that are not bleeding.

Spenco 2nd Skin is a hydrogel (96% water, 4% polyethylene oxide) that's a great field dressing for open blisters and burns. It soaks up fluids and reduces pain and friction.

Skin-closure strips. Butterfly (Johnson & Johnson), Steri-Strip (3M), Curi-strips (Kendall), and Coverstrip Closures (Beiersdorf). These sterile strips can often be used in lieu of stitches to close cuts. They'll stay on longer if you apply *tincture of benzoin* to the skin on either side of the wound and let it dry until it becomes "sticky." (*Warning:* Benzoin is an organic solvent—don't let it come into contact with the wound itself.) *Caution:* Skin closures are best reserved for "clean," relatively superficial wounds. Deep, jagged lacerations are best treated in a medical facility.

Silvadene cream is the preferred topical preparation for burns (do not apply it to facial burns, however).

Silver nitrate sticks are used to cauterize nosebleeds.

Dressings and bandages should be stored in a watertight plastic container to ensure that they don't get wet.

MEDICINES

"No families take so little medicine as those of doctors, except those of apothecaries."

—Oliver Wendell Holmes, *Medical Essays*

100 aspirin, acetaminophen, or ibuprofen tablets

10 meclizine tablets, 25 mg

*4 Transderm Scop discs

20 diphenhydramine (Benadryl) tablets, 25 mg

30 Imodium tablets

*10 Phenergan suppositories, 25 mg

*30 Darvocet N-100 tablets

*15 Tylox tablets

30 melatonin tablets, 3 mg

*40 penicillin V potassium tablets, 250 mg

*30 amoxicillin tablets, 250 mg

*20 Duricef (cefadroxil) capsules, 500 mg

*20 Bactrim DS (TMP-SMX) tablets

*#30 acetazolamide tablets, 250 mg

*#16 Decadron tablets, 4 mg

*#26 nifedipine tablets, 20 mg

Otic Domeboro, 2 oz

Maalox, Mylanta, or other antacid, 5 oz

Calamine or Caladryl lotion, 8 oz

12 Domeboro tablets

*sulfacetamide 10% ophthalmic drops, 10 cc

tetrahydrozoline eye-drops 0.05%, ½ oz

miconazole cream 2%, ½ oz

hydrocortisone 1.0% cream, 60 gram tube

*Cortisporin otic solution, 10 cc bottle

sunscreen, SPF 15 or greater, 8 oz

zinc oxide, 1 oz

Cavit, 7 gram tube

*dimenhydrinate (Dramamine)

Lotrimin (clotrimazole) cream 1%, 30 grams

*Lidex (fluocinonide) 0.05% cream, 60 grams

*20 Pepcid tablets, 20 mg

*2 EpiPen Autoinjectors

35 prednisone tablets, 20 mg

30 metronidazole tablets, 250 mg

#&Auralgan, 10 cc

&Rehydralyte, two 8 oz bottles

&Pedialyte, two 8 oz bottles

personal medications

*Prescription medications
#Include only if you are traveling to high altitude (above 8,000 feet).
&Include if you have small children in your party.

> *"A desire to take medicine is, perhaps, the greatest feature which distinguishes man from other animals."*
>
> —Sir William Osler, *Science*

Meclizine and *Transderm Scop* prevent motion sickness.

Diphenhydramine (Benadryl) should always be on hand for allergic reactions and to control severe itching from poison ivy or other causes.

Imodium is a nonprescription antidiarrheal.

Phenergan (promethazine) suppositories will put the stops to nausea and vomiting.

Darvocet N-100 is a narcotic analgesic for moderately severe pain.

Melatonin is nature's sleeping pill.

Penicillin V potassium is penicillin—the drug of choice for dental infections and strep throat. *Amoxicillin* is effective in treating urinary-tract infections, middle-ear infections, and sinus infections. *Duricef* is effective against staph and strep bacteria and in treating wound infections and other soft-tissue infections. It can be substituted for penicillin for people allergic to penicillin. *Bactrim DS* is an antibiotic that is especially useful in treating urinary-tract infections.

Acetazolamide and *Decadron* are useful in treating mountain sickness.

Calamine dries weeping, itching poison ivy rashes. One or two *Domeboro* tablets can be added to a pint of water to make Burow's solution, an astringent, drying solution.

Sulfacetamide 10% ophthalmic drops are used to treat conjunctivitis.

Tetrahydrozoline drops (e.g., Visine) soothe eyes reddened by smoke or sun.

Miconazole cream (Micatin and others) cures athlete's foot.

Cortisporin otic solution is used to treat swimmer's ear.

Zinc oxide is a physical sunblock.

Cavit is a dental paste for emergency repair of lost crowns and fillings.

Lotrimin cream can be used to treat athlete's foot and ringworm.

Lidex is a potent topical anti-inflammatory steroid for treating severe rashes. (Never apply to the face.)

Pepcid is an antihistamine that blocks the flow of acid through the stomach lining.

Tylox is a potent narcotic analgesic.

Insect sting kits (e.g., EpiPen) contain a prefilled syringe of adrenaline for self-treatment of severe insect sting reactions. If you're allergic to bees, don't leave home without one.

Prednisone is an anti-inflammatory steroid used to treat severe poison ivy rashes and other forms of dermatitis.

Auralgan drops reduce the pain of middle-ear infections.

Rehydralyte is an oral electrolyte rehydration solution for children.

Pedialyte is an oral electrolyte maintenance solution for children.

MISCELLANEOUS

2 instant cold packs
2 elastic (Ace) bandages, 3" and 6"
bulb irrigating syringe, 60 cc
triangular bandage
6 large safety pins
2 tongue blades
scissors
tweezers
No. 3 stainless steel scalpel handle
Nos. 10, 11, and 20 scalpel blades, 3 of each
needlenose pliers
Sawyer Extractor snake venom suction device
spare eyeglasses
signal mirror
magnifying glass
penlight flashlight
waterproof matches
Sam splint
2 Merocel nasal tampons
insect repellent
moleskin
thermometer
single-edge razor
water-purification tablets (e.g., Potable Aqua, Globaline, Halazone)
dental first-aid kit (see Chapter 20)

Elastic (Ace) bandages are good for wrapping sprains and applying compression to large, bleeding wounds.

Triangular bandage. A large muslin bandage can be used as a shoulder sling, turban bandage for head wounds, or to secure splints to fractured extremities.

Safety pins have many uses: securing slings and splints, closing large wounds, holding the tongue out of the back of the throat when the jaw is badly broken.

Tongue blades make good temporary splints for fractured fingers.

Needlenose pliers for removing fishhooks.

The Extractor is a snake venom suctioning device available from Sawyer Products, Safety Harbor, FL.

This is a comprehensive list. Which of these items you actually need in your kit depends on the number of people in your group, their ages and their health, the level of medical expertise in the group, the expected risk of injury or illness during the trek, the duration of the trek, and the maximum distance you will be from medical help at any point during the trek.

The equipment in the kit should be consistent with the skills of the most medically sophisticated member of the group. There is no point in packing hemostats and scalpels if no member of the group has ever seen the inside of an operating room. On the other hand, a qualified physician would probably like to see some intravenous solutions and injectable medications included in the kit.

The kit as described would be a load to lug around on a long trek. One way around that problem is to have each member of the group carry his or her own personal medications, as well as a portion of the medical kit.

A KIT-WITHIN-A-KIT

The president is followed wherever he goes by a naval officer lugging a "black box" containing nuclear weapons codes. Unless you have someone like that to carry around your medical kit, you'll probably elect to leave it in camp when you set out upcountry each morning. But you *can* pack a small first aid kit. Store the following items in a small, waterproof case in your pocket or in a fanny pack:

    antiseptic solution, 1 oz

    6 adhesive bandage strips

    4 skin-closure strips

    4 sterile gauze dressings, 4" × 4"

    waterproof adhesive tape, ½"

    waterproof matches

    triangular bandage

    aspirin/ibuprofen/acetaminophen tablets

    snake venom suction device (if you are in snake country)

It is also a good idea to carry the following items on your person at all times:

    identification, including a list of medical problems, allergies, and medications

    bandanna (doubles as a bandage or sling)

    coins for telephone

    cord

    Swiss Army knife

    2 safety pins

"Half the modern drugs could well be thrown out the window, except that the birds might eat them."

—Martin H. Fischer, *Fischerisms*

EMERGENCY TREATMENT PROCEDURES

Few of the medical problems you are likely to encounter in the wild will be of the life- or limb-threatening variety. Most illnesses and injuries can be approached in a relaxed, deliberate manner. On the other hand, opportunities abound in the wilderness for even the most savvy outdoors enthusiast to become desperately ill or injured, and in critical situations, you will have to respond quickly and instinctively to prevent loss of limb or life. This book contains a wealth of information on a wide range of medical emergencies, but if you or a comrade suddenly starts to choke on a piece of steak or go into shock after being stung by a bee or falling from a cliff and rupturing your spleen, you may not have time to sit down and study the relevant text. In immediate life-threatening situations, where minutes or seconds count, you should instead refer to the following Emergency Treatment Procedures. They provide step-by-step instructions on how to deal with the most critical medical emergencies. Then, after you have stabilized your patient and she is no longer in acute distress, take the time to carefully read the more detailed information provided in the body of the book. If you decide that her condition is unstable, read Chapter 25, "Wilderness Evacuation Techniques," to learn how to prepare her for evacuation to a hospital.

SHOCK

✤ **Signs and Symptoms**
- Victim anxious, apprehensive
- Skin pale, cool, and clammy
- Pulse rapid and thready
- Breathing rapid and shallow

✤ **Treatment Steps**
1. Check the ABCs: *a*irway, *b*reathing, and *c*irculation (see Chapter 1, page 4).
2. Stabilize any obvious injury, e.g., control bleeding (see Chapter 1), stabilize chest injuries (see Chapter 6), assess head and spinal injuries (see Chapter 5), and splint fractures (see Chapter 4).
3. Place the victim on her back with her head low and her legs elevated above heart level. If she has a chest injury, place her in a semi-sitting position. Move her as gently and as little as possible.
4. Loosen tight clothing so that she can breathe more easily.
5. Cover her with blankets and offer her warm fluids by mouth if she is alert.
6. Constantly monitor her skin condition, pulse, breathing pattern, urine output, and her state of alertness.
7. Send someone for help.
8. Refer to Chapter 1 for more information on treating shock.

CHOKING

❖ **Signs of Choking**
  • The victim turns blue and grabs his throat.
  • He may make high-pitched, screechy sounds, or be totally unable to speak.

❖ **Treatment Steps**
  If victim is standing or sitting, and conscious:
  1. Perform the Heimlich maneuver:
     a. Stand behind him and wrap your arms around his waist.
     b. Place one fist thumb side in on the center of the victim's stomach between the rib cage and the navel. Grab your fist with your other hand and pull up and in sharply, using 5 quick thrusts.
     c. Repeat the series of 5 quick thrusts until the airway is cleared or he loses consciousness.
  2. If he loses consciousness, open his mouth by grasping the tongue and lower jaw and lifting up. Then, insert the index finger of your other hand alongside the cheek to the base of the tongue. Hook the finger behind the object and remove it from the mouth.
  3. Give a series of mouth-to-mouth breaths.
  4. If you can't ventilate the lungs, perform 6 to 10 abdominal thrusts; repeat the finger sweep and the mouth-to-mouth ventilations.
  5. Repeat the sequence of Heimlich maneuver, finger sweep, and mouth-to-mouth breathing until the airway is cleared.

  The victim is lying on the ground unconscious:
  1. Place him on his back, and kneel astride his thighs.
  2. Place the heel of one hand against his abdomen just above the navel, and put the other hand over the first.
  3. Press into the abdomen with a quick upward thrust.
  4. Repeat the Heimlich maneuver, finger sweep, ventilation sequence as necessary.

  You are alone and choking:
  Perform the Heimlich maneuver on yourself. Make a fist with one hand, and place the thumb side on your abdomen just above the navel. Grab the fist with the other hand, and press inward and upward in a quick, sharp, thrusting motion. If this doesn't work, press your abdomen across any firm surface, such as a tree stump or a log.

  (Refer to pages 5–8 for more information on choking.)

SEVERE BLEEDING

1. Apply firm pressure directly over the wound with a sterile dressing pad or the cleanest cloth material at hand.
2. Raise the part as high above heart level as possible.
3. Place the victim on his back with his head low and legs above heart level.
4. If you cannot control bleeding from an extremity wound by applying firm pressure, consider using a tourniquet. But keep in mind that tourniquets are dangerous: Don't use one unless you are willing to sacrifice the limb to save the victim.
5. When the bleeding stops, cleanse and dress the wound as described on pages 15–18.

CHEMICAL BURNS TO THE EYE

Caustic substances (especially alkali) can cause severe injury. Symptoms include pain, tearing, redness, and spasm of the eyelids.

✤ **Treatment**

1. Irrigate the affected area with a continuous stream of water for at least 10 minutes; remove particulate material with a cotton swab, and make sure you thoroughly irrigate the insides of both lids.
2. If the substance is an acid, continue the irrigation for 1 hour. If it is an alkali, irrigate the eye continuously until the patient arrives at a hospital.
3. Instill a drop of sulfacetamide 10% in the eye every 4 hours for 24 hours.

ANAPHYLACTIC SHOCK (SEVERE ALLERGIC REACTION)

✤ **Signs and Symptoms**
  - Anxiety
  - Hives
  - Facial swelling
  - Difficulty breathing
  - Wheezing
  - Collapse

✤ Treatment

1. Place the patient in a supine position.
2. If you have an insect-sting kit or an EpiPen, inject 0.3 mg (0.15 mg for a small child) of adrenaline into her thigh.
3. Give Benadryl, 50 mg by mouth.
4. Give another adrenaline injection if there is no significant improvement in 15 minutes.
5. Call for help.

UNRESPONSIVE PERSON

1. Call her name, shake her, pinch her. If she doesn't respond, proceed to step 2.
2. Open her airway using the jaw-thrust technique: Put your fingers under each side of her jaw and lift it up and forward without tilting her head back (see page 4).
3. Check her mouth and throat and remove any obstruction.
4. Check for breathing: Listen for breath sounds and watch for chest movement. If she is not breathing, give 2 quick mouth-to-mouth breaths before proceeding to step 5.
5. Check for pulse: Put your index and middle fingers over her windpipe and slide them down alongside the neck muscle to feel for a pulse. If you don't find one, start CPR (see pages 8–10).
6. If she is unconscious but is breathing and has a detectable pulse and no signs of serious head, neck, chest, back, or abdominal injury, roll her onto her left side to prevent her from choking on her tongue or vomit. Place her right hand under her cheek to support her head and flex her right knee and hip at right angles to keep her from rolling onto her stomach.
7. Monitor her breathing and pulse while you call for help.
8. If she is *not* breathing but does have a pulse, give her 16 mouth-to-mouth ventilations every minute. Check her pulse once every minute, and start CPR if you cannot detect one.

NEAR-DROWNING

1. Remove the victim from the water as quickly as possible (splint the neck if you suspect a neck injury).
2. If he is not breathing, use the jaw-thrust technique to open his airway (see page 4), clear any debris from his airway, and start mouth-to-mouth ventilation while still in the water. If he has no pulse, start chest compressions as soon as you can place him on a firm surface.
3. Rewarm him if he is hypothermic.
4. Continue CPR (see pages 8–10) until he revives or emergency personnel take over.

HYPOTHERMIA

1. Check the *ABCs* (see Chapter 1). Check her respirations and pulse and make sure she has a clear airway (see Chapter 1). If she is pulseless and not breathing, start CPR. Do *not* perform CPR if she has any pulse and respirations, no matter how feeble. If she is found floating face-down, treat her as a near-drowning victim.
2. Examine her from head to toe. CAUTION! Fixed and dilated pupils are not a reliable sign of death in a hypothermia victim.
3. Get her into a shelter, remove her wet clothing, gently dry her skin, and cover her with blankets or a sleeping bag.
4. Apply hot packs to her neck, armpits, trunk, and groin, or have two people get undressed from the waist up, get into bed with her, and maintain close chest-to-chest contact. Be careful not to burn her skin, and do *not* apply heat to any other areas.
5. Don't give her alcohol or any other drink unless she is alert.
6. See Chapter 8 for more information about hypothermia.

GLOSSARY OF MEDICAL TERMS

ABCs. Airway, Breathing, and Circulation.

Abrasion. An area of the body where the superficial layer of skin has been sheared off by mechanical trauma.

Abscess. A localized collection of pus in a cavity formed by the disintegration of tissues.

Acidosis. An abnormal state caused by a surplus of acids or deficiency of bases in the blood and tissues.

Aerophobia. The morbid fear of air or being up in the air.

Analgesic. A medication that relieves pain.

Anaphylaxis. A severe allergic reaction characterized by respiratory compromise and circulatory collapse.

Antibodies. A serum protein produced by lymph tissue in response to exposure to a foreign object.

Antimotility agent. Medication designed to slow contractions of the intestinal muscles.

Antivenin. An antitoxic serum for venom, especially snake venom.

Apneic spells. Periods of time when a person is not breathing.

Appendicitis. Inflammation of the appendix.

Arc burn. Corneal burn caused by exposure of the cornea to an arc welder's torch.

Aspirate. To breathe stomach contents into the lungs.

Auricle. The ear flap.

Avulsion. The tearing away of part of a structure.

Bacteremia. The presence of bacteria in the blood.

Basal cell carcinoma. A form of skin cancer.

Bile. A fluid secreted by the liver and poured into the intestine.

Body position sensors. Specialized nerve endings around the joints that relay data to the brain regarding the body's position.

BSA. Body surface area.

Bubo. Inflammatory swelling of a lymph gland due to the absorption of infective material.

Buddy splint. A splint made by taping an injured finger or toe to an uninjured adjacent finger or toe.

Callus (See also **Corn.**) An area of skin thickened as a result of friction or pressure.

Cc. Cubic centimeter. A liquid measure equivalent to a milliliter (ml, $\frac{1}{1000}$ liter).

Cellulitis. An infection of the loose, subcutaneous tissues.

Cervical spine. The neck portion of the spine.

Chilblains (Pernio). Localized itching and painful redness on the fingers, toes, or ears caused by cold, damp weather.

Cholecystitis. Inflammation of the gall bladder.

Chronic sprain. Permanent stretching of the ligaments supporting a joint.

Circumferential burn. A burn that encircles the trunk or a limb.

CMS. Circulation, motor function, and sensation.

Cock-up splint. A splint made to immobilize the wrist in a position of extension.

Colic. Severe, cramping pain caused by stretching of a hollow structure.

Colitis. Inflammation of the colon.

Colon. The terminal segment of the intestinal tract.

Compress. A pad or bolster of folded linen or other material applied to a body part.

Compression dressing. A bulky, multilayered dressing used to cover large, open wounds or to stabilize skeletal injuries.

Concussion. A transient disruption of brain function following blunt head trauma.

Conjunctiva. The delicate, translucent membrane that lines the inner surface of the eyelids and the exposed surface of the eyeballs. *Conjunctivitis* is the inflammation of the conjunctiva.

Contusion. A bruise.

Corn. A painful callus between the toes.

Cornea. The transparent, very sensitive outer part of the eye in front of the pupil and iris.

Crepitus. The grating sound made by the rubbing together of the ends of a fractured bone. *Subcutaneous crepitus* is the tactile sensation imparted when gas bubbles in the skin are stroked with the fingertips.

Croup. A viral infection of the larynx, trachea, and bronchi in children 6 months to 3 years of age.

Crown. The part of the tooth that extends above the gums.

Debride. To remove foreign matter and devitalized tissue from a wound.

Dentin. The hard substance of the tooth surrounding the pulp.

Dermatitis. Inflammation of the skin.

Diaphragm. The muscular partition separating the chest and abdomen.

Dislocation. The disruption of a bony joint.

Distal. Remote from any point of anatomic reference. (See also **Proximal.**)

Diverticulum. An abnormal patch or pouch created by the herniation of the intestinal lining at a defect in the muscular area. *Diverticulitis* is the inflammation of a diverticulum.

Drowning. Death by asphyxia following submersion.

Dry drowning. Drowning in which spasms of the vocal cords prevent aspiration of water into the lungs.

Duodenum. The first part of the small intestine.

Ecchymoses. Leakage of blood under the skin, manifested as "black and blue" marks.

Ectopic pregnancy. A pregnancy in which the fertilized egg implants and starts to develop outside of the uterus, usually in the Fallopian tube ("tubal pregnancy").

Enamel. The hard, white material that covers the dentin of the teeth.

Epidural hematoma. A collection of blood between the brain and the skull.

Epiglottitis. Inflammation of the epiglottis, the "trap door" that covers the trachea during swallowing.

Eschar. A dry scab formed on the skin as a result of a burn, frostbite, or corrosive action.

Exsanguination. The complete draining of blood from the body.

Extracellular fluid. Fluid outside of the cells.

Feathering burns. A fern-like pattern on the skin caused by lightning. Not a true burn.

Fecal impaction. A mass of hard stool in the rectum.

Flail chest. An unstable chest segment caused by two or more fractures in each of three or more consecutive ribs.

Flash burn. A burn produced by very brief exposure to radiant heat of high intensity.

Flatus. Gas generated in the stomach or bowels.

Foreign body granuloma. A small inflammatory nodule under the skin in reaction to a foreign object.

Fracture. A broken bone. (See also **Open fracture.**)

Friction burn (or "rope" burn). A burn caused by the friction generated by a rope being pulled through the hands.

Frostbite. Tissue injury or death caused by exposure to subfreezing cold.

Frostnip. Cold injury characterized by reversible numbness and blanching of the tissue.

Full-thickness burn. A burn involving all of the skin layers.

Gallbladder. A sac under the liver that stores and secretes bile.

Gallstone (biliary) colic. Intense, spasmodic upper abdominal pain, usually associated with the presence of a stone in the gall bladder.

Giardia. A one-celled (protozoan) animal that parasitizes animals and humans, causing gastrointestinal distress.

Gingivae. The gums.

Globe. The eyeball.

Glomerulonephritis. Inflammation of the kidneys sometimes following impetigo.

Granuloma. A small, round, fleshy mass in a wound.

Greenstick fracture. An incomplete fracture of long bones; usually seen in children.

Heat edema. A form of heat illness characterized by swelling of the hands, feet, ankles, and legs, caused by hormonal fluctuating and dilation of blood vessels.

Heat exhaustion (heat prostration/heat collapse). A mild form of heat illness characterized by weakness, headache, vomiting, sweating, muscle cramps, and collapse.

Heatstroke. Lethargy, weakness, confusion, elevated body temperature, and collapse due to high ambient temperatures; usually seen in elderly people.

Heat syncope. Loss of consciousness in an unacclimated person exposed to hot, humid conditions.

Heimlich maneuver. A maneuver used to clear the upper airway of a choking victim.

Hematoma. A collection of blood.

Hematuria. Blood in the urine.

Hemolysis. Breakdown of the red blood cells.

Hemopneumothorax. Blood and air in the chest cavity.

Hemorrhoid. A varicose vein of the rectum or anus.

Hemothorax. A collection of blood in the chest cavity.

Hernia. A protrusion of a part through the structure that normally contains it, as in herniation of intestine through the abdominal wall.

High-altitude cerebral edema. Swelling of the brain at high altitude, leading to nausea, vomiting, headache, and loss of coordination.

High-altitude flatus expulsion. Flatus caused by expansion of intestinal gas at high elevation.

High-altitude illness. Any of several illness resulting from reduced oxygen in the air (and thus, in the blood) at high elevations. (See also **High-altitude pulmonary edema; High-altitude cerebral edema;**

High-altitude flatus expulsion.) **High-altitude pulmonary edema (HAPE).** Accumulation of fluid in the lungs at high elevations.

Humerus. The upper arm bone.

Hydrophobia. Fear of water.

Hypercarbia. Excess carbon dioxide in the blood.

Hyperdration. A group of related disorders often experienced by people ascending to elevations over 8,000 feet.

Hypertonic. A solution with a higher solute concentration than blood plasma.

Hyphema. Bleeding into the anterior chamber of the eye.

Hypotension. Low blood pressure.

Hypothermia. Cooling of the body's core temperature below 95°F.

Hypotonic. A solution with a lower solute concentration than blood plasma.

Hypoxemia. A deficiency of oxygen in the blood.

Immersion. The state of being in the water. (See also **Submersion.**) *Immersion syndrome* is sudden death after immersion in cold water.

Impetigo. A bacterial skin disease.

Intestinal hernia. Protrusion of a loop or knuckle of intestine through an abnormal opening in the abdominal wall.

Iris. The circular pigmented membrane behind the cornea.

Kiesselbach's area. An area in the anterior part of the nasal septum that is richly supplied with capillaries.

Labyrinthitis. Inflammation of the inner ear.

Laceration. A wound made by tearing.

Large-bowel obstruction. A blockage of the large bowel.

Lens. The transparent, biconvex body of the eye that refracts in-coming light rays and focuses them on the retina. A *dislocated lens* is a lens that has been displaced from its normal position.

Lumbar. Pertaining to the lower back.

Lyme disease. Infection with the tick-borne bacterium *Borrelia burgdorferi,* so named because it was first reported near Lyme, Connecticut.

Maceration. The softening of a solid by soaking.

Malignant melanoma. A tumor made up of melanin-containing cells.

Melanin. The dark pigment of the skin and hair.

Melanocytes. Cells that synthesize melanin.

Melanosomes. Pigment particles in the pigment-producing cells (melanocytes).

Meningitis. Inflammation or infection of the membranes that line the brain and spinal cord *(meninges).*

Mesenteric thrombosis. A blood clot in the artery which supplies the intestine.

Metatarsal. One of the long bones of the foot.

Murphy's sign. The inability to take a deep breath when an examiner's fingers are pressed up under the lower right ribs.

Myofascial pain-dysfunction syndrome (MPD). A sign of gallbladder inflammation.

Near-drowning. At least temporary survival after being submersed.

Necrotic. Adjective used to describe devitalized (dead) tissue.

Neurotoxin. A substance that is poisonous to nerve tissue.

Open dislocation. A dislocation in which there is a wound over the joint.

Open fracture. A fracture in which bone is visible through an open wound.

Orbital. Pertaining to the eye socket.

Ossicles. The small, sound-conducting bones of the middle ear; the malleus, incus, and stapes.

Osteomyelitis. Bacterial infection of a bone.

Otitis externa. Inflammation of the external ear.

Otitis media. Inflammation of the middle ear.

Otoliths. Calcium carbonate crystals that line the membranous labyrinth of the inner ear.

Pancreas. An organ situated behind the stomach that produces insulin and digestive enzymes.

Partial-thickness burn. A burn that does not involve the full skin thickness.

Percuss. To strike a part with short, sharp blows to diagnose the condition of the parts below by the sound produced.

Periapical periodontitis. Inflammation of the supporting structures near the root of a tooth.

Pericoronitis. Inflammation of the gums of a partially erupted tooth.

Periodic breathing. Waxing and waning cycles of heavy breathing interspersed with intervals of no breathing.

Periorbital. Referring to the area surrounding the eye socket.

Peritoneal cavity. The abdominal cavity.

Peritoneum. The membrane that lines the walls of the abdominal cavity and the abdominal organs. *Peritonitis* is an inflammation of the peritoneum.

Petechiae. Small, round, purplish red spots caused by bleeding under the surface of the skin.

Phalanx. One of the long bones of the fingers and toes.

Photoallergy. An allergic sensitivity to light after exposure to a photoallergen.

Photosensitizers. Chemicals that cause an exaggerated response to sunlight.

Phototoxicity. A severe sunburn mediated by exposure to a photo-sensitizing chemical.

Phytophotodermatitis. An allergic rash or severe sunburn resulting from combined exposure to certain plants and sunlight.

Plasma. The fluid portion of the blood.

Pneumothorax. An accumulation of air in the chest cavity.

Postimmersion syndrome. Severe shortness of breath minutes to hours after being pulled out of the water. (Also called "secondary drowning.")

Priapism. A sustained penile erection.

Prodrome. A premonitory symptom indicating the onset of a disease.

Prolapse. The falling down or slipping of a body part or organ.

Prophylaxis. The prevention of disease.

Proximal. Closer to any anatomic point of reference. (See also **Distal.**)

Pulmonary embolus. A blood clot that has traveled through the venous system and lodged in the lung.

Pulp. The connective tissue in the central cavity of the tooth. *Pulpitis* is the inflammation of pulp.

Pyrogen. A fever-producing substance.

Rabies. An infectious disease of animals, transmitted to humans through the bite of an infected animal. *Furious rabies* is a form of the disease in which the victim is extremely excited.

Reduce. To restore a fractured bone or dislocated joint to its normal alignment.

Reducible hernia. A hernia that can be pushed back into the abdominal cavity.

Reflectivity. The degree to which a surface reflects light.

Retina. The inner lining of the back chamber of the eye. A *detached retina* is a retina that peels away from the back of the

eye due to fluid in the eye's back chamber.

Rewarming shock. Shock that results when externally applied heat causes the blood vessels of the skin and extremities to dilate and fill with warm blood from the body's core.

RICE. Rest, Ice, Compression, Elevation.

Rickettsia. A genus of bacteria that live inside the cells of lice, fleas, ticks, and mites.

Root. The part of a tooth below the gum line.

Salmonella. A genus of bacteria that causes disease in humans, including gastroenteritis.

Scapula. The shoulder blade.

Sclera. The "white" of the eye.

Sentinel pile. Localized swelling near an anal fissure.

Separated cartilage. Disruption of the cartilage linkage between the bony rib and the sternum (breastbone).

Sepsis. The presence of bacteria or their toxins in the blood or tissues.

Shallow-water blackout. Loss of consciousness after hyperventilating before swimming underwater.

Shigella. A genus of bacteria that can cause dysentery.

Shock. The breakdown of vital functions that follows collapse of the circulation.

Sitz bath. A hot bath taken in the sitting position.

Small-bowel obstruction. Blockage of the small bowel by tumor, scar from previous abdominal surgery, hernias, or other causes.

Solar keratoses. Scaly, rough, white thickenings on the skin caused by chronic exposure to the sun.

Solar retinitis. Inflammation of the retina caused by staring at the sun.

Sprain. Stretching or tearing injury to the ligaments that support a joint.

Squamous cell carcinoma. A form of skin cancer.

Strain. An injury to the musculo-tendinous unit resulting from sudden overstretching of the muscle or sudden increase in the tension within the unit.

Strangulated hernia. An irreducible hernia in which the blood supply is compromised; gangrene ensues if the hernia is not reduced promptly.

Stricture. A narrowing of a hollow structure, such as the esophagus.

Subdural hematoma. A collection of blood between the brain and its protective covering (the dura).

Submersion. The state of being under the water. (See also **Immersion.**)

Sun protection factor. A measure of the protection against ultraviolet light provided by sunscreen.

Surfactant. A surface tension–lowering substance that coats the

inner surface of the lung and prevents the small air cells from collapsing.

Swimmer's ear. See **Otitis externa.**

Sympathetic nervous system. A special network of nerves supplying the heart and blood vessels.

Tenesmus. Ineffectual and painful straining at stool or urination.

Tension pneumothorax. The accumulation of air under pressure in the chest cavity, which increases to the point of shock.

Thermoregulatory center. The part of the brain that acts as a thermostat in regulating body temperature.

Torus fracture. An incomplete fracture of a child's bone in which the bone kinks or wrinkles without breaking all the way through.

Toxin. A poison.

Traction. The act of pulling on a limb to reduce a fracture.

Trench foot. A condition in which the feet

become cold, waxy, pulseless, and numb after prolonged immersion in cold water. (Also called "immersion foot.")

Triage. The sorting of victims into prioritized groups.

Ureter. The tube that conveys urine from the kidney to the bladder.

UVA. Ultraviolet light of 320 to 400 nanometers wavelength.

UVB. Ultraviolet light of 290 to 320 nanometers wavelength.

UVC. Ultraviolet light of 270 to 290 nanometers wavelength.

Vasoconstriction. The diminution of caliber of vessels leading to decreased blood flow to a part.

Vasomotor. Affecting the caliber of a blood vessel.

Vector. A carrier that transfers an infective agent from one host to another.

Ventricular fibrillation. A condition in which the heart muscle twitches and there is no effective contraction of the pumping chamber (ventricle).

Vertigo. A hallucination of movement; a sensation of the world spinning around the patient.

Vestibular system. The three semicircular canals and the otoliths in the inner ear that play a key role in maintaining body position balance.

Volvulus. Twisting and knotting of the bowel leading to obstruction.

Wet drowning. Drowning in which water enters and fills the lung.

Windburn. Aggravation of sunburn by the drying effect of wind.

Wrist drop. Inability to extend the wrist or fingers after injury to the radial nerve, often seen after fractures of the long bone of the upper arm (humerus).

Xiphoid process. A sword-shaped (xiphoid) cartilage-covered piece of bone that projects downward from the lower sternum.

INDEX